THE ILLUSTRIOUS
LADY

THE ILLUSTRIOUS LADY

A Biography of
Barbara Villiers, Countess of Castlemaine
and Duchess of Cleveland

by

ELIZABETH HAMILTON

HAMISH HAMILTON
LONDON

First published in Great Britain 1980
by Hamish Hamilton Ltd
Garden House 57-59 Long Acre London WC2E 9JZ

Copyright © 1980 by Elizabeth Hamilton

British Library Cataloguing in Publication Data
Hamilton, Elizabeth, *Lady, b. 1928*
The illustrious lady.
1. Castlemaine, Barbara Palmer, *Countess of*
2. Charles II, King of England - Relationship
with women 3. Favorites, Royal - Biography
4. Mistresses - England - Biography
942.0'6'60924   DA447.C/
ISBN 0 241 10310 X

Printed in Great Britain
by Ebenezer Baylis & Son Ltd
The Trinity Press, Worcester, and London

CONTENTS

ILLUSTRATIONS

between pages 120 *and* 121

WILLIAM VILLIERS, 2ND VISCOUNT GRANDISON
School of Van Dyck.   Reproduced by permission of the National Trust
at Hardwick Hall.
BARBARA VILLIERS LATER DUCHESS OF CLEVELAND
By Sir Peter Lely.   Reproduced by kind permission of the Mint
Museum, Charlotte, North Carolina.
GEORGE VILLIERS, 2ND DUKE OF BUCKINGHAM
By John Michael Wright.   Reproduced by kind permission of the Earl
of Malmesbury.
PHILIP STANHOPE, 2ND EARL OF CHESTERFIELD
By Sir Peter Lely.   Reproduced by kind permission of Lord Melbourne.
ROGER PALMER, 1ST EARL OF CASTLEMAINE, WITH HIS SECRETARY
Venetian School.   Reproduced by kind permission of the Earl of Powis.
KING CHARLES II
By Simon Verelst.   From the collection at Parham Park, Sussex.
EDWARD HYDE, 1ST EARL OF CLARENDON
After A. Hanneman.   Reproduced by permission of the National
Portrait Gallery.
SIR HENRY BENNET, 1ST EARL OF ARLINGTON
After Lely.   Reproduced by permission of the National Portrait Gallery.
BAPTIST MAY IN 1662
By John Greenhill.   Reproduced by kind permission of the National
Trust, the Rotunda, Ickworth.
BARBARA VILLIERS, DUCHESS OF CLEVELAND
By John Michael Wright.   Reproduced by kind permission of the Earl
of Lisburne.
QUEEN CATHERINE
Miniature by Samuel Cooper.   Reproduced by gracious permission of
Her Majesty the Queen.
BARBARA VILLIERS, DUCHESS OF CLEVELAND
Miniature by Samuel Cooper.   Reproduced by gracious permission of
Her Majesty the Queen.
KING CHARLES II
Chalk drawing by Samuel Cooper.   Reproduced by gracious permission
of Her Majesty the Queen.
FRANCES STUART, DUCHESS OF RICHMOND
Miniature by Samuel Cooper.   Reproduced by gracious permission of
Her Majesty the Queen.

LOUISE DE KÉROUALLE (detail)
By Simon Verelst. From the collection at Parham Park, Sussex.

MOLL DAVIES
By Sir Peter Lely. Reproduced by kind permission of the Earl of
Bradford.

NELL GWYNN
Engraving after Henri Gascars. Reproduced by kind permission of the
National Portrait Gallery.

JACOB HALL
Artist unknown. Reproduced by kind permission of F. T. Dent Esq.

WILLIAM WYCHERLEY
Mezzotint by I. Smith after Lely. Reproduced by kind permission of
the National Portrait Gallery.

ISABELLA BENNET, 1ST DUCHESS OF GRAFTON
Lely Studio. Reproduced by kind permission of the National Trust,
the Rotunda, Ickworth.

HENRY FITZROY, 1ST DUKE OF GRAFTON
Lely Studio. Reproduced by kind permission of the National Trust,
the Rotunda, Ickworth.

LADY ANNE PALMER IN 1663, LATER COUNTESS OF SUSSEX
Portrait on copper by T. Johnson. Reproduced by kind permission of
Lt.-Col. P. D. S. Palmer.

LADY CHARLOTTE FITZROY, LATER COUNTESS OF LICHFIELD
By Sir Peter Lely. Reproduced by kind permission of the York City
Art Gallery.

JAMES II WHEN DUKE OF YORK
By Sir Peter Lely. Reproduced by kind permission of the National
Portrait Gallery.

ANNE HYDE, DUCHESS OF YORK (detail)
By Sir Peter Lely. Reproduced by kind permission of the Scottish
National Portrait Gallery.

THOMAS, 1ST BARON CLIFFORD OF CHUDLEIGH
By Samuel Cooper. Reproduced by kind permission of Lord Clifford
of Chudleigh.

RALPH, 1ST DUKE OF MONTAGU
By Benedetto Gennari. Reproduced by kind permission of His Grace
the Duke of Buccleuch and Queensberry.

THE ROYAL PROGRESS BY WATER FROM HAMPTON COURT TO
WHITEHALL IN AUGUST 1662
Reproduced by permission of the Master and Fellows, Magdalene
College, Cambridge.

BRIDGEWATER HOUSE, FORMERLY KNOWN AS BERKSHIRE HOUSE AND
CLEVELAND HOUSE, SOUTH FRONT
Etching, about 1700. Reproduced by courtesy of the Trustees of
the British Museum.

MAP OF LONDON 1658. BERKSHIRE HOUSE IS ON THE TOP LEFT, OPPOSITE
ST JAMES'S PALACE
Detail of map by William Faithorne. G.L.C. Map Collection.

ACKNOWLEDGEMENTS

I should like to express my thanks to the librarians and staff of the Bodleian Library, the British Library, the London Library and the Warwickshire County Library, also to Dr Kitching and the staff at the Public Record Office. I am grateful to Dr Levi Fox for allowing me to quote from Sir Francis Fane's Commonplace Book, and to the Librarian and staff of the Shakespeare Centre at Stratford-on-Avon for their courtesy and help. My thanks are due to Miss Rosemary Ashbee, the Archivist at Williams and Glyn's Bank Limited, for showing me the relevant ledgers. I should also like to thank His Grace the Duke of Grafton and Colonel Palmer for their readiness to talk about their families, as well as Sir Oliver Millar and Dr Malcolm Rogers who gave me invaluable help in selecting portraits for the illustrations. As usual my husband has given much thought and time to correcting the typescript and proofs, as has Caroline Tonson Rye of Hamish Hamilton.

It is impossible to acknowledge adequately my debt to the many scholars who have worked on the reign of Charles II. The notes and select bibliography at the end of the book do something to show how much I have benefited from other people's research, also from previous biographers of the Duchess of Cleveland and Charles II, and in particular from the fine scholarship that went into the production of the Robert Latham and William Matthews edition of Samuel Pepys's diary, as well as E. S. de Beer's edition of John Evelyn's diary and correspondence. The quotations from Samuel Pepys's diary are reprinted by permission of A. D. Peters & Co. Ltd.

CHAPTER ONE

THE SILKEN HEIRS

O N A Monday morning in October 1639, Hyde Park in London was the scene of a hard-fought duel between two young Lords of the English Court. Their quarrel was concerned with a fourteen-year-old heiress whose fortune was estimated at £20,000 a year. Mary Bayning was the granddaughter of one of the first of the great City tycoons who had amassed a fortune through the management of shrewd mercantile enterprises all over the navigable world. The young men who were prepared to risk their lives in the forbidden activity of duelling came of a different background. They were creatures of the Court, and the handsome and pious Lord Grandison, who wished to gain Mary's hand in marriage, was a member of the famous Villiers family brought to the fore in the reign of James I by the spectacular Duke of Buckingham. Lord Newark, Grandison's challenger, was Mary's brother-in-law; only a month before he had lost his wife, the young and rich Cecilia who had borne him two daughters. He had perhaps suspected that Grandison had his eye on the Bayning family fortunes rather than on Mary herself, but a reckless readiness to sacrifice his life gave sufficient proof of the suitor's sincerity.

Although no blood was spilt, Lord Newark had the worst of the fight and conceded victory. Within a week the two young men were reconciled, and Mary had made it clear that her affection was settled. At the mature age of fourteen she was considered old enough to know her own mind. Lord Grandison lost no time in marrying her before anyone else should have a chance to snatch away the rich prize. Within a year Mary had given birth to a daughter, Barbara Villiers, a child whose family connections and rich fortunes seemed likely to provide her with a life of plenty and privilege. The Duke of Buckingham's ability to make himself acceptable to kings had brought power and riches to many members of his family; his brothers and half-brothers had all married well and their wives were much favoured by James I—they helped to make his days pass pleasantly as they accompanied him 'in honourable fashion' out hunting, at table, and in his carriage. Buckingham's sister, Susan Villiers, became Mistress of the Robes to Queen Henrietta Maria, wife of Charles I, while her husband William Feilding found himself raised to the peerage as Earl of Denbigh; he later became an admiral despite a singular lack of nautical experience.

While the Duke's relations were swept into lucrative places in the wake of his unprecedented rise to power, gathering titles and perquisites, patents for gold and silver thread, enviable posts as Grooms of the Bedchamber and Keepers of the Royal Parks, Mary Bayning's grandfather had bought his way into the realms of the titled by paying £1,500 for one of the earliest baronetcies. In 1628 he laid out an extortionate £15,000 in order to become a viscount—some said at Buckingham's instigation, and somewhat against his inclinations, although he could well afford the price. During the thirties he augmented his capital by extensive moneylending, or usury, to use the more common contemporary term. He and his son Paul numbered at least ten earls among their clients, and syndicates engaged in ambitious schemes to drain land in the fens borrowed over £60,000 on mortgage.

Members of the Villiers family found favour at Court by virtue of their grace and ability to charm, but Paul Bayning made himself useful in terms of hard cash with the large loans Charles I so urgently needed to make him independent of his troublesome Parliament. And while few of the Villiers family strayed far from the Court, Viscount Bayning travelled abroad to gain experience and education:

> Not like our silken heirs, who only bound
> Their knowledge in the sphere of hawk and hound

as one adulatory versifier put it. Everywhere he went, Bayning created a good impression; he studied at Oxford and was beginning to devote large sums to charitable causes. He seemed destined for a distinguished career, but he died in 1638 soon after returning from his travels. He had already proved himself a considerable benefactor of his own college at Oxford, Christ Church, and the scholars marked his death with nearly thirty elegies dedicated to his young widow:

> Thus big with foreign praises he's come home
> But all was only here to find a tomb.

Lord Bayning had no male heirs, and his death brought to an end the title that had been purchased for such an inflated price. His widow was quickly acquired by the Herberts of Wilton for Philip, Lord Herbert, later 5th Earl of Pembroke, and there was no lack of bidders for the profitable wardship of his daughters who were each 'sold' for £10,000. The main part of the Bayning fortune went to Aubrey, 20th Earl of Oxford, who had wisely married Anne Bayning when she was only ten years old. The fact that the Baynings could still be classed among the *nouveaux riches* mattered little to Herbert, Oxford or Grandison, for it was always wise to inject more money into noble families burdened with property, titles to live up to, and innumerable lesser relations to care for.

In November 1640 Lord and Lady Grandison's infant daughter was christened at St Margaret's, Westminster. She was named after her grandmother, Barbara St John, who came of an ancient family and was related to the Marquess of Winchester. It was her uncle, Oliver St John, who had stipulated that the Grandison title should be passed down to her heirs. It might have seemed that everything was set fair for the young couple and their newly christened daughter. But already, in the autumn of 1640, the prospect had begun to darken for all those who moved in exclusive circles. That summer the Scots had crossed the Tweed and inflicted a humiliating defeat on the English at Newburn. By the terms of the Treaty of Ripon the Scots remained in Northumberland receiving a large sum for every day of their stay.

On his return from the north Charles I drove through the streets of London with his Queen and some of his children, among them his heir, Charles Prince of Wales. The Prince was now a lively dark-countenanced ten-year-old, sternly nurtured in the Anglican morality and piety which his father deemed essential in one who was to become God's deputy on earth. The royal cavalcade was greeted by cheering crowds, but the mood of the new Parliament which met for the first time in November was far from friendly. Many of the King's supporters had not been returned in the keenly-fought elections, and there was little chance that Members would do anything to satisfy the King's urgent need for money until many grievances had been aired. There were tense scenes in the House; Archbishop Laud was taken into custody, the Earl of Strafford was arrested and imprisoned in the Tower while proceedings for impeachment were initiated against other ministers, some of whom fled summarily to France. In the new year there was mounting unrest in the capital, and hostile crowds milled around the Palace and the Parliament House as Strafford's trial drew towards its gruesome conclusion.

Throughout the summer and autumn of 1641 the situation continued to deteriorate amid deepening bitterness between the King and his Parliament. Early in 1642 the Queen left for Holland, ostensibly bent on taking her eldest daughter Mary to be married to William, heir to the Prince of Orange, but secretly determined to raise money and troops for her husband's cause. After she had gone, the King committed the irretrievable blunder of abandoning the capital. He went first to Theobalds, taking the Prince of Wales with him, and then rode on to York hoping to attract supporters as he went. Viscount Grandison was among those who accompanied him, for as a member of the favoured Villiers family he felt that no other course was open to him. 'The very obligations of gratitude to the King of my house are such as my life is but due sacrifice' was how he put it.

The King's hopes of gaining the large munitions store at Hull were foiled when the Governor closed the gates of the city against him. With this setback his hopes of equipping an army began to recede. He had left behind him in London the administrative machinery which might have helped him raise money from his subjects. As it was he had to rely on the friends who had already reduced their resources by earlier loans and gifts. Grandison was among the first to come to his aid by raising and equipping a regiment, although it was no easy task to persuade men to leave their homes at harvest time. The provision of horses was another problem, as Sir Edmund Verney, for one, appreciated. 'I shall shortly send for my coach mares,' he told his steward, adding that when his mare had foaled, the foal was to be knocked on the head and the mare taken to the house, for he could not spare her that summer.

The royal standard was raised at Nottingham on August 22, and on September 9 the Earl of Essex, in command of a rather uncoordinated army of Parliamentarians, marched north to link up with other rebels in the Midlands. Fearful of the enemy's superior numbers, the King withdrew to the Welsh marches, arresting prominent Puritans in the towns he passed through. Grandison led his troop in a lightning raid on Nantwich where he searched the houses of disaffected gentry and annexed their horses. He was typical of many young men who had joined the King's forces and who now spent their days with Prince Rupert, drilling the cavalry in the water-meadows beside the Severn. Most of them were as handsome and as dashing as Prince Rupert himself, but Grandison, though he too possessed these qualities, was in addition so unusually pious that in the opinion of his friend Edward Hyde, 'the court or camp could not show a more faultless person'. His only sin was that he had indulged in duelling in more peaceful times, otherwise, Hyde believed, his justice and integrity were so deeply rooted that nothing could corrupt him; unlike most other people he remained unaffected by the barbarities of war and never once swerved from his principles.

At the battle of Edgehill in October 1642 Grandison's regiment was positioned on the left wing of the King's forces under Lord Wilmot's command. When Prince Rupert's men surged off after the enemy, their horses, well-schooled but unused to war, proved difficult to hold in the heat of the moment; Grandison was among those who managed to reassemble about 200 horses; one of his men recaptured the King's standard. As the King fell back to Oxford, his leisurely march towards London having been halted at Turnham Green, some of the younger Royalists made it clear that they did not intend to spend the winter in idleness. Unready to concede that Rupert held the monopoly in military victories, the Lords Digby, Wilmot and Grandison led an assault on Marlborough with the aim of cutting one of London's main supply lines. On 5 December 1642, after some difficulty, they succeeded in entering the long main street of the town through an inn yard. Grandison then pressed on with his men to Winchester where he expected to find friends and reinforcements. The town was full of 'malignant spirits', to quote a parliamentary propagandist, but the promised supplies predictably failed to materialize, so that Grandison found himself without equipment or provisions to withstand a siege. Making up for royalist inefficiency with courage and enthusiasm, Grandison marched out to do battle with Sir William Waller's advancing forces, but he was driven violently back within the city walls after a fierce skirmish. As usual he behaved impeccably, surrendering at the right time to avoid bloodshed and to obtain better terms for his men. *The Parliamentary Chronicle* had reported that at Marlborough some of the Royalists had acted like 'lustful bloody thieves', but Colonel Fiennes sent a despatch from Winchester admitting that if there had been any pillaging there, it had all been on the parliamentary side, while the men under Grandison's command had shown admirable restraint.

Grandison was imprisoned with his officers at Portsmouth, but before the end of the year he managed to escape, rejoining the King at Oxford where by now crowds of Royalists and their families had gravitated. There were times when the realities of war seemed far away as 'the beauty, wit and flirtation of Whitehall began to enliven the sedate precincts of the Muses', and the only Parliament was 'the rattle-headed Parliament of ladies'. The King dined on capons, partridges, larks and pippin tart, while the ladies paraded through the college quadrangles in their finery. Although for a while the King had to wear purple mourning to mark the death of his mother-in-law, Marie de Medici, nobody could pretend that he was broken-hearted about this particular bereavement. The Queen was still abroad, but he had with him the Prince of Wales, whose careful education had been interrupted by the exigencies of war. Already the young Charles had begun to show signs of deviating from the princely standard of behaviour which his father had planned for him. Charles I saw all monarchs, and himself in particular, as superior beings, half-way between men and the angels, although it may be that his philosophical theory sprang from the deep psychological need of a small man to set himself up on a pedestal, distancing taller mortals. The young Prince, disconcertingly, seemed set to follow a different pattern; he had inherited the Gallic vivacity of his mother and the energetic worldliness of his grandfather Henri IV who had sired a large number of children by a variety of mistresses. Even though he was not yet thirteen, the Prince had begun to show a predilection for the opposite sex, and on one occasion his austere father had administered a sharp blow on his head with a staff, having observed him in church peering through the curtains at a group of ladies in the neighbouring pew.

It is probable that Grandison was reunited with his wife and daughter at Oxford, but in the summer he set off with Prince Rupert in the hope of joining up with Royalist forces from the West Country. Grandison, who now enjoyed the rank of colonel-general, was in command of a brigade consisting of six regiments. Before the end of July Rupert's forces had made contact with the western army, and plans were formed to capture Bristol and its much-needed port. On July 26 the general assault took place, but the Cornish to the south of the city anticipated the plan in their enthusiasm, and did not wait for the two demi-cannons which were to have signalled the attack. Grandison's brigade had been assigned the task of storming Prior's fort, but thanks to the early start the scaling-ladders had not yet arrived, and although the soldiers cheerfully followed their leader into the ditch below the fort, they were soon beaten back by shot and stones hurled down by the defenders. Grandison, who showed great courage throughout the day, persuaded his men to return, and when they were forced to retreat again, he 'took horse to fetch them up a third time, which they obeyed very willingly, following even to the very ditch'. Meanwhile some of the enemy had come down from the fort and one of them shot Grandison in the leg. He refused to have his wound dressed until there was definite news that the outer defences of the town had been breached.

Grandison was taken back to Oxford where he remained until the gangrene which had developed in his wound brought his brief but noble life to an end. Many years later his daughter raised a fine marble monument at Christ Church to commemorate his admirable character and gallant exploits. By then, through an adroit manipulation of her inherited gifts— the Villiers beauty and charm and the Bayning business flair—she found herself in a position to afford this extravagant demonstration of filial respect, but in the autumn of 1643 the eighteen-year-old widow and her three-year-old daughter were forced to live in much reduced circumstances.

CHAPTER TWO

THE TRIBE OF FORTUNE

THE WAR continued, with its sad wastage of life and talent, its bloodshed, pillaging and hardship, taking its toll of the young and privileged men who had lived in and around the Court in the previous decade. The Villiers family, in common with many others, was much depleted by the holocaust. The Earl of Denbigh, husband of Susan Villiers, fell at the battle of Birmingham, and in 1648, when the King was a prisoner at Carisbrooke Castle, the 2nd Duke of Buckingham's exquisite brother Francis was killed at Kingston-on-Thames, defending himself bravely with his back against an elm tree in a foolhardy exploit organized by his elder brother George. It was in this year that Barbara's mother re-married, allying herself once again with a member of the Villiers family, her husband's cousin Charles, 2nd Earl of Anglesea. The union brought about little change in her material circumstances, for such estates as the Earl had inherited were all sequestered, while her own lay in eastern counties under parliamentary control. The rents which would have come to her in happier times were earmarked for the state, and many of the loans granted by her father to help with the fen drainage schemes had never been recovered. Before his death Lord Grandison had several times petitioned the Lords for an enquiry into the ownership of reclaimed lands in the fens, and he had asked that while the cause was under consideration no division of land should be made among the commoners. In 1645 Lady Grandison petitioned again with her stepfather and her uncle Lord Dacre, requesting that the cause which had been interrupted by 'the great affairs of the kingdom' should be revived and a final determination made. But as time went on all hopes of recovering her father's money became increasingly remote.

After the King's execution in 1649 the outlook for all Royalists was more unpromising than ever and every family had to decide for itself how it could best survive under the new regime. Some gravitated to Henrietta Maria's Court in Paris, others joined the new King in Jersey, but the majority remained in England making the best of bad circumstances and awaiting better times. Cromwell shrewdly made it clear to men of property that they would be allowed to enjoy their possessions, if only in a limited way, provided they lived quietly and made no trouble. Already heavily penalized for their royalist allegiance, many landowners felt that their only chance was to lie low and avoid further punishment. It was the young men with little to lose who added spice to a humdrum life by working secretly for the King's cause. They found it convenient to live in the capital, along with other cavaliers who preferred the anonymity of the metropolis to the provinces, where petty officials often made it their business to harass acknowledged Royalists. Although their means were limited and they were bereft of the privileges and power which their fathers had enjoyed, they could at least meet and converse with their friends. The playhouses were closed and public performances of all kinds were discouraged, but the *virtuosi* musicians of the late King's reign were often invited to private *musicales* where they gave recitals accompanied by the high-born ladies they themselves had tutored. The royalist men were able to foregather in the taverns, and in their less drunken moments could practise the well-turned 'ayres' and songs which were relics of the old days at Court.

The Angleseas were among the Royalists who decided that their best course was to settle in London. Although Barbara was brought up in the country until her early teens, she later joined her mother and stepfather at their house on Ludgate Hill. At first she appeared in society in 'a very plain country dress', but in spite of the fact that extravagant clothes were frowned upon during the interregnum, she soon assumed an outfit which was much more suited to 'the gaiety and mode of the town'. This, in Abel Boyer's opinion, added 'a new lustre to that blooming beauty of which she had as great a share as any lady of her time'.

Barbara's good looks and excellent connections provided her with an instant entrée into royalist circles in London where the Villiers family, although depleted by the war, was still much to the fore. George, the 2nd Duke of Buckingham, had joined the King in exile, but several of Barbara's aunts and uncles and cousins were still in England. Many of her relations were involved in active resistance to the government; her uncle, Edward Villiers, was one of the founder members of the Sealed Knot, the official underground movement, and her cousin Alan Brodrick was enlisted into the select ranks after the failure of the Penruddock rising in 1655. He had been recommended by the Countess of Morton, herself a Villiers before her marriage. Edward Hyde, the King's chief adviser in exile, was also connected with the Villiers family through his first wife. He regarded Edward Villiers—'honest Ned'—as one of his most trusted agents.

Ned Villiers and his sister Barbara had both allied themselves with members of the ubiquitous Howard family thus becoming part of a network that included the Dukes of Norfolk as well as the Earls of Suffolk and Berkshire. Barbara had married in 1650 James Howard, Earl of Suffolk, while Edward had wed the Earl's youngest sister Frances. On the death of Penelope Bayning, the Earl of Pembroke had married Catherine Villiers thus extending even further the tentacles of a family that had once been described as 'the tribe of fortune'. Now misfortune might have been a more suitable word to describe their collective situation. Like all other Royalists they had suffered the usual fines and sequestrations; Lord Fairfax had been granted most of the Duke of Buckingham's property in Yorkshire, and Viscount Grandison, who had inherited his brother's title, arrived in Dunkirk in 1657 penniless and without a pass. Alan Brodrick asked Edward Hyde to write to Grandison's mother, Lady Villiers, begging her to send her son two suits of clothes, but Hyde was afraid it might prove dangerous for her to receive a letter from him. Besides, he knew that her fortune was 'never so large as some thought it to be' and now, as a result of her losses, it was quite inadequate to cater for her own needs, let alone provide for her destitute son.

For the younger members of royalist society there was little to do except to snatch what pleasure was available to them. Unless they were involved in the cloak-and-dagger world of the underground movement, with its ciphers and secret letters hidden under floorboards and in the linings of hatbands, they could find little better occupations than carousing and falling in love. The uncertainty of the future seemed to lend an urgency to their self-indulgence. King Charles I had encouraged his courtiers to be chivalrous and dignified, and there had been more than a tinge of puritanism in his attitude. By contrast the children of his courtiers were reacting not only against the severe moral climate of the fifties, but also against the pallid philosophy of their fathers. In this, King Charles II and his childhood friend, the 2nd Duke of Buckingham, were typical of their generation. Buckingham was a brilliant mimic and he entertained the King endlessly with imitations of his father, picking out the over-seriousness and cold piety which Charles II had quite failed to inherit. Edward Hyde, as austere in outlook as the old King, naturally disapproved of such flippancy, as he did of all excess; he would certainly have made no effort to help Lord Grandison in Dunkirk had he not heard that the imprisoned peer had recently put some restraint on himself and retreated from 'that licence to which he had been too much and too long indulgent'.

Bereft of a career at Court or in public service of any kind, the new generation of Royalists sought consolation in the close companionship that often springs up among those who find themselves out of favour with the current government. Barbara Villiers found plenty of other girls in a similar situation to her own. There were the four daughters of the 2nd Duke of Hamilton who like Barbara's father had died as the result of a wound sustained in the King's service, and the eldest, Lady Anne, became one of Barbara's closest friends. Lady Elizabeth Howard, a niece of Barbara's uncle-in-law the Earl of Suffolk, was another member of the fast-living set which attracted all the high-born pleasure-seekers. Barbara herself, by virtue of her birth and background, was inevitably drawn towards the wilder fringe of royalist society. It was soon clear that she had not inherited her father's exemplary character, even though she was amply endowed with the Villiers beauty. In later years it was said that from her earliest childhood she had shown signs of an unusual lasciviousness, and whether this was true or not, she certainly began to attract the attention of 'divers young gentlemen of the town' soon after her arrival in London. She possessed the same kind of magnetism as her cousin the 2nd Duke of Buckingham, of whom it was said that 'if he did but cross a room, all eyes were turned to follow him'. In addition she was as striking as the Duke's younger brother Francis, who had been judged a youth of 'rare beauty and comeliness of person'. She was to be described on more than one occasion as the finest woman of her age, with her auburn hair, her voluptuous figure and her dark blue eyes. The 1st Duke of Buckingham's eyes, which were of a similar colour, have been described as 'the dark blue eyes of the highly-sexed'.

In spite of all her many attractions, Barbara's marriage prospects were bleak. Any young man hoping for advancement was more likely to seek the hand of one of Cromwell's daughters, or the eligible heiress of a parliamentary general rather than the pretty but penniless child of a Royalist long since dead. But this did not mean there was to be no flirtation or falling in love, and it was not long before Barbara embarked on an amorous career that was to last for fifty years and earn her such uncomplimentary names as whore and concubine. Later, when she became mature and seasoned by experience, she grew more calculating, but when she lost her heart to a young widower who arrived in London in the autumn of 1656, she made no attempt to curb the warmth of her passion. Her approach was artless and uncontrolled and she could not hide her jealousy. The man who won her affection, Philip, 2nd Earl of Chesterfield, had, like herself, been bereft of his father when he was only a few years old. Brought up in England by his grandparents, and later in Holland where his mother had been appointed governess to Princess Mary, he had travelled in France and Italy before returning to make a profitable marriage with the eldest daughter of the Earl of Northumberland. After the death of his wife he had again travelled on the Continent, and now, having overcome his grief, he was bent on finding another heiress to augment his fortunes and restore the brief happiness he had found with Lady Anne Percy.

CHAPTER THREE

LOVE ON LUDGATE HILL

THE EARL of Chesterfield was more than likely to cause a stir among the ladies when he appeared in England in the autumn of 1656. He was already much travelled and had undergone a succession of unusual adventures, including a session in the pest-house at Marseilles. He was good-looking, with 'a very agreeable face and a fine head of hair', and several young girls of a royalist background were soon deeply in love with him. He himself, though not averse to indulging in a variety of flirtations concurrently, was not as yet ready to make a marriage unless it brought him some of the advantages he had lost with the death of his first wife. His father-in-law, the Earl of Northumberland, had retained in the new body politic the position of Lord High Admiral which he had enjoyed under Charles I, and Chesterfield now set his sights on the daughter of General Fairfax, who had commanded the parliamentary forces at Naseby with such distinction.

During his absence on the Continent, one of Chesterfield's uncles had seized his estate and he was warned that if he returned to England he would be imprisoned on a trumped-up charge of owing £10,000. He had been forced to live in great poverty and at one time had nearly died of a fever in a lonely cottage, surviving with the help of a Jesuit who took pity on him and afterwards paid for his journey to Paris. It was then that he received the news of his grandfather's death and learnt that he could return to England to take over his estate in Derbyshire.

The outlook for Royalists was now bleaker than ever. In 1655 Penruddock's rising had all too easily been quelled, but the fact that it had happened at all gave the Supreme Magistrate good cause to consolidate his position with the help of repressive measures. Ten major-generals were appointed to ensure the security of the country. A new force of militia was raised with the help of a Decimation Tax charged at ten per cent of the income of all those with royalist affinities. Cromwell's thoughts also turned to the more distant future, taking into account the fact that he himself was not immortal. He had not as yet found any satisfactory way of securing the succession, and his own ill-health added an urgency to any meditations on the subject. There was some speculation as to whether he would annexe for himself the title of king or even of emperor, but he was wise enough to realize that such a move would arouse more unpopularity than it was worth. He was rumoured to have said that 'he was now an old man and cared not for wearing a feather in his cap'. The idea that he could found a dynasty more securely by marrying his daughters to men of aristocratic background was often in his thoughts, and when Chesterfield returned to England he treated the young Earl with unexpected civility, offering him his daughter Frances with a dowry of £20,000 and the promise of a military appointment. Chesterfield, however, felt unable to accept this remarkable offer, and not surprisingly his temerity soon turned all Cromwell's kindness to hatred. Frances, in any case, had a mind of her own, and a determination that matched her father's. She had fallen in love with Lord Warwick's grandson, Robert Rich, and refused to consider any other suitor. Cromwell disapproved of her choice, particularly as Rich was said to be 'given to play and such-like things'. But Frances had her way, and her wedding was celebrated at Whitehall on an un-puritanical scale, with music provided by an orchestra which included forty ungodly violins.

Chesterfield meanwhile pursued his own plan of marrying Mary Fairfax whose father after some disagreements about government policy had retired to his Yorkshire home at Nun Appleton to savour the pleasures of a country life. Mary was a charming girl, serious-minded and intelligent rather than good-looking:

> For she, to higher beauties rais'd,
> Disdains to be for lesser prais'd

as her tutor Andrew Marvell politely put it. The thought of enjoying his estates in comfort drove Chesterfield to the verge of matrimony. His banns were called twice at St Martin-in-the-Fields, and his future seemed settled until all his plans were disrupted by the arrival on the scene of the 2nd Duke of Buckingham. Cold-shouldered out of the King's councils by the disapproving Hyde, the Duke had made his way back to England, bent on restoring his financial position. Having learned that loyalty to the exiled King could only lead to penury, he had decided to regain the Villiers property granted to Fairfax by marrying the eligible Mary. The match had been mooted several years before, and there had even been talk of him annexing one of Cromwell's daughters—becoming 'Cromwell's groom to get his estate' as one commentator put it. As soon as Buckingham appeared at Nun Appleton the whole Fairfax family seemed to be swept off its feet; attractive though Chesterfield was he could not compete with the dazzling Villiers charm. The audacity of his behaviour surprised everybody, including Edward Hyde. 'I was one of those who did not till this very minute believe that Fairfax would or could have given his daughter to my Lord of Buckingham', he confessed.

Chesterfield had a right to feel incredulous when he found that his bride had been taken from him virtually at the altar. He consoled himself by entering wholeheartedly into the heady pleasures of the town, much to the disapproval of Lady Essex, his pious sister-in-law. 'My Lord, these courses must needs undo your person, fortune, and reputation', she warned him; 'for out of those wild persons' company you will not be esteemed, you will lose your most considerable friends, and at last make your own life miserable, and, which is the saddest of all, ruin your own soul; for be confident that those momentary pleasures will have an end, and a sad one too . . . You have a person which might make you and a virtuous wife happy; you have wit, fortune, and all desirable things in this world, and you abuse them all . . .' Philip made a half-hearted attempt to defend himself. 'The world is strangely given to lying,' he told her.

The truth was that the young Earl had taken the town by storm; and Barbara Villiers had not escaped his attentions. He wrote to her from his estate at Bretby in Derbyshire, accusing her of coldness and complaining that the hundreds of miles that lay between them had done nothing but exacerbate his distemper;

No, Madam, the idea I have of your perfections is too glorious to be shadowed either by absence or time; and if I should never more see the sun, yet I should not cease from admiring his light; therefore do not seek to darken my weak sense by endeavouring to make me adore you less:

> For if you decree, that I must die,
> Falling is nobler, than retiring,
> And in the glory of aspiring
> It is brave to tumble from the sky.

This sally into verse evidently removed whatever remained of the coldness which had irked the ardent Philip, and soon Barbara herself was writing in a vein that showed she was completely vanquished:

I sent you yesterday a letter that I think might convince you that I loved nothing besides yourself, nor will I ever, though you should hate me; but if you should, I would never give you the trouble of telling you how much I loved you, but keep it to myself till it had broke my heart.

Her feelings were fanned by jealousy, for she knew that she was not by any means the only object of his affections. 'I am never so well pleased as when I am with you', she told him, 'though I find you are better when you are with other ladies; for you were yesterday all the afternoon with the person I am most jealous of, and I know I have so little merit that I am suspicious you love all women better than myself.'

Barbara's youthful infatuation for a young man whose reputation as a rake was becoming firmly established, naturally caused concern to her family. Chesterfield's sister-in-law had become increasingly worried about his behaviour:

> You treat all the mad drinking lords, you swear, you game and commit all the extravagances incident to untamed youths . . . and the worst of all is, I hear there is a handsome young lady (to both your shames) with child by you.

This Chesterfield denied, and he told his sister-in-law 'to forbear censuring on my account one of the most virtuous persons living'. When such rumours even reached Lady Essex, who lived in seclusion and who knew little about what went on in the world, it was not surprising that reports of what she described as his 'exceeding wildness' were circulating in town. Lady Anglesea evidently did all she could to discourage her daughter, but this did not prevent the headstrong Barbara from making her own arrangements. Her friend Lady Anne Hamilton, who was as infatuated with Philip as she was herself, was a fellow-plotter, and when Barbara wrote to him she told him that she and Lady Anne were 'just now abed together a-contriving how to have your company this afternoon'—a confession which has prompted some commentators to accuse both girls of lesbianism. Their thoughts, however, were all devoted to the irresistible Earl. 'If you deserve this favour', she told him, 'you will come and seek us at Ludgate Hill, about three a-clock at Butler's shop where we will expect you.'

Nobody knows whether the assignation on Ludgate Hill ever took place, but it is certain that Lady Anne's mother allowed her no further chances. 'I came just now from the Duchess of Hamilton', Barbara reported to Philip, 'and where I found, to my great affliction, that the Lady Anne was sent to Windsor, and the world says you are the occasion of it. I am sorry to hear that the having a kindness for you is so great a crime that people are to suffer for it.' From Windsor Lady Anne managed to communicate with the forbidden Earl by letter. 'I thought fit to send you this advertisement, that you may give me some Adieus with your eyes, since it is to be done no other way.'

Lady Anglesea was not wise enough to send Barbara out of London, perhaps because, for a while at least, Chesterfield removed himself to Tunbridge Wells, where he tasted the waters and indulged in other equally therapeutic pleasures. Barbara was relieved to hear from him, since this proved that he still had time to think of her even though the

Spa was frequented by 'a great plenty' of fine ladies. And when he returned to London, nothing was straightforward. He had assured Lady Anne that he had quite given up making love to five or six ladies at a time, but Barbara knew too well that she could not claim all his affection. He had added to his list of conquests her aunt's niece Lady Elizabeth Howard, who wrote to him suggesting a secret rendezvous at the Old Exchange. Despite all his protestations, Barbara was still, for Philip, one of many, and his letters tended to be a trifle over-literary in style—'I hope this letter will be so fortunate as to kiss your hands, and yet I envy it a happiness I want myself' is a fair example. But there is no doubting the intensity of Barbara's feelings, and everything she wrote pulsated with passion. Nothing deterred her. 'I would fain have had the happiness to have seen you at church this day, but I was not suffered to go', she told him; in her frustration she was ready to take the bold step of visiting him at his own lodgings—she did not wait to be invited:

> It is ever my ill fortune to be disappointed of what I most desire, for this afternoon I did promise to myself the satisfaction of your company; but I fear I am disappointed, which I assure you is no small affliction to me; but I hope the fates may yet be so kind as to let me see you about five o'clock; if you will be at your private lodgings at Lincoln's Inn fields, I will endeavour to come.

The only thing that mattered to her now was that she should see him, and she loved him without any restraint—nor was she afraid to tell him so. 'The joy I had of being with you the last night has made me do nothing but dream of you, and my life is never pleasant to me but when I am with you or talking of you.'

In 1657 when the affair was at its height Philip was removed to the Tower accused of wounding Captain Whalley in a duel. He wrote to the worried Lady Essex describing his trouble as nothing more than 'a little disaster' and assuring her that he hoped to be released before the next Quarter Sessions. There was in any case a young man by the name of Roger Palmer who was able to benefit by Philip's incarceration in the Tower. He had fallen deeply in love with Barbara and was determined to make an honest woman of her. His father, Sir James, who had been a Gentleman of the Bedchamber to James I and a favoured friend of Charles I, had suffered the usual fines and depredations, and the fact that Roger had fallen under the spell of a young lady with a tarnished reputation seemed to him the final misfortune. As Abel Boyer put it, 'having strong surmises of the misfortunes that would attend this match, he used all the arguments that paternal affection could suggest to dissuade his son from prosecuting his suit in that way, adding that if he resolved to marry her he foresaw he would be one of the most miserable men in the world'.

Without his father's blessing Roger was unable to embark on matrimony, for he had little money and no chance of gaining any, since life was becoming more precarious than ever for young men of royalist pedigree.

CHAPTER FOUR

MRS PALMER

DURING THE summer of 1658 Royalist hopes seemed to have reached their nadir. The resistance movement lacked unity and strong leadership, and a planned rising in the spring had been foiled almost before it had a chance to become anything but a ripple of talk among the conspirators. After a sadly ineffective showing in London a number of royalist supporters were arrested, including John Mordaunt, a cousin of Alan Brodrick. Edward Villiers, always cautious, had taken the precaution of leaving the capital, and he and his fellow members of the Sealed Knot made it clear that they would not advocate any large-scale rising until help from abroad had actually reached English shores. On the Continent Edward Hyde felt close to despair; he had little faith in the King's supporters and was not afraid to say so. 'They rarely confer together or send advice', he wrote, '. . . but seem so heart-broken as only to wait for some extraordinary act of Providence; if the King were to land tomorrow in England with as good an army as can be hoped for, he would be overpowered as he was at Worcester, while men sit still and wait for the effect of the first battle.'

The death of Oliver Cromwell in the autumn brought none of the expected benefits, and Richard Cromwell stepped into his father's place as if he were the heir to a long-established dynasty. However by the New Year the situation had begun to change for the better as it became clear that Richard lacked his father's strength of character. 'Dick Cromwell . . . sits like an ape on horseback', one of the King's correspondents told him. The obstreperous army chiefs forced him to recall the remnants of the Long Parliament and a Council of State was set up. John Mordaunt urged the King to make capital out of the increasing confusion before the opportunity passed, and attempts were made to strengthen the royalist organization in every county in England. Impatient of the Sealed Knot's perpetual caution, Charles II authorized in the spring of 1659 a new organization called the Great Trust, with Mordaunt, whom he created a viscount, as the leading spirit.

Meanwhile, in spite of parental disapproval, Roger Palmer continued to pay his court to Barbara Villiers. His father had died in 1658 and he was now in a position to take up his modest inheritance. It is probable that Lady Anglesea gave him every encouragement. His royalist pedigree was impeccable, he was sober and steady, and he had been educated at Eton and Cambridge before being admitted to the Inner Temple. Although possibly a trifle dull, he was the kind of suitor any mother would prefer to the perfidious Chesterfield. And so on 14 April 1659, at the age of twenty-four, he married the eighteen-year-old Barbara at St Gregory's, a church built against the walls of the old St Paul's Cathedral, a short way from the Angleseas' house on Ludgate Hill.

It was not long before Roger had to face the fact that there had been some wisdom in his father's warnings—an admission that no young man particularly likes to make. Barbara showed little sign of altering her way of life and she went on seeing Philip. 'The discourses of the world must make me a little more circumspect' she had told him early in their rela-tionship, but however careful she managed to be, it was not long before her husband began to realize what was going on. He threatened to remove her from the capital, probably with the intention of taking her to Dorney Court, the fine half-timbered manor house near Windsor which his half-brother Philip had inherited from their father. Before she left, Barbara wrote a hasty note which may or may not have been an invitation to elopement. It certainly indicates that her marriage so far was hardly proving a success:

> My Lord,
>   Since I saw you, I have been at home, and I find the *mounser* in a very ill humour, for he says he is resolved never to bring me to town again, and that nobody shall see me when I am in the country. I would not have you come today, for that would displease him more; but send me word presently what you would advise me to do, for I am ready and willing to go all over the world with you, and I will obey your commands, that am whilst I live,
>
> > Yours.

Not long afterwards Barbara succumbed to an attack of smallpox. When Chesterfield heard the news he expressed incredulity; he told her that the knowledge she was ill should have been enough to make him sick as well, but he did not find himself ready as yet for another world. 'I am confident', he wrote, 'that if I did go to heaven before you, I should want something there till you came.' Although he had himself survived an attack of the disease some years before and could not make the fear of infection his excuse, he did not rush to visit her. 'Had I thought that my coming to town could either have been serviceable or acceptable to your ladyship, you should certainly have seen at London, not at the bottom of a letter, Madam, your most faithful humble servant,

C.' Probably by this time Barbara was already on the mend, and she made a complete recovery, her beauty unimpaired. As for Chesterfield himself, he had more important matters to attend to than his sick mistress. It was on such young men, 'the new sprung-up Cavaliers' that the King now had to rely, men who were often loquacious and indiscreet, irresponsible because they had never shouldered responsibility, debauched because they had no other outlets. Few of them were cast in a heroic mould, and Chesterfield was more at home making love to a variety of ladies than mustering support for the King in distant Derbyshire. Raising a regiment was not his style; he had up to now exercised his talents in a rather different sphere, indulging, for example, in such pleasures as writing a suitable message for his mistress on the bottom of a chamber pot:

> Narcisse, se mirant en l'onde
> Vit la plus belle chose du monde.
>
> Narcissus, looking at himself in the water,
> Saw the most beautiful thing in the world.

He described his fine house at Bretby as his hermitage, making everybody believe that it was situated in the heart of the wild and rugged Peak District when in fact it stood in a green and fertile valley. 'I am now dismally alone,' he told one of the ladies he had left behind, adding, 'how often do I wish to have you again in my arms, how often do I please myself with the thoughts of the joys we have had . . . I would put off my journeys, my business, or anything to have you here.'

Chesterfield's efforts at organizing resistance were desultory. It was in any case difficult to raise men in the summer months when work was available in the fields for 2s 6d a day. He went so far as to send loyal messages to the King in June, and communicated with other royalist gentlemen in his county. Mordaunt who had himself made a rapid visit to the Continent to discuss plans with the King, assumed that Chesterfield would join with Lord Byron to lead the rebellion in Nottinghamshire and Derbyshire.

August 1, 1659, had been chosen as the day when the Royalists would stage a national uprising. But as usual the government was well aware of the impending danger. The familiar process of arrests and questioning began; all gatherings were banned, the militia was strengthened and horses were commandeered. By the beginning of August many Royalists were already in prison and General Booth's isolated success in Cheshire was not supported by any of the neighbouring counties. Chesterfield had been arrested, not for the first time that year, and taken to Derby gaol.

The London prisons were full to overflowing, and to relieve the over-crowding, many Royalists were let out on bail. Chesterfield was anxious that the Council of State should be reminded of his plight:

> I have been a prisoner six times this year, and am now confined at Derby, though I never was yet accused of anything, and I have found that all my former commitments were only grounded on suspicions, wherefore I do entreat you to move the Council that I may either come out upon bail, or have a speedy trial.

His plea was quickly answered, for on September 2 the Captain of the Troop for the county of Derby was ordered to send the Earl up to London in safe custody. On October 5 the Committee for Examinations ordered his release on parole on his own security of £10,000.

Although for many Royalists the spell of close confinement in the Tower or at Newgate had proved to be brief, they had during that time been given an unprecedented opportunity to meet and discuss future plans. The summer rising had been a disappointment but many lessons had been learned, and it was now possible to evaluate the efforts of the royalist gentry with a view to choosing leaders for the future. Mordaunt was busy sifting through reports concerning imprisoned Royalists whose support was 'highly to be cherished'. Philip Howard, a member of the Catholic branch of the Howard family, and commonly known as the Cardinal of Norfolk, had reported favourably on Chesterfield's behaviour during the summer, so that he was now invited to join the Trust. 'The north needs a person of quality to raise forces and conduct them', Mordaunt told the King.

Mordaunt was working hard to rebuild the Trust, discarding those who had been lukewarm in their support, and trying to persuade others to join him. But he was a tactless man, arrogant and over-sensitive to criticism, and he tended to alienate more people than he attracted. The King, in his instructions to the Trust, had stressed the need for unity, but members were continually falling out with one another, and Brodrick and Mordaunt were always at odds. The King still encouraged Brodrick to work for him in spite of Mordaunt's monotonous warnings that his cousin was too indiscreet to be trusted. At this stage the King felt reluctant to reject any willing offers of help, and if Brodrick and Mordaunt were unable to work together he was happy to let them go their own ways.

After all the disasters of the summer royalist prospects began to improve steadily, and by the new year the King's affairs showed 'so cheerful a face' that the resistance movement began to gain renewed impetus. The uneasy alliance between the Army and the Rump now showed signs of breaking down altogether and the country seemed to be approaching a state of

anarchy. There were scenes in the City reminiscent of the days when
the late King had been locked in a struggle with his Parliament; the
apprentices rioted, and the mob milled around the Parliament House,
demonstrating against the activities of the Army. Monck, although still
expressing loyalty to the civilian authority, had begun to march south
from Scotland with his troops, but nobody yet knew what his real
intentions were.

Feeling at last that hope was truly justified, many Royalists who had
lain low for years now came forward, eager to demonstrate their loyalty.
For the first time they could visualize a future that might bring them
prosperity and preferment. Roger Palmer knew that he must look for a
profitable position at Court if the King were restored, for he was under
no illusions now about the woman he had married or about the money
he would need to give her the kind of life she liked to lead. Gambling on
the possibility of a Restoration, he donated £1,000 to the King's cause.
And through his wife's cousin Brodrick he was provided with a chance
to bring himself to the King's notice at this most opportune of moments.

Alan Brodrick had been working hard to build up his own group of
intelligence agents, enlisting the help of his friends and relations. By
great good fortune Roger Palmer's sister Catherine was married to Mar-
maduke Darrell, whose brother Henry held an important post as principal clerk of the Council of State. Brodrick persuaded Henry Darrell to
pass secret information to Catherine, which she was able to impart to
Roger without arousing suspicion. In this way letters could be intercepted and, even more important, Brodrick was now able to pass on the
details of debates in the Council. It was not surprising that he wrote to
the King on 3 February 1660 in a state of excitement, telling him that
it had 'pleased Almighty God to vouchsafe me an opportunity, almost
equal to my prayers, for the advancement of your Majesty's service in
discovering Councils of State'. He described his new under-cover agents
in glowing terms. Loyalty to the Crown, he explained, ran in the blood;
Roger's father had been a Deputy Chancellor of the Order of the Garter
in addition to all his other positions at Court. The Palmers had suffered
cruelly at the hands of the Parliamentarians—Dorney Court had been
plundered by the soldiery and Sir James Palmer's precious collection of
miniatures summarily annexed by the Surveyor-General. In addition
Sir James had raised a troop of horse during the war at his own expense
and it was estimated that he had spent over £7,000 on his services to the
Crown. With all this in mind, Roger's contribution of £1,000 could be
seen as a considerable sacrifice. 'I must presume to whisper to your
Lordship his condition', Brodrick wrote to Hyde; 'a gay wife and great
expense to a slender fortune in possession, the main of his estate being
in lease for some years to come.'

The King showed himself suitably appreciative. Brodrick had described the new agents as 'persons of great worth and fidelity, hereditary servants to your Crown, by a long series of ancestors'. In reply the King assured Brodrick that he was very well pleased 'to find so much zeal and affection to run in the blood'. To Roger he wrote that he was fully aware that he had 'more than one title to my kindness'. It was evident that the King's interest had been aroused, not only by the qualifications of the worthy Roger, but also by the mention of his wife, who had by now gained the reputation of being one of the most beautiful and the most exciting of all the royalist ladies in London.

CHAPTER FIVE

OUR COUSIN VILLIERS

THE KING'S Court was now at Brussels, and in the spring of 1660 there was a virulent outbreak of smallpox in Flanders, so that it was important to choose messengers from England who had already had the disease. But it was becoming increasingly difficult to find Royalists who were free to cross the Channel, for many of them were working hard for the King's cause, and others, like Roger Palmer, had immersed themselves in the forthcoming elections in the hope of achieving a Parliament loyal to the Crown. Hyde, devoting himself as ever to his master's affairs, found the growing volume of correspondence at times overwhelming; he told Brodrick a trifle petulantly that the King made matters more confusing than ever by addressing his letters using the first letter only of the recipients' names. He could as a result only guess that one of the letters was destined for Roger Palmer 'the husband of our cousin Villiers' as he put it. 'I would never get so much information from you upon several questions I have asked you', he added. Hyde's sense of annoyance was increased by the fact that the King seemed to know far more about the Palmers, and his cousin Barbara in particular, than he did himself. The fact that Mrs Palmer was a young woman of exceptional beauty mattered little to Hyde, but knowing his master's predilections he should not have been surprised that at least one fact about her past life had lodged in the royal mind. 'It seems that the King knows more of it than I do,' he wrote, 'for he told me this day that she had had the smallpox.'

It is probable that Barbara Palmer was at this moment the only member of Brodrick's group who could be spared to carry messages to the King, and now that a restoration had become so unexpectedly imminent, it was certainly politic to have a representative in Brussels. The trusting Roger may have appreciated the advantages of sending a member of the family to the exiled Court, but in spite of all the warnings he had been given he apparently failed to foresee just how much success his wife was likely to achieve. Nothing definite is known about the steps that were taken to convey Barbara Palmer to the Continent, or what were the real reasons for the decision, but it is generally agreed that she did visit the

King, and that he succumbed to her charms without undue delay. He was by now something of a connoisseur of female beauty—he had been credited with sixteen mistresses, an estimate which he himself modestly disclaimed, although flattered that he was thought capable of such a total. Nobody disputed the fact that Barbara was beautiful, and it was equally certain that she was no longer innocent, for she had been schooled in the world of royalist society where nobody thought too much about the future or worried themselves unduly about the consequences of their own actions.

Since January, Barbara's lover had been out of England. Philip had been forced to leave the country after a duel in which he had killed Francis Woolley, the son of one of Charles I's chaplains. The quarrel had arisen, not as might have been expected, over a woman, but on the subject of an unsatisfactory mare that had changed hands for the then inordinate sum of £18. Unable to use up his energies playing the responsible rôle which had been assigned to him as a member of the Trust, Philip had taken up residence in Paris, where he flirted dangerously with the Parisian beauties, while at the same time keeping in touch with his old loves in London. 'Tell me what you think', he demanded of one of them, 'nay tell me what you dream, and whether you must marry your rich neighbour or my lord mare [sic] this winter.' He kept in touch with Barbara, but she knew that she was not the only one to be privileged with his letters, and her loyalty to him did not prove strong enough to resist the flattering attentions of a King—and particularly of a King who seemed likely to regain his throne in the fairly near future.

King or not, Charles II was attractive enough to conquer a woman in his own right. Tall and very dark, with an amenable disposition and a humorous outlook on life, he seemed to possess an unlimited capacity for enjoyment. His susceptibility where women were concerned had given Edward Hyde much cause for concern over the years. Fortunately most of his mistresses—Lady Byron, described by Pepys as 'the King's seventeenth whore abroad', Catherine Pegge and Lady Shannon, to name but a few—had appeared on the scene for a short while only, vanishing into obscurity once they had served their purpose. It was the King's first love, the dark-eyed Lucy Walter, who refused to be cast aside or to be parted from her son. Hyde felt little sympathy towards women who tried to exercise some kind of a hold over the King. Of Lucy Walter he had written irascibly to the Earl of Ormonde in 1657, 'there is much talk here of a certain lady who is at Brussels and many shrewd discourses which will quickly get into England; pray let her go to some other place'.

To prevent 'shrewd discourses' from reaching England proved to be one of Hyde's most difficult tasks. Cromwell's agents did not miss any opportunity of sending back accounts of the whoring, drinking and swearing indulged in by the exiled Cavaliers. In Madrid they believed that Oliver Cromwell would have been ousted long before if only the King had refrained from visiting theatres on the Lord's Day and indulging in other pleasures which were bound to offend the Presbyterians. But it was always Hyde's hope that the King would 'outlive all those scandals and give the world evidence of another temper of mind'. As he put it in 1657, 'We must always remember that Kings are of the same mould as other men, and must have the same time to be made perfect.'

There was still a possibility that marriage might help to bring out the King's latent nobility, and many attempts had been made to ally him with a good woman who would provide him with material prosperity and the blessing of legitimate heirs. There had been talk of marrying him, for expediency's sake, to the Marquis of Argyll's daughter, Lady Anne Campbell, 'a gentlewoman of rare parts and education'. The sober Edward Villiers had even gone so far as to suggest an alliance with Cromwell's daughter Frances, and Fatima Lambert had also been mooted, if not for the King at least for one of his brothers. His mother had been one of the most persistent match-makers, throwing him together on every possible occasion with her niece, the Grande Mademoiselle, whose fortune could have abolished his penury at a stroke, but whose rather grotesque appearance did nothing to win his heart. The King's first cousin Sophie, one of Elizabeth of Bohemia's lively daughters, had at one time aroused his interest, but she had hung back, probably wary of his reputation. She absented herself from the Court as soon as he seemed too forthcoming, with the rather unconvincing excuse that she had a painful corn on her toe. Cardinal Mazarin's beautiful niece, Hortense Mancini, had also been discussed, as well as Henrietta of Orange, and a daughter of the Duke of Lorraine.

Now that the King seemed likely to woo as a reigning monarch rather than as a penniless exile it was as well that nothing had come of any of these schemes, and the last thing that Hyde wanted at this moment was to see him become entangled with a woman. Hyde had spent so many years struggling to keep the King away from the Queen Mother and her Louvrian party that he could only view with apprehension the arrival in Brussels at this inopportune moment of a forceful and intelligent young woman of outstanding beauty. He no doubt did his best to ensure that no rumours of the King's new conquest reached the outside world, and it is possible that Barbara herself tried to be circumspect as she had in the early days of her affair with Philip. All the same, whispers of this latest development were soon circulating in England and before long reached Chesterfield in Paris. He wrote to her expressing shock and amazement.

2

The privilege of loving '5 or 6 at a time' was one that he reserved for himself, and he felt distressed to think that she could prove unfaithful, not only to her husband—that he could understand—but also to himself. He begged her to send him her portrait by way of consolation, 'for then I shall have something that is like you, and yet unchangeable'.

Mystery shrouds Barbara's movements in April and May 1660. Some chroniclers have stated that she returned to England after the King, or even crossed from Holland with him. The most common theory, and the most convincing, is that she preceded him and was awaiting him on his return. Had she appeared when the King, on Monck's advice, made a hasty move to Breda, or had she accompanied him to the Hague when the Dutch invited him there, her presence would have caused a proliferation of gossip, and would certainly have been noted by the observant Samuel Pepys along with other details such as the nature of the King's breakfast and the behaviour of the royal dog.

If Barbara did return to England in April she would have found the country already in a state of pleasurable anticipation. In the Declaration of Breda, the King had promised clemency to all his opponents with the exception of those directly responsible for his father's death, and this had given courage to the waverers, heightening the ardour of Royalists whose spirits had already been raised by favourable election results. The new Parliament answered the letters carried to England by Mordaunt and Grenville with a resolution containing the words that the King had waited so long to hear. 'It is necessary, first of all . . . to restore the King to his people.'

In recent years the spring weather had brought bitter winds that encouraged epidemics, preventing the transport of goods by river and causing an endless increase in the price of commodities, particularly of coal. The summer of 1659 had seen much cattle sickness and consequent hardship among the people. Now, as if to prove to everyone that the Almighty was in favour of the King's return, the weather turned fine and warm—as good an omen as anyone could ask for. Maypoles, the source of much innocent and traditional pleasure until they were banned in the interregnum, now came out of storage; at Deal, they flew the King's flag from the top of the poles for good measure. In Pepys's opinion May Day would be remembered as the happiest there had been for many a year.

There was a temporary alarm when Lambert escaped from the Tower and made for the Midlands. For a short while the 'Phanatiques' held their heads high, until Lambert was defeated and captured at Daventry. The uncertainties of the past months seemed to vanish at a stroke. Every new development was greeted with bells, bonfires, and feasting. 'The calamities of 18 years have now pulled the visor from a blinded world', the Earl of Berkshire told the King. Everybody, from the Lord Mayor to the milkmaid, was talking about the return of the King. For the Royalists the long era of fear and secrecy was over. At last, as Lady Willoughby told Hyde, she would be able to write plainly and without a cipher, the words, 'God Save the King'.

At the Palace of Whitehall attempts were being made to trace the King's possessions, many of which had been sold—it was said that Elizabeth Cromwell had been storing some of them in a warehouse. Mrs Monck was much in evidence, and had taken it upon herself to provide the King's linen, assuring everybody that as it was her old trade she knew what she was doing and would be able to cut the expenses by half. Most Royalists were doing everything they could to ensure their own future, writing to remind the King of the hardships they had suffered on his behalf, establishing themselves in lodgings as near the Palace as possible and making preparations to set off for the coast the moment the news came that the King had left Holland.

Roger Palmer was one of those who could look forward to the future with confidence. He had caught the King's attention at just the right moment, unlike the unfortunate John Mordaunt who had begun to realize that he had 'run all these risques' only to see others overtake him in the King's favour. Roger had been returned to Parliament as a member for Windsor, and it was evident that he would need to find himself lodgings in the vicinity of Westminster. A house in King Street, backing onto the Privy Garden at Whitehall Palace, became available when Cromwell's cousin Edward Whalley fled to New England on hearing that he was to be exempt from the general pardon. It would have been hard to imagine a more convenient site, placed as it was between the Palace and the Parliament House, and the ease with which he gained possession may have surprised even Roger himself, although he was unlikely to quarrel with the good fortune which had given him such a good start in the scramble for preferment.

The King rode into London with his brothers on May 29, his birthday, wearing a dark cloth suit which stood out by virtue of its plainness from all the bright velvets and taffetas, the gold and silver trimmings affected by those who accompanied him. The route from Canterbury had been lined with people and strewn with flowers, 'like one continued street wonderfully inhabited'. As the King rode over London Bridge, bare-headed, church bells rang, trumpets sounded and there was music, publicly played for the first time for years. The enthusiasm of the crowd was likened to the joy of emancipated slaves. It seemed as if the age of austerity was over; the streets were hung with tapestry, the fountains ran with wine. Men and women had decked themselves out in the finest clothes they could find. Ladies who crowded onto every

balcony filled their eyes 'with a beloved spectacle of which they had
been so long deprived'.

Few people had ever seen their monarch before. He had left England
a sweet-faced boy, with eyes that were dark and lustrous, shining black
hair, 'not frizzled but curling into large rings and very ornamental'.
Now the humiliations of exile had left their mark; his hair was streaked
with grey and his face was thin and lined, although his expression softened
when he spoke. Those who could remember his father's remote and
dignified air were pleasantly surprised by his easy affability and unosten-
tatious appearance. When he went to the Banqueting House he was
wearing a plain stuff suit and a plume of red feathers and he listened
patiently to loyal addresses from both Houses of Parliament, perhaps
recalling the days when he had sat in the same hall as a child, watching
his parents perform in lavish masques—dancing in tinselled costumes,
or descending from the ceiling on a cloud. He told Members that he
intended to preserve the laws and liberties of his people and the Protestant religion, and that he would be ready to grant whatever requests his
people were to make. For the time being, however, he was beginning to
feel the effects of his journey. He confessed that he was so tired he was
scarcely able to speak and so having allowed every member of the Lords
and Commons to kiss his hand, he excused himself from a service he
should have attended in the Abbey and retired to bed.

Throughout the night huge bonfires blazed in the streets, consuming
effigies of Cromwell, and the King's health was drunk incessantly. Of
the King himself nothing more was seen. His more pious subjects liked
to think that he spent the night in 'sedate and sweet repose'. Writing
more than a century and a half later, Mrs Jameson asserted that he
retired with Mrs Palmer to Sir Samuel Morland's house in Vauxhall, a
theory convincingly demolished by a later biographer who pointed out
that Morland did not obtain the lease of his house for another fifteen
years. The Earl of Dartmouth, who added a characteristic note to Bishop
Burnet's account, stated categorically that the King 'had' Mrs Palmer
on his first night in London. For, as J. H. Jesse put it, while Roger
Palmer had already made himself acceptable by his loans, his lady had
made herself more than acceptable by her charms. Abel Boyer was equally
definite, writing as he did less than a century after the event; 'this lady',
he stated, 'was prepared for his bed the very first night he lay at Whitehall . . . seduced from her loyalty to her husband and enticed into the
arms of the happily restored Prince'.

CHAPTER SIX

THE RETURN OF THE KING

HOW SOON Roger Palmer realized that his house in King Street had its convenience for others besides himself is a matter for speculation, but it is certain that in whatever manner the King spent his first night at Whitehall, the next morning he had to face up to the realities of ruling a country which for eleven years had kept him away from its shores. On behalf of the peers, the Earl of Manchester had expressed joy at the King's safe return and at the substitution of the rightful sovereign with his royal sceptre for the rule of strangers with a rod of iron. But once the loyal greetings had been made, everybody's thoughts turned towards the new monarch's choice of counsellors and servants. On the one hand the King was faced with Royalists clamouring for rewards and retribution, and on the other with those who had flourished under the Protectorate, but who had accepted in good faith the King's promises of forgiveness and a general pardon. For every Royalist eager to regain confiscated lands and old honours, there was a Parliamentarian fearful of losing property or of forfeiting a place held for years, often with distinction.

While maintaining his usual air of charming approachability, the King was inwardly disillusioned by the exhibition of selfishness and greed which followed the first enthusiastic welcome. When he stopped at Canterbury on his way to London he had been subjected to a jostling crowd of Royalists, all unashamedly pressing their own particular claims to his bounty. At the same time Monck had handed him a list of people recommended for places of trust, and he could see at a glance that it contained only a few royalist names. Charles characteristically pocketed the list without revealing his dismay, later handing it to Hyde who equally characteristically commented that most of the names had been included 'to satisfy the foul and unruly inclination of Mrs Monck'. Although in Brodrick's opinion, Mrs Monck was 'an extreme good woman', Hyde was sure that she came into the same category as ladies like the Queen Mother who were inclined to 'rule the roost'. After all those years when the King had commanded no more real power than the Doge of Venice, he had now become sovereign indeed, and Hyde, having steered him towards this almost unbelievable restoration, had no intention of allowing him to fall under any influence but his own. The King was to rule with the help of Hyde in conjunction with his Council and his Parliament, and without the intercession of any woman—his mother, Mrs Monck or any other.

Many royalist claims were genuine and worthy of recognition. They ranged from those of the grandees who computed their losses at thousands of pounds, down to the humblest of petitioners. One widow, for example, claimed £300 for recent expenses incurred carting ammunition between Tower Wharf and the stores, as well as debts dating back to the late King's time, which with the loss of horses and the high price of hay had left her much impoverished. One petitioner described how he had been 'imprisoned, thrice plundered, sequestered, trepanned and decimated'. The search for employment was as intense as the desire for repayment of debts. One Francis Bowles begged for the Mastership of the Tents; he pointed out that his father and grandfather had been involved in similar work, and he himself had supported the King's cause, being stripped and left for dead at Edgehill. There were far too many petitioners and far too few jobs available, and the situation was complicated by the fact that many Royalists who were most deserving on account of their consistent loyalty were at the same time the least qualified for administrative posts. Those who had retired to their estates in the hope of keeping out of trouble were no more experienced than others who had stayed on in London, turning to drink and debauchery by way of an outlet in a world which denied them the chance to prove themselves. John Mordaunt, who had lost many friends as a result of his untiring efforts to bring back the King by force, had early seen the way things might go. 'I shall not be amazed if I have no fortune at Court', he told his wife, 'for there is chance in that, and few upright persons grow great.'

Hyde insisted that the King must honour the promises enshrined in the Declaration of Breda. Having little faith in the young Royalists who had grown up in troubled times, he gathered round the King a group of sound and on the whole elderly advisers who had gained their practical experience of administration either in the late King's reign or during the interregnum. Preference was given to those who had held the principal offices at the exiled Court. Hyde himself kept his post as Chancellor, relying heavily on Sir Edward Nicholas as Secretary of State, and entrusting the Earl of Southampton, a balanced and reliable Royalist who had stayed in England during the interregnum, with the vital job of Lord Treasurer. Those Parliamentarians who had helped bring back the King were, however, given their just reward. Monck was made Captain-General for life, and his friend, William Morrice, became the second Secretary of State, while Ashley Cooper who had turned his

coat and joined the Parliamentarians in 1644 was appointed Chancellor
of the Exchequer before many months had elapsed.

Experience in exile had taught the King that prevarication could bring
its own reward. Tempting though it had been at times to throw in his lot
with the more active resistance leaders, it seemed now that he had been
right to await events rather than to spill the blood of his supporters in
ill-prepared schemes for a restoration by force rather than by invitation.
Playing off both wings of the underground movement against each other
had formed a habit which was to die hard. He had learnt to dissimulate,
to abandon his principles in the interests of expediency, something his
father had never done and his brother would never bring himself to do.
It was in Scotland that he had first revealed this propensity, as the Scots
themselves had realised:

> We did both sinfully entangle and engage the nation, ourselves, and
> that poor, young prince . . . making him sign and swear a Covenant,
> which we knew from clear and demonstrable reasons he hated in his
> heart . . . He sinfully complied with what we, most sinfully, pressed
> upon him . . . In this he was not so constant to his principles as his
> father.

During the summer months of 1660 the King's tactics worked well.
So long as there were still places to dispense and hope remained that
debts would be paid, petitioners were happy to succumb to his charm and
trust in the future. His policy was to listen patiently, refraining with
infinite courtesy from interrupting, or making vague promises which it
was Hyde's task to break. He thus deflected hatred from himself with the
result that, as Hyde put it, 'those who murmured at the ingratitude of the
King conceived a deadly hate against his ministers'.

Like everybody else, members of the Villiers and Howard families
found themselves caught up in the scramble for preferment as they
struggled to regain the power and position they had enjoyed during the
reigns of James I and Charles I. The fact that Hyde had Villiers connections might have augured well for the family if the Chancellor had
not chosen to select his ministry for their merit rather than their family
background. It was more than unfortunate that Hyde particularly disliked the 2nd Duke of Buckingham whom he had always seen as a bad
influence over the King. The Duke's temporary abandonment of the
royalist cause and his marriage to Mary Fairfax would not necessarily
have counted against him—it was Hyde's antipathy that weighed most
heavily in the scales. The Montagu family, almost as widespread as the
Howards, seemed in a far better position, even though several of its
members had joined the Parliamentary ranks. Edward Montagu, created
Earl of Sandwich for his services in securing the fleet for the King, was

allowed to keep his naval command as Admiral of the narrow seas. His cousin Edward Montagu, Earl of Manchester, although he had fought against Charles I as a parliamentary general, now secured the vital appointment of Lord Chamberlain which gave him an *ex officio* seat on the Council, as well as an overall control of the Household and its many appointments. Such good fortune falling to the lot of men who had actively opposed the King naturally caused dissatisfaction to others who had forfeited their wealth and security in the King's cause, and even more so to the younger generation who had worked hard and undergone imprisonment on account of their activities in the resistance movement.

Edward Villiers deservedly fared better than some, and Hyde evidently saw to it that 'honest Ned' received at least a minor reward in the shape of a post as Knight-Marshal of the Household and a grant of the Manor and Royal House at Richmond. Roger Palmer was less fortunate; reminding the King that he had 'promoted the royal cause at the utmost hazard to life and great loss of fortune', he requested the Marshalship of the King's Bench Prison, but he had to wait several years before his modest wish was granted. Sir Robert Howard, perhaps one of the most able Royalists of the King's generation, had been knighted in a field near Banbury for his gallantry in an encounter with the rebels in 1644, imprisoned at Windsor Castle, and finally invited to join the Trust. His family had remained loyal to the King, his sister Mary had spent several weeks in the Tower under suspicion of being implicated in the summer rising of 1659, and yet in the first hand-out of places all he received was the position of Sergeant-Painter to the King. Just before the Restoration he had printed a collection of his own poems, described by one critic as 'productions of a freezing mediocrity', but although he carefully pointed out that his 'Panegyrick to the King' had been composed during his enforced sojourn at Windsor Castle, there was no niche waiting for him in the new administration.

To find a way of securing the King's favour without recourse to Hyde seemed to many Royalists the best way of insuring against the future. The Chancellor, for all his strict control over affairs of state, had never been capable of governing the King in his leisure hours. When the day's work was done Hyde set off for home, leaving the King to pursue his own pleasures, and Mrs Hyde was actively discouraged from seeking any contact with the corrupting elements of Court life. Since many of them were barred from the corridors of power, the young Royalists of the King's own generation soon began to ease themselves into the circle of brilliant and amusing people which was already forming round the King, foregathering in the evenings, walking with him in the Park and helping him to enjoy his new-found affluence. In Bishop Burnet's opinion, the best way of keeping on good terms with the King was 'the being easy and the making everything easy to him'. There were plenty of people in the summer of 1660 who were prepared to meet his needs. As day after brilliant day passed in the unbroken summer weather, there seemed to be an endless succession of 'festivals and no fasts', and Evelyn thought it strange, after the soberness of earlier days, to see the colourful crowds in the Park and the King himself walking there 'amidst an abundance of gallantry'. Sometimes, after the dust and heat of the day, the whole Court would go down to Whitehall steps and embark on the river. A mass of boats followed the royal barge; there were fireworks, and magnificent 'collations' eaten to the sound of music with instruments and voices.

Having so carefully 'prepared' Barbara for the King's bed, the Villiers family was not slow to follow up its success. The Palmers' house, strategically situated just across the garden from the King's apartments, could be seen as a useful rallying point for all those who had not as yet found their place in the Palace itself. On July 13 Roger and Barbara felt confident enough of their favour with the King to invite him with his two brothers to a musical party in King Street. Working late at Lord Sandwich's house, Pepys became aware of the 'great doings of music' next door, and when he had finished his work he and Lord Sandwich stood for a long while listening 'at the old door that did go into those lodgings'. Pepys had heard that the King's brothers, the Dukes of York and Gloucester, were interested in the pretty Madam Palmer—so much so that they had 'a fancy to make her husband a cuckold'. It was to be a good many months before he and others guessed the real truth.

Soon there were other entertainments besides the *musicale*. One evening in August the King had a 'divertissement of dancing on the ropes before him in the great hall at Whitehall', and this was probably the first entertainment staged in the Hall after the King's return. The masons and carpenters received orders to put up timbers for ropes and degrees for the spectators, so that members of his Court could enjoy the incredible skill of the dancers who had been a familiar sight in the towns where he had lived in exile. He appointed three official acrobats, including the oustandingly handsome and skilful Jacob Hall, and granted patents to Sir William Davenant and Thomas Killigrew to form two theatrical companies. He opened negotiations with foreign musicians, including an Italian opera company that he intended to import, complete with all their scenery and *machine mutationi*.

The King was gifted with unusual energy; unlike many of his friends he was able to rise early however late he had been up the night before, and when he took his dogs out in the Park he usually outstripped those who accompanied him. Sometimes he indulged in a game of tennis

2*

before breakfast, but by the end of the day he was as full of life as ever. His mental alertness surprised those who had feared that he would prove incapable of turning his mind to business. 'We see what he can do when he is resolved', observers had noted when he had visited Fuenterrabia for the Franco-Spanish peace negotiations. Once his interest was aroused he would become completely absorbed, staying on 'as long as his ministers had work for him'.

During the first summer the new administration inspired confidence with its efficient disbandment of the army and its punctual payment of arrears. Its tolerant policies were underlined when, in August, Parliament passed the Act of Indemnity, and the King took the opportunity, since the mood of the Commons seemed so amicable, to remind Members that he was still living on the money they had sent over to him in Holland—'and I thank you for it', he had the grace to add. He told them that he had not been able to give his brother a single shilling or to entertain others as he would have liked to do. 'And that which troubles me most,' he went on, 'is to see so many of you come to see me at Whitehall and think you must go somewhere else to seek your dinner.' This well-phrased appeal produced a sum of over £1,000,000 per annum which seemed more than adequate to a man who for so long had lived on a pittance.

In spite of all the serious work that remained to be done and the problems that were still unsolved, the atmosphere of 'joy and jubilee' continued throughout the summer until in September the popular and promising Duke of Gloucester sickened and died of smallpox. The Court went into deep mourning for six weeks, and the theatres which had just opened were closed down again for several days. The King was stricken with grief, so much so that people were surprised by the depth of feeling he revealed. Then came the disconcerting revelation that the Duke of York, 'always of an amorous disposition', had been secretly married in Brussels to the Chancellor's daughter Anne Hyde who was now expecting his child. Hyde had disapproved strongly when Anne left the security of home to go on a 'gadding journey' to Princess Mary's Court in Holland and now, appalled by her behaviour, which justified all his fears, he threatened to turn her out of the house as a strumpet. The King viewed the situation with amused tolerance and told his brother concisely that he must drink as he had brewed. As for James himself, Pepys was told that he was 'sorry for his lying with my Lord Chancellor's daughter', which was not surprising now that he was surrounded by women who were far more beautiful than the heavy-featured Anne. There was for example Mrs Palmer, and on October 14 Pepys saw the Duke in Whitehall Chapel talking to her 'very wantonly through the hangings that part the King's closet where the ladies sit'. Such

behaviour was not becoming in a man whose wife was due to give birth
in ten days' time.

Although it was evident that Barbara Palmer was never far from the
royal party, Pepys for one did not yet associate her name with the King's.
She was expecting her first child in February, and towards the
end of the year it seems that she began to stay in the background, leaving
the gossips to discuss other matters such as the King's marriage with
Catherine of Braganza, the Portuguese Infanta. Many people had hoped
that the King would select a Protestant wife from among his own subjects, but he informed Hyde himself that he was unable to find any
among them who 'pleased him to that end'. If he wanted beauty he did
not have far to look, but none of his subjects was able to bring him in
her dowry trading facilities in the Caribbean and the town of Tangier
which dominated the Mediterranean, not to mention £500,000 in cash.

The French favoured the match, while the Spanish did everything
they could to discourage it. One story circulating around London had
the Spanish Ambassador scattering seditious literature from a window
onto a group of ladies so that they could read how Catherine was deformed
and suffered from many diseases. There were certainly rumours that she
was incapable of bearing children, and Hyde was later accused of favouring the match in the hope that she might indeed prove infertile in which
case one of his own grandchildren would inherit the Crown. He himself
vehemently denied the charge, reminding everyone that the match had
first been mooted in 1644 when Catherine was a child of six, and insisting
that it was the Earl of Manchester who had now revived the idea. Not
that Hyde disapproved of the choice, for he knew that Catherine was by
nature devoid of what he described as that 'meddling activity which
many times made those of that religion troublesome and restless when
they came into a country where another religion was practised'. Hyde
was of course referring to the Queen Mother whose strong personality
had in his opinion been the cause of many of the old King's problems.
His unpaternal reaction to his daughter's marriage with the heir to the
throne may well have been caused by the fear that people would accuse
him of the very crime which he himself most condemned—the attempt
to gain power with the help of female influence.

The pro-Spanish Earl of Bristol was doing all he could to discredit
Catherine; he had even made a journey to Parma to cast an eye over two
princesses either of whom might have provided a suitable alternative.
But having viewed them on their way to church he had to admit that
they had little chance of gaining the heart of a King 'by whom personal
beauty was so much valued', since one was corpulent and the other
excessively ugly. The Queen Mother, for once agreeing with Hyde,
approved of the Portuguese match. She knew that Catherine was a

conscientious Catholic and she hurried over to England with Henrietta, better known as Minette, to do what she could to promote Charles's marriage and disrupt James's. As it was, she found that the Portuguese match was well under way, and she had to accept the fact that her son James had irrevocably attached himself to the Hyde family. Like everyone else who needed money she was forced to treat Hyde with respect. She managed to greet him with a cheerful countenance, although he himself was sure that her 'implacable displeasure remained', and she even brought herself to receive her new daughter-in-law during her visit to England.

The death of the King's sister Princess Mary cast a gloom over the royal Christmas. She had been ill for five days with smallpox, measles or the spotted fever, 'the physicians disagreeing whether'. There was further anxiety when Henrietta, the King's last surviving sister, fell dangerously sick on the way back to France with her mother. The prospect of yet another tragedy caused the poet Andrew Marvell to beg that the Almighty would 'stay his hand from further severity in that royal family whereon the nation's well-being and well-fare is so much concerned'. Minette recovered and continued on her way, but bereavement, anxiety and the slow ebb of popularity had already taken the bloom off the first ecstasy of the Restoration, and there were some who believed that the King was already being made to pay for his frivolity and devotion to pleasure. He came hurrying back from the family parting at Portsmouth to deal with a rising of the Fifth Monarchy men, described variously as 'discontented schismatics', 'desperate fellows' or 'fierce enthusiasts'. The rebels, led by a wine-cooper named Venner, turned the season of Epiphany into a brief episode of terror. Aldersgate, Cheapside and Threadneedle Street rang with the cry of 'No King but Christ'. The self-styled soldiers of King Jesus vowed never to sheathe the sword till 'His Kingdom should be made triumphant' and the powers of the world no more than 'a hissing and a curse'. But after fighting it out with the trained bands they were finally overcome in the neighbourhood of Cripplegate.

Venner's rising was only a minor outbreak but it introduced the first serious feeling of uncertainty since the return of the King, providing ammunition for those propagandists who believed that he had been too tolerant to his enemies. The new Parliament which met in May 1661 was more belligerently cavalier in outlook than its predecessor, and the King had to remind Members that he was still under an obligation to honour promises solemnly made at Breda. The parliamentary session opened on May 8 and in his speech he imparted news which he believed the assembled Members would be glad to hear. He said that everybody had been telling him for a long while that it was time he married, and now he was now able to inform them that he had finally selected the Portuguese Princess whose name had been coupled with his so long ago. He realized that there might be some criticism on religious grounds, but, he told Members, if he were to wait for the perfect match, they would live to see him an old bachelor.

Although some people did murmur that the King would be better married to a Protestant, the size of Catherine's probable dowry tended to overcome all scruples, and everybody agreed that the sooner he settled down to matrimony the better. On June 30 the Portuguese Ambassador was summoned to Whitehall; the King greeted him with great ceremony, treated him to a large dinner and sent him on his way to Lisbon, expressing the hope that he would speedily return with a satisfactory settlement. Having done his duty, the King did not allow the prospect of marriage vows to darken the rest of the summer. There were times when Hyde, now raised to the peerage as Earl of Clarendon, noticed that the King looked 'perplexed and full of thoughts', but for the most part he seemed bent on forgetting all his cares and of extracting the maximum enjoyment from his last months of freedom.

CHAPTER SEVEN

THE JOVIAL CREW

O N 25 FEBRUARY 1661 Barbara Palmer gave birth to a daughter. Her husband seemed happy to acknowledge the child; he showed her great affection and took her down to Dorney where that year a new porch was added to the church. She was christened Anne. Although she had blue eyes like her mother, some people thought she bore a remarkable resemblance to the Earl of Chesterfield. Others were quick to point out that her birth took place almost exactly nine months after the King's first night in London. Such theories and calculations gained impetus when Barbara Palmer recovered quickly from her accouchement and took her place openly at the King's side on every possible occasion.

On April 20, just three days before the coronation, Pepys saw Barbara Palmer when he went to a performance at the Cockpit Theatre of *The Humorous Lieutenant* by Beaumont and Fletcher. 'My pleasure was great', he noted in his diary, 'to see . . . so many beauties, but above all Mrs Palmer with whom the King doth discover a good deal of familiarity.' On July 23 when he saw her at the Theatre Royal in Vere Street, he referred to her for the first time as the King's mistress. The diarist was completely smitten with her beauty. The badness of the play or the incompetence of the actors mattered little provided he was able to catch a glimpse of her. 'I sat before Mrs Palmer, the King's mistress, and filled my eyes with her, which much pleased me', he wrote. One evening in August he took his wife to see *The Jovial Crew* by Richard Brome which he described as a 'play full of mirth'. The King, the Duke and Duchess of York and 'Madame Palmer' were all there, and Mrs Pepys 'to her great content had her full sight of them all'. In September when they saw *Bartholomew Fair* they sat as close as possible to the royal brothers, but as usual Barbara Palmer was the main attraction. 'I can never enough admire her beauty', Pepys confessed.

Some people optimistically prophesied that once the novelty had worn off, the King would put his pleasures into perspective and would settle down to a more sober way of life. But as yet there was less sign than ever of the reformation that so many hoped to see. He played tennis, went to parties, sailed down the river in the fine yacht presented to him by the Dutch East India Company, and took part in races with other pleasure-boats. Thanks to his patronage the theatre, viewed by many of his subjects as a breeding-ground of vice, had become the focus of the fashionable world. The King's Company under Killigrew's management, and the Duke's Company under Davenant's, were by now well established in converted tennis-courts in Vere Street and Lincoln's Inn Fields. The magnificent perspective scenery, the lavish costumes, and the music which was introduced on every possible pretext, came as a revelation to a younger generation which had been starved of dramatic entertainment. The attraction was even greater now that the theatres sported 'women-actors as beyond sea'. During his exile the King had become used to seeing ladies on the stage, and he no doubt encouraged the innovation. The Restoration audience was in no mood to appreciate the skills of actors who had long ago shed their boyish charm:

> For to speak truth, men act, that are between
> Forty and fifty, wenches of fifteen;
> With bone so large and nerve so incompliant
> When you call Desdemona, enter giant.

Desdemona had in fact been played by a woman before the end of 1660, and by the summer of 1661 several actresses were beginning to make a name for themselves. The new dramatists took to writing parts specially for them, often giving them a chance to dress up as boys so that they could show off their legs to good advantage. Dancing became an integral part of most performances, and the women players tended to be judged on their ability to execute the brilliant and complicated jig without which no comedy seemed complete. It was not surprising that when the players went down to Oxford to perform in the taverns during the summer season of 1661, the women 'made the scholars mad, run after them, take ill courses'.

Inevitably the theatres were blamed for inciting their courtly audiences and encouraging lechery, which was only one of the many depravities that seemed to be on the increase. Pepys listed the vices of the Court as 'swearing, drinking and whoring', and the sad fact was that the King seemed to be leading the way. Evelyn was pained to observe, during the revelry at Court on Twelfth Night in 1662, that it was the King himself who opened the proceedings by throwing the dice, letting £100 speedily slip from his grasp. 'Sorry I am', Evelyn had to say, 'that such a wretched custom as play to that excess should be countenanced in a Court which ought to be an example of virtue to the rest of the kingdom.' It was becoming apparent that the reaction against Puritanism had gone too far. The old fear was voiced that men were growing effeminate, imitating women with their long periwigs and 'short wide breeches like petticoats', while the women were all the time growing more masculine—riding, tippling and playing at cards just as deeply as the men. Clarendon accurately prophesied that people would turn to debauchery in the hope of finding favour with the King and he put the point uncompromisingly in his speech at the dissolution of Parliament:

> If the old reproaches of Cavalier, and Roundhead and Malignant be committed to the grave, let us not find more significant and better words to signify worse things. Let not piety and godliness grow into terms of reproach.

Clarendon genuinely feared the effects of a reaction against republican authority, and the association of loyalty with 'profligate excesses'. He was not alone; on April 6 a Canon of Christ Church had the temerity to preach before the King on the subject of adultery, although his text had not given him too much justification for introducing this topic. Many others were saying openly that the money the King had gained by the unpopular measure of ceding Dunkirk to the French was being squandered on idle amusements, and particularly on his mistress. There had been rumours as far back as the summer of 1661 that Mrs Palmer was with child, and in the new year of 1662 the truth had become all too apparent. It was also clear that the unfortunate Roger had become a husband only in name. In spite of the fact that negotiations for his marriage had gone ahead, the King showed no sign of overcoming his infatuation. Most people were beginning to accept the fact that his levity was more than a veneer of youthful high spirits, and it was significant that when he was described in a collect for the Parliament as 'our most religious King', the phrase caused a ripple of amusement. Clarendon might have gone on hoping, against all the evidence, that the King would in the end extricate himself from his youthful companions and self-indulgent way of life, even if the change of heart was slow in coming. There was still a last chance that a good wife might be able to work the miracle; one encouraging rumour had it that when his mistress asked him what he expected her to do on the arrival of the Queen, he replied, 'You must stick to your husband as I intend to stick to my wife.' While the rest of the world waited, fearful or fascinated, to see what effect the arrival of the Portuguese Infanta would have on the King's relationship with Barbara Palmer, Clarendon worked diligently to prevent her usurping Catherine's position in advance. He had not put all his efforts into obtaining a shy and retiring Queen only to allow a woman who traded on her beauty to exercise an unconstitutional hold over the King. For him women with their gossiping ways were nothing but a hindrance to those who steered the ship of state. 'There are so many avenues where women and others hearken' was a typical complaint.

Clarendon was still troubled by petitioners, and particularly by old Cavaliers who grew more importunate the more they began to realise they might never be repaid for all they had lent and lost during the Civil War. The Earl of Worcester, for example, pestered him with his constant reminders that Charles I had promised him land worth £40,000. 'As troublesome as you take him to be', Clarendon told the King, 'he is an angel in comparison of his wife, and his brother John, who torment me every day.' The prospect of a Queen had given new encouragement to the place-hunters, who were already jostling for lucrative places in the Household. Whether through her niece's intervention or not, Barbara, Countess of Suffolk, had been named as a probable Lady of the Bedchamber, and the Catholic Philip Howard had a good chance of being chosen as her chaplain. Although several of Mrs Palmer's relations had played a prominent part in the coronation—the Earl of Suffolk had acted as Earl Marshal, another uncle, the Earl of Oxford, had carried the sword of state, and her cousin the Duke of Buckingham had borne the orb—the Chancellor saw to it that none of them gained any material benefits as a result of her influence. The Duke of Buckingham, by virtue of his own charm and persistence, had so far proved the most successful, and in April 1662 he was admitted to the Privy Council; Sir Robert Howard, ambitious and astute, had made valuable use of the contracts that came his way, in his capacity of Sergeant-Painter, for redecorating the royal Palaces and coaches, and for gilding and painting yachts and barges. He had acquired the profitable post of Clerk of the Patents in Chancery, and when appointed to the Committee charged with examining the claims of those wishing to recover goods and money appropriated during the interregnum, he had seen to it that his family's valuable right to collect fines known as the Green Wax had been swiftly renewed. The fines were levied by the sheriffs whose documents were sealed with green wax. Among the first to appreciate the potential of the theatre as a propaganda machine, he had invested money in Killigrew's company, advancing, in December 1661, a quarter of the cost of a new playhouse to be built on a site in Bridges Street. But most of the Howards and Villiers had neither the money nor the financial acumen to better their prospects in such ways, and they still looked to Barbara Palmer as their best advocate.

Although her hold over the King was so strong that there were doubts as to whether he would be able to detach himself from her once he was married, it was as well to ensure her position at Court alongside her aunt in the Bedchamber. The first step was to see that she was admitted to the ranks of the titled. The King was prepared to co-operate; he was just as anxious as anybody else to make sure that Barbara would have plenty of opportunity to frequent the Court after the arrival of the Queen. The problem was to persuade Clarendon and his cronies to prepare the warrant. In this the King was prepared to show them that for all their experience and administrative expertise, they were his servants rather than his masters. Writing to Sir William Morrice, one of the Secretaries of State, on October 16, the King requested that a warrant should be prepared with the date blank, 'for Mr Roger Palmer to be an Irish Earl, to him and the heirs of his body gotten on Barbara Palmer his now wife'. The King added a peremptory postscript. 'Let me have it as soon as you can—C.' The King's servants were in no hurry to comply with this particular order, and let it lie on the table for at least a month. On the morning of November 8, he demanded a warrant creating Palmer Baron of Limerick and Earl of Castlemaine. 'And let me have it before dinner', he added. Pepys saw the Patent at the Privy Seal Office on December 7 and did not fail to notice that it was only Lady Castlemaine's heirs who were to be honoured, 'the reason whereof everybody knows', Pepys added. The long-suffering Palmer was himself no longer under any illusions. Although he always regarded Anne as his own child, he knew that he had lost his wife, gaining in return the earldom of a distant village in County Kerry, while as a small compensation his half-brother was granted a knighthood and the appointment of Cupbearer to the King.

Roger Palmer did not assume his title for some while, knowing too well the price he had paid for it and, to quote Clarendon, 'the brand of such a nobility'. Clarendon, for his part, was more determined than ever to block the advancement of the woman he from now on never referred to except, with more than a touch of sarcasm, as 'the Lady'.

CHAPTER EIGHT

THE QUEEN AND THE ENCHANTRESS

THE KING, writing dutifully to his future wife in the summer of 1661, had told her that he longed to see her 'beloved person' in his kingdoms. When confronted with her portrait he said rather more guardedly that 'such a person could not be unhandsome'. In Portugal Catherine began to prepare herself for the new life which lay ahead of her. Before her betrothal she had hardly been allowed to leave the royal palace, and even now her excursions were limited to some sedate visits to the shrines of local saints. She practised walking in high-heeled shoes in the English fashion, and waited for the fleet under the Earl of Sandwich's command which had been sent to fetch her.

In England the Court was already divided between those who hoped to find favour with the new Queen, and others who suspected that the easiest road to success lay in courting the King's mistress. On January 22 Pepys wrote, 'There are factions, (private ones at Court) about Madam Palmer. What it is about I know not, but it is something about the King's favour to her, now that the Queen is coming'. Pepys had evidently got wind of the controversy concerning the new Countess's appointment as a Lady of the Bedchamber. The Duchess of York sided with her father, all her ladies followed suit, and many others who had made up to the Countess when her position had seemed unassailable now shunned her. The Duke of Buckingham's sister, the widowed Duchess of Richmond, compared her publicly to Jane Shore, and expressed the hope that she would come to the same end, for Jane had been Edward IV's mistress and had ended her life in poverty— legend had it that her body had finally been flung on a dunghill.

Lady Castlemaine went on visiting the theatre and in general showed a marked reluctance to quit the centre of the stage. Her beauty was unimpaired despite her condition, which destroyed the hope that the King might succeed in detaching himself from her before the Queen's arrival. In May she announced that she intended the birth of her child to take place at Hampton Court, an event which seemed likely to coincide with the royal honeymoon in the same Palace. Lady Sandwich confided in Pepys on May 14 that she was afraid 'my Lady Castlemaine will keep in still with the King'. Pepys, for his part, was afraid that she would not, and fervently hoped that she would, 'for I love her well', he wrote.

On Sunday April 13, after celebrating Mass, Catherine set out from Lisbon. Her journey was stormy and she was miserably seasick. She passed the time in her own cabin, listening to Lord Sandwich's music and hardly ever appearing on deck. Meanwhile, in England, the royal apartments were being refurbished with a fine bed presented by the States of Holland, a looking-glass provided by the Queen Mother, and a multitude of pictures. Every day crowds of people left London for Portsmouth to make sure they would be there in time to watch the Queen's fleet sail in. The King was working hard to clear any outstanding matters, so that all Acts of Parliament could be passed before he left town. Members did not altogether appreciate being made to 'huddle' over business in a succession of late-night sittings, and they would probably have felt even less willing had they known that in spite of all the hard work they were expected to do, the King still found time to dine with Lady Castlemaine every night when work was finished.

Pepys heard about all the goings-on in King Street from Sarah, Lord Sandwich's housekeeper. Although in Pepys's description she was old and very painful she proved to be a fertile source of information, and it was she who told him the famous story about the King's behaviour on the very evening that his Queen arrived within sight of English shores. The event had been marked by the firing of a salvo of guns from the Tower, and most Londoners celebrated by lighting a bonfire outside their door. There was, however, no bonfire outside Lady Castlemaine's house and as Sarah told Pepys, 'the King and she did send for a pair of scales and weighed one another; and she, being with child, was said to be the heaviest'.

After one more long session which lasted until nine o'clock in the evening, the King announced the prorogation and left immediately for Guildford where he spent what remained of the night. Lady Castlemaine stayed behind, and for several days she was so disconsolate that she did not leave the house. When Pepys went to the theatre to see *The French Dancing Master* he had one of his much prized sightings, and he spent the evening as usual gazing at her, although his pleasure was spoiled 'to see her look dejectedly and slighted by people already'.

At least the Queen was greeted at her lodgings in Portsmouth by Barbara Castlemaine's aunt, the Countess of Suffolk, which seemed to ensure that the family stood a chance of dominating the new Household. Clarendon, however, still did his best to control the King's actions, even though he himself had remained in London, and he had seen to it that a Bishop was in attendance at Portsmouth. 'He must marry you before you go to bed', Clarendon bluntly told the King. As it was Charles felt so sleepy after managing to snatch only two hours rest at Guildford that he did not feel tempted to consummate the union, and Catherine was suffering from a sore throat so was no more enthusiastic than he was. But the King was pleasantly surprised by his bride's appearance and was relieved to find that she did not suffer from any deformities. There was nothing about her, he assured Clarendon 'that in the least degree can shock one'. She was slim and small and inclined to paint her face in the Mediterranean fashion. One report described her as 'short, but lovely, fair and black-eyed', although it had to be admitted that with 'her teeth wronging her mouth by sticking out a little too much' she was no great beauty. The King told Clarendon that he was confident their two humours would agree very well together, and in a later letter he wrote encouragingly, 'I think I must be the worst person living (which I hope I am not) if I be not a good husband'. When the royal couple returned to London most people were overjoyed to see that they appeared to take great pleasure in each other's company; at Hampton Court those who saw the Queen found her handsome and discreet, and thought the King seemed pleased with her, which, as Pepys noted, was likely to put 'Madam Castlemaine's nose out of joint'.

Although it seemed that Lady Castlemaine did not intend to carry out her threat of giving birth to the King's child at Hampton Court, there were many people who still felt uneasy about the situation. Sir John Reresby, the Yorkshire diarist and M.P., was of the opinion that it was 'very discernable that the King was not much enamoured of his bride'. Certainly the new Queen, brought up in what almost amounted to a nunnery, and lacking the good looks possessed by other women he had known, 'had little about her capable to make the King forget his inclinations to the Countess of Castlemaine'. The Earl of Chesterfield was one of those who could have wished that Catherine had the power to wean the King away from his former love, for he himself had never been able to eradicate his affection for Barbara, and had written to her as late as 1661 in his old romantically passionate vein:

> Let me not live, if I did believe that all the women on earth could give me so great an affliction as I have suffered by your displeasure . . . do not suffer one to perish who desires only to live upon your account. Besides, naturally I hate dying, and it is one of the last things I would do to show my passion.

Chesterfield knew too well that his road to favour was barred by the King's jealousy of his past association with Barbara. If the mistress were to be superseded, there was no doubt that his own prospects might be brighter. He could not, however, feel too optimistic; although he had been told that Catherine was devout and discreet and had beautiful hands and excellent eyes, he had to admit that 'when all was said and done, this would hardly be likely to make things run in the right channel; but, if it should, I suppose our Court will require new modelling, and then the profession of an honest man's friendship will signify more than it does at present'. Pepys would have agreed. He had an argument with his aunt who had tried to make out that the Queen was good-looking —but then Pepys tended to disagree with his aunt on principle. 'If my nose is handsome, then is hers', he said. He reserved his admiration for Lady Castlemaine; on May 21, as he walked across the Privy Garden he saw 'the finest smocks and linen petticoats of my Lady Castlemaine laced with rich lace at the bottom, that mine eyes ever beheld; it did me good to look at them'.

For a while the King 'carried things decently'. He remained at Hampton Court with his wife, and was so kind to her that she showed unmistakable signs of falling for the dark-countenanced man whose language she scarcely understood. Lady Castlemaine was left alone, awaiting the birth of her child, and it was impossible for the King to visit her. With the Court away, Whitehall and Westminster were almost deserted, much to the chagrin of the tradesmen, whose livelihood was badly affected. Nobody knows whether Roger, like everybody else, had decided to leave town, but in any case, as soon as Barbara gave birth to a son, he asserted his right to have the child christened in the Catholic faith, to which he had recently been converted, a move which Abel Boyer attributed to 'the misfortunes of his bed'. Six days later, the King came up to London for a second ceremony which was held at St Margaret's, Westminster, and performed this time by an Anglican clergyman rather than a priest, with a proviso that the child had not been previously christened. The King and the Countess of Suffolk stood as sponsors and the child was named Charles Palmer, Lord Limerick.

The second ceremony provoked a violent quarrel between the Lady and her husband. Flying into one of the rages for which she was to become famous, she removed herself to her uncle's house at Richmond, taking with her everything she could lay her hands on, every dish and cloth, all her plate and jewels and most of the King Street servants. Roger admitted defeat, left as he was with a virtually empty house and no staff except the porter, the only minion she had the grace to leave behind. At the end of July there were rumours that he was planning to leave for France with the intention of entering a monastery. He took the wise precaution of executing a bond with his wife's relations, the Earl and Countess of Suffolk and her uncle Lord Grandison, binding them with the sum of £10,000 to indemnify him 'from all and every manner of debts, contracts, sum and sums of money now due, or that shall grow due from any contract or bargain made by the Right Honourable Barbara Countess of Castlemaine or by any person or persons authorized by her'. As far as the family was concerned, £10,000 was a small guarantee, provided they could keep their exotic advocate available for the King's use.

Some said that the Lady's rage was simulated and that her decampment to Richmond had been accomplished simply to make it easier for the King to visit her so long as he remained at Hampton Court. It would have been unwise, at this stage, to be too blatant, for he was still hoping to have his mistress included in his wife's list of Household appointments before the Court returned to London. He had so far behaved with such discretion that for a brief time Catherine believed he had fallen in love with her just as she had fallen for him. The torment she endured when she became aware that there was another woman in his life is almost unimaginable. In all probability the King was not unmoved by the suffering he knew he would be bound to inflict on her; sometimes his face was clouded, and those who had the temerity to remind him of his conjugal duties were likely to find that he was extremely touchy on the point.

The list of posts in the new Household remained in suspension, for the King refused to confirm any appointments until Lady Castlemaine's nomination had been accepted. When he handed Catherine a list which included the mistress's name, she showed more awareness of the situation than he had bargained for and promptly crossed it off. The King, who could be adamant when he chose, equally promptly restored it. Already, after only two months of marriage, the couple found themselves facing an uncomfortable impasse. Pepys heard that 'the King was angry and the Queen discontented a whole day and night upon it', but that as a result of it the King had promised to have nothing more to do with Lady Castlemaine. This Pepys viewed with scepticism. 'I cannot believe', he wrote in his diary, 'that the King can fling her off so, he loving her too well.' He expounded this theory in a letter to Lady Sandwich, referring to the mistress as 'the lady I admire'.

It appeared that while the King had been away meeting his mother who had come over to England to meet her new daughter-in-law, 'malicious persons', named by some as Portuguese priests and friars, had taken it upon themselves to enlighten the Queen who so far had been unaware of the King's infidelity; she had up to then treated Lady Castlemaine graciously and only a few days before had even allowed her to kiss her hand. The King returned from Portsmouth to be told that his wife had vowed never to see Lady Castlemaine again; not only would

she not allow her in the Household—she refused to admit any of her
relations either. Her reaction produced an atmosphere of coldness, even
though the situation eased slightly when the King promised to end his
relationship with the Lady. As the Venetian Resident in England, Fran-
cesco Giavarina, put it to the Doge, 'if the old Queen does not arrange
matters, as is expected, the bride will not be happily placed in her relations with the King'. For once in his life Clarendon may well have
wished that Henrietta Maria could exercise some control over her
son.

The Queen had good enough cause to feel unhappy without discovering that her husband's affection was already settled on another
woman. Her health was not good; she had no appetite and the English
water seemed to her like 'so much poison'. She was totally confused by
the crowds of new faces around her, and altogether she was so out of
sorts that at one time they feared she was sickening for smallpox. When
she showed some signs of recovery, however, the King seemed pleased
and he took her out on the river in a gondola which had been sent as a
present from the Doge. Then he himself fell ill for a while, and when
Clarendon reported to Ormonde that the King had completely recovered,
he could not resist adding, 'I wish he were free from all *other*'.

As soon as he sensed that the Queen was in a better mood, Charles
decided to introduce the Lady into her presence himself. Catherine
immediately fell into a faint, much to his annoyance, and he callously
dismissed this show of distress as an act of defiance. He complained
to Clarendon about her perverseness and bad temper, not to mention
the uncooperative attitude of the Portuguese attendants she had brought
with her. They did nothing but complain about, among other things, the
nastiness of London's drinking water, recalling with nostalgia the sweet
mountain streams which were piped in aqueducts to Lisbon. They
were shocked by the free and easy manners of the English Court, while
the English for their part were repulsed by the Portuguese with their
ugly faces, their quaint old-fashioned dress and their excruciating
'Portugal music'. With their elementary English and prim outlook,
they were of course quite incapable of appreciating the esoteric jokes
and witty exchanges which were the delight of the King and his circle
of friends.

Everyone had known that there would inevitably be misunderstand-
ings between two people who had been brought up in different tradi-
tions and with little knowledge of one another's language. Giavarina
sagely pointed out that England's 'remarkable climate' was unlikely to
suit anyone from a warmer country, and particularly the Queen, with
her delicate constitution. The general hope was that given a little time,
the royal couple like the King's father and mother would overcome their

differences and learn to love each other after all the turmoil of their early life together. But so far neither of them had been prepared to make concessions, and the King showed an unexpected streak of obstinacy in his unswerving determination to introduce his paramour into his wife's Household. Having failed to quell his Queen, he asked Clarendon to intervene, but the Chancellor felt inclined to demur, saying that the task was 'too delicate a province for so plain-dealing a man'. All the same he agreed to take a message to the Queen telling her that the King was firm in his intention of appointing Lady Castlemaine, that he promised to see that she behaved herself with suitable humility, and that he would expect and exact from his wife a complete conformity with his wishes in this matter.

Clarendon did his best; he told the Queen that he felt sure she must have seen more instances of iniquity in her own country 'than this cold region could afford'—it was midsummer at the time and very hot, which must have lent less weight to his argument. The Queen 'blushingly and tearfully replied that she had at least not expected her husband to be already engaged in his affection to another lady'. Clarendon heavily expressed his disbelief that she was so completely innocent as to imagine that the King, in the full vigour of his youth, would have remained ignorant of the opposite sex. He advised her to treat the whole matter with as much good humour as possible, but she greeted the suggestion that she should allow the Lady to become one of her Household with an outburst of rage, and threatened to return to Lisbon at once.

Clarendon also offered fatherly advice to the King, reminding him of the censorious remarks he had once made himself about monarchs who allowed their whores to live at Court—a custom that might be acceptable abroad, but which was considered an odious Continental habit by the English. Certainly, Clarendon pointed out, it was the best way of breaking the hearts of his friends and of losing the affections of his people. The King listened patiently with only a few of 'those little interruptions which were natural to him', and Clarendon was able to report to his friend the Duke of Ormonde, that he had conducted three or four long conferences with the King 'with better temper than before'. He had to admit that the Lady had been down to Hampton Court the same evening. 'I cannot tell you there was no discomposure', he wrote, but he was able to add, 'I am not out of all hope, and that is all I can yet say'.

The Chancellor's hope that matters were beginning to stabilize was disappointed when the King provoked a quarrel almost as spectacular as the great fracas forty years previously when his father had dismissed Henrietta Maria's French attendants. Charles now told Catherine that he had decided to send all her servants back to Portugal, and when she threatened to return to Lisbon with them he said he very much doubted whether her mother would have her. In spite of all her protests he sent the Portuguese away forthwith, allowing her to keep the decrepit Countess of Penalva, some priests and a few kitchen maids. He would have liked to dispense with her cacophonous musicians, but in the end he allowed them to stay.

Having sent away most of her servants, the King made his plans to take the Queen back to London with her attenuated train. On August 23 they left Hampton Court by barge and were met with a rapturous welcome as they neared Westminster. The river was crowded with vessels dressed and adorned; the spectacle, according to Evelyn, outdid the Venetian ceremony on Ascension Day when the whole city went out to espouse the Adriatic.

For Pepys, waiting among the crowds that had gathered on shore at the Palace, it was far more important to station himself where he could gaze on Lady Castlemaine rather than jostle for a first glimpse of the Queen. 'That which pleased me best', he wrote, 'was that my Lady Castlemaine stood over against us upon a piece of White-hall—where I glutted myself with looking on her.' She had returned to London from Richmond to be in residence for the King's return, and Pepys thought it strange to see that her husband was near her; they walked up and down without taking the slightest notice of one another—'only, at first entry, he put off his hat and she made him a very civil salute'. But both of them 'now and then would take their child, which the nurse held in her arms, and dandle it'. Pepys did not fail to notice that when one of the scaffolds built for spectators suddenly collapsed, it was Lady Castlemaine of all the grand women present, who spontaneously ran down among the rabble to comfort an injured child, 'which methought was so noble'. He noticed, too, that the Lady talked for a long while to a gentleman who was booted and spurred; she was hatless, and to protect her hair, she borrowed her companion's hat, 'which was but an ordinary one . . . But methought it became her mightily, as everything else do'.

Although Pepys had eyes only for the superb Lady Castlemaine, it was the Queen that most people had come to see. For a few days after her arrival everything seemed calm, but once the lull was over it was not difficult to tell which way things would go. Clarendon's friend Daniel O'Neill wrote to the faithful Duke of Ormonde in Ireland that he felt it was 'impossible for the King to endure the insolency of the dame . . . we that see it can hardly credit our eyes . . . Our Master is seldom abed after six, always ready before seven and constantly before eight in the dame's chamber where he is until nine, the rest of the day is hardly spent out of her company somewhere or other'. Less than three weeks after the Queen's arrival in London on September 9, Clarendon himself told Ormonde 'all things are bad with reference to the Lady'. When Pepys visited the Presence Chamber he found that Lady Castlemaine, and not the Queen, was the main focus of attention. At more informal gatherings the Queen always sat 'untaken notice of', while a large crowd gathered round her rival. She was forced to see the Lady riding in the royal coach, and there were many rumours that the mistress was to be assigned lodgings within the Palace. Even the Queen's servants seemed to pay more attention to Lady Castlemaine than they did to herself, and the little foreign Queen had to face the sad and humiliating fact that there was 'an universal mirth in all company but hers'.

Soon after meeting his wife the King had written to his mother-in-law telling her that he was 'the happiest man in the world and the most enamoured'. Now there was no denying that only three months later the first rapture had worn off—if it had ever really existed. As the cynical Chesterfield had put it when writing about another newly-married couple, 'a small prophet may easily foretell the term of such a happiness and I fancy the unsanctified enjoyments are of more duration'. Certainly the insignificant Queen was no match for the magnificent Castlemaine, in the face of whose rages even a King was prepared to quail. At times it seemed as though she was becoming resigned to the situation, for on September 13 O'Neill wrote, 'The Queen all this week has been in a very good humour and shows no more concernment at what she daily sees than if she were insensible.' This behaviour caused alarm to her supporters, and particularly to Clarendon, who was sure that if Catherine maintained an attitude of coldness and disapproval, the King would in the end be the first to capitulate. Father Talbot, a young priest who had gained the Queen's confidence and who was able to speak to her in Spanish, tried to warn her of the dangers of giving up the fight; he fed her with long stories about the Lady's iniquity, describing her as an enchantress—a word which for Catherine seemed to have alarming overtones, for, as O'Neill told Ormonde, it was 'much used among the lovers in Spain' and had sinister implications. Greatly alarmed, the Queen reported the conversation to the King, who in his turn told the Lady. She immediately went into one of her rages, complained bitterly about Father Talbot's ingratitude, and pressed 'all passionately' to have him removed from Court. As a result of the incident, the Queen's position was worse than ever, for the fact that she had disclosed the details of her talk with Talbot made even her friends wary and 'the world so shy of her that all that had any kindness for her shun her' as O'Neill put it, making sure that from now on anything he wrote in his letters to Ormonde on the subject of Lady Castlemaine was put into cipher.

As the Queen's isolation deepened, her lack of friends broke her

spirit, and like everybody else she began to make up to Lady Castlemaine, realizing that this was the quickest way to gain the King's
approval. Her 'excess of condescension' filled the Chancellor with dismay, and for the first time he and his friends had to admit that they
were no longer in the commanding position they had enjoyed since the
Restoration. They had done all they could to guard against the introduction of undesirable female influences into the King's councils, but
they had underestimated the ability of the enchanting Lady.

CHAPTER NINE

THE HOUSE IN KING STREET

IF THE Queen was prepared to face her troubles with resignation and a show of 'masculine courage', Clarendon for his part was determined to continue the fight. He had always regarded it as his sacred duty, entrusted to him by the previous King, to protect the young Charles from his enemies and from all the evil influences that threatened to destroy his moral fibre. As the Chancellor put it to Edward Nicholas, 'it is our parts to use our utmost endeavour to prevent the King's doing anything that is amiss, but when it is done to make the best of it, and to be sure to do what is our duty'. Hyde now saw his duty as a dogged refusal to sign any warrants for titles or money which included the Lady's name. He shunned her, never visiting her or any of her friends, and openly lamenting that the gallant Grandison had bred such a daughter. This attitude was described by Burnet as 'maintaining the decencies of virtue in a very solemn manner', and there was little doubt that although his stand was morally sound it was not at all wise.

At a younger age the King had submitted to his governor's tutelage without complaint, and the two men had for years maintained a deep and mutual loyalty. When an attempt was made during the interregnum to blacken the Chancellor's name with the accusation that he had received £4,000 as an intelligence agent in Thurloe's pay, the King had dismissed the suggestion with contempt. He respected his old servant's extreme rectitude and relied on him heavily to deal with administrative problems. In the days of exile, if Hyde ever succeeded in taking a few days' leave with his much neglected family, the King would soon write urging him to return as fast as his gouty feet would let him. His absence always caused endless inconvenience; on one occasion when he went away and took the book of inscriptions, subscriptions and superscriptions with him, there was consternation as nobody else knew how to address a letter to Don Juan, the Spanish Governor in the Netherlands.

It had been natural and fitting that the King should honour with the highest office a man who had stood by him in all the difficulties and humiliations of exile. There had been times in those days when Hyde had needed sleep so badly and had felt so cold for lack of firing that he could hardly sit up and hold a pen. 'The life we lead is unpleasant', he had told Nicholas, 'and bread and water in some secure corner would be a great relief.' Although nowadays his work-load was not much lighter, the Chancellor could at least enjoy the benefits of material comfort as well as the kudos of high office. But he could no longer expect the King to defer to him in everything as he had done when he was still a boy, and it was not surprising that already signs had appeared of a growing independence on the part of the monarch. Clarendon was not afraid to remind the King that he must not allow himself to be 'governed', but it came as something of a shock to realize that he himself could be classed as one of those unconstitutional influences he so decried; he had after all no mandate to remain the King's chief counsellor for life, and Charles had a right to grow tired of elderly advisers who failed to move with the times. Clarendon's manner, in Burnet's opinion, was altogether too 'magisterial'; like the nurse who treats her former charges as if they are still in the nursery, he was inclined to forget that the King had grown up and was rapidly becoming a shrewd politician and an excellent chairman of the Council, able to delegate the trivia and leave his own mind free to ponder more weighty matters.

A confrontation was bound to come and it was the Lady who provided the excuse. The King had responded angrily to any suggestion that he allowed her to influence his decisions—he was 'new chafed with being governed' as Clarendon put it. Exasperated by the nagging efforts of Clarendon's clique to block Lady Castlemaine's appointment, he turned on Alan Brodrick who had recently weighed in with advice, warning him that he would meddle at his peril. Nobody, he wrote, had the power to thwart him in his intention of including Lady Castlemaine in his wife's Household. 'I am resolved to go through with this matter, let what will come on it . . . whosoever I find to be my Lady Castlemaine's enemy in this matter, I do promise, upon my word, to be his enemy as long as I live.' Clarendon no doubt pictured the Lady at his elbow, dictating the words and strengthening his resolve. This may have been so, but the truth was that the King was capable of asserting himself whether the mistress was behind him or not. Nothing would make him break promises uttered in good faith to a lady, and in any case he had gone too far in the matter to withdraw. Were he to do so, the Lady would be treated with contempt while his own honour would suffer so much that he would become 'ridiculous to the world, and be thought too in pupilage under a governor'.

In opposing the Lady, the Chancellor gave the King an opportunity to break free from the bonds which had already become constricting. He also cut himself off from the circle of intimate friends where the leaders of the future were doing their best to monopolize the King's favour. Change was in the air, and Lady Castlemaine had provided the encouraging proof that it was possible to oppose the Chancellor without alienating the King. She had become so confident that she was heard freely expressing her opinion of the Chancellor in a crowd of people in the Queen's Chamber, not scrupling to remark that she hoped to see his head on the stake outside Westminster Hall along with the regicides. 'I dare say', O'Neill told Ormonde, 'she says no less to the King for there is no limit to her power nor his fondness. It's happy her parts does not answer else she would make mad work.'

The Chancellor and his friends made their greatest mistake in acknowledging the Lady's physical attractions but failing to recognize her intelligence, her instinctive knowledge of the workings of the Court, and her inbred ability to move at ease in royal circles. Pepys was nearer the mark when he refused to label her a common whore; he found there was such an air about her that he was ready to go anywhere in the hope of seeing her—he even braved the discordant Portuguese music in the Queen's Chapel to catch a glimpse of her. The King himself believed that Clarendon should have been able to appreciate the Lady's aristocratic claim to a place in the Queen's Household. He reminded the Chancellor that she was a member of the distinguished Villiers family and had just as much right to be included as the Countess of Suffolk or anybody else. Other mistresses like Elizabeth Weaver, an actress who played secondary roles in the theatre and whom the King had 'spoiled' soon after his arrival in England, were in quite a different category. The Lady outclassed them all in her power not only to capture the King's affection but also to dominate and manipulate his circle of friends. Gradually the Chancellor's enemies were drawn to the house in King Street, knowing that the King was certain to be there. Lady Castlemaine was an excellent hostess, and they could be sure of a good supper, plenty of witty conversation and the chance to make themselves amenable to the King.

At first Clarendon thought that the King's companions were no more than confidants of his pleasure, although this in itself was enough to break the hearts of his older friends. 'He seeks for his satisfaction and delight in other company, which do not love him as well as you and I do', Clarendon told Ormonde. Pepys also found it hard to believe that Lady Castlemaine and her faction did anything more 'than to debauch the King', but many people were beginning to suspect that she was cleverer than anyone had thought and might in the end prove capable of wielding untold influence in the courts of power. After a while even Clarendon's friends came to realize that they had underestimated the Lady's ability. 'We that are gentle spectators', O'Neill told Ormonde, 'have subject enough of raillery, but the apprehension of the consequence spoils our mirth, giving my wife such fits of the spleen as will oblige me to make away for Ireland with her.'

O'Neill suspected that the Lady had been behind the move to dismiss the Portuguese retainers. He told Ormonde that she was now pressing the King to send away the Countess of Penalva; this would mean depriving the Queen of the companion who had been 'bred with her and indeed that she cannot well live without, for she is not only her confidant but cooks her breakfast and what she eats between meals she dresses'. There was little doubt that the Lady was organizing the Queen's establishment to suit herself, in partnership with her aunt the Countess of Suffolk, who added to her other responsibilities the task of arranging the nightly rendezvous between the King and her niece. 'Already the La. Castlemaine and her kindred stomach much the stay of the Countess of Panalva', O'Neill reported, and, he added, the King was 'tormented with the discontents of that fury that will not be appeased because the Countess of Panalva stays'.

Increasingly people began to face the fact that Lady Castlemaine was not only acting as the King's paramour but was also playing 'a high game'. In Spain the Duke of Medina heard with interest that those who naturally favoured his country, among them the Earl of Bristol, were always to be seen in her company. According to Clarendon, the Earl of Bristol 'left no way unattempted to render himself gracious to the King, by saying and doing all that might be acceptable unto him, and contriving such meetings and jollities as he was pleased with'. O'Neill observed that the King and the Lady were regularly invited to Bristol's out-of-town house. 'Twice a week they are at Wimbledon, the master of which is much in grace', he told Ormonde. Sir Henry Bennet, another champion of the Spanish, was also thought to cultivate the Lady's favour, if rather less openly. When the post of Ambassador to France became vacant, Bennet managed to persuade the Lady to plead for him with the King, and his name was suggested, even though it was known that he was no lover of France. The French Ambassador in England, the Comte d'Estrades, was appalled at the very idea, particularly as he knew it was supported by what he described as 'the cabal opposed to the Chancellor's'. On this occasion the opposition of the French King had been enough to secure the appointment of Clarendon's candidate, Lord Holles.

Outwardly, Sir Henry Bennet maintained cordial relations with the Chancellor, while continuing his courtship of the King Street cabal. But by the beginning of August 1662 Giavarina could clearly define two power-groups. He explained to the Doge that the Chancellor supported the Queen while the Earl of Bristol and Sir Henry Bennet, who stood high in the King's favour, as well as other influential people, supported the Countess of Castlemaine. 'What is more important,' he added, 'the King seems to incline to that side and refuses to gratify the Queen by forbidding the Countess the Court.' O'Neill went further and voiced a suspicion that the Montagu family block, headed by the Lord Chamberlain, was moving over into the Villiers enclave. O'Neill's hatred of the Earl of Manchester was second only to his dislike of the Lady. The Montagu nephews, Edward and Ralph, with their sister Elizabeth, who were the children of Lord Montagu of Boughton, were all ambitious and ready to seize any opportunity of advancement. It was Edward Montagu who had acted as mediator between the King and his cousin Edward, now Lord Sandwich, thus securing the loyalty of the fleet. He had also brought the first news of the Queen's arrival off the English coast, and he was now established prominently at Court as the Queen's Master of the Horse while his brother Ralph held the same position in the Duchess of York's Household. O'Neill did not care for the way Edward was behaving and he told Ormonde he was sure that 'ungrateful Montagu, Master of the Horse, is deep in this cabal against the Chancellor of England'. Lord Sandwich too seemed to be veering in the same direction. When the Lady gave a ball at her house in October, the Earl, along with the King, was one of the guests—he no longer had to stand outside listening to the music as he and Pepys had done in the summer of 1660.

Even the closely observant O'Neill found it hard to say for certain where Bennet's loyalties lay. 'How far Sir Henry Bennet is in their design I cannot learn', he wrote, 'but I doubt more than he should, for he and Montagu are very good friends.' O'Neill believed that Father Talbot would never have had the misfortune of being banished from Court if his friend Bennet had not 'quitted his care'.

The Duke of Buckingham was another prominent figure whose activities were viewed with distrust. As an old enemy of Clarendon he was a natural denizen of his cousin's house in King Street. He had quickly worked his way back into favour after the Restoration, ignoring the King's initial coldness and insinuating himself into the boot of the royal coach as it drove away from Dover and keeping close to the front of the procession on the road to London. The King tended to regard him as a brother, for he and the first Duke's other children had been brought up in the royal nursery after their father's assassination. With his outstanding gift of mimicry Buckingham was an asset in any company. Sometimes he would portray an unsuspecting victim who was actually in the room, reproducing mannerisms and tone of voice with unbelievable accuracy. He had perfected an impersonation of Clarendon, which Charles found particularly amusing. All the same, in spite of the King's affection for him, Buckingham's hopes of obtaining high office were bound

3

to remain unfulfilled so long as his old enemy remained Lord Chancellor.

The new cabal was united in its hatred of Clarendon, and its members were also drawn together by a mutual interest in the cause of religious toleration. Since the Venner rising the attitude of the Cavalier Parliament had hardened against nonconformists of all kinds. The Act of Uniformity, passed earlier in the year, had been designed to root out of the Church all those who could not accept every article of its doctrines. In the summer of 1662 many Protestant dissenters resigned their benefices rather than be forced to take the 'test' of their loyalty to the established Church. The Catholics too were affected by the current attitude of intolerance, and all nonconformists were seeking out ways of lessening the effects of the new Act. Many of the King's friends were either men of Catholic leanings like Bristol and Bennet, or had been bred up in the Presbyterian tradition like the Montagus. Buckingham, despite his reputation for inconsistency, firmly espoused the nonconformist cause throughout his whole career; as he put it himself 'when he was in drink he was for the episcopacy, but when serious and sober for the fanatiques'. And the King, by nature a tolerant man, had little difficulty in appreciating their point of view. But in order to keep Parliament in a good mood in the hope of gaining increased financial grants, he had been forced into accepting the Act of Uniformity against his deepest inclinations.

The King himself had no objection to the reappearance in English churches of 'singing men in surplices', but unlike his father he would never have gone to war to preserve the altar rail, the Anglican prayerbook, or the right to bow at the name of Jesus. He extracted from his religion, as he did from life in general, the maximum amount of enjoyment, making sure that the services he attended were made palatable by the introduction of a full-blooded orchestra wherever possible. Thus Evelyn was scandalized when he counted twenty-four violins which interpolated their evil sound at every pause in the service, 'after the French fantastical light way, better suiting a tavern or playhouse than a church'. The King saw no reason to be ashamed of such a musical accompaniment. He told Burnet that 'he could not think God would make a man miserable for taking a little pleasure on the way'. Like many other people, Charles fashioned God after his own image, and as a result he saw the Almighty as a supremely benign and easy-going individual. He was happy to refrain from mystical meditation, to mind his own religious business and let God, the priests and the sectarians do likewise. So long as the dissenters allowed him to govern the country peaceably he was prepared to let them worship as they pleased, and when Bristol and others put pressure on him to espouse the nonconformist cause, they were speaking to the converted.

From June 1662 meetings were held in Lord Manchester's lodgings to discuss the possibility of reversing some of the more drastic provisos of the Act of Uniformity. The Lady immersed herself energetically in the campaign to help the Presbyterian clergy who were being turned out of their parishes in large numbers. 'You will hardly believe it', O'Neill told Ormonde, 'but it's very true, that the powerful Lady is . . . the fiercest solicitor these ejected Ministers have.' It was ironical that the adulterous Lady Castlemaine should champion the cause of the Presbyterian clergy whose attitude to the sins of the flesh was so unequivocal. Less out of keeping was her support of the move to loosen Clarendon's tight hold on the administration. Before they could make their presence felt in the government, Bristol and his friends needed at least one man in a position of real power who could be relied upon to give them his support. It seemed to them that Sir Edward Nicholas was ripe for replacement. He was just on seventy—Giavarina described him as 'old and uncapable'—and although he was an experienced administrator there were good grounds for asking him to make way for a younger man. The King bribed him generously and he retired without bitterness, optimistically believing that his son would succeed him as Secretary of State. He withdrew to the country to prepare himself for a better world, and his place was speedily bestowed on Sir Henry Bennet.

Clarendon had once been Bennet's friend, but from now on he defined the Secretary as a master of backstairs intrigue, who carried on most of his business in private and never spoke at the Council table unless it was to whisper in his neighbour's ear something detrimental about the member who had just spoken. One of his first acts on taking over the Secretary's lodgings at Whitehall was to make a door that led straight out onto the private stairs going up to the King's apartments. At the same time those less biased than Clarendon could see that Bennet was well qualified for his new task. An aloof and striking figure with a black patch on his face that covered a wound sustained in the civil war, he had a slightly saturnine appearance but could be charming when he chose. Unlike the Chancellor, who was inclined to be insular, he spoke several languages fluently, and he was an experienced diplomat, having served as British Ambassador in Spain. Clarendon had made the mistake of opposing Bennet's appointment to the lucrative place of Postmaster-General. This had offended the King, and O'Neill had prophesied accurately that as a result Charles would think up 'another design that Henry Bennet will find more his advantage in and that will less please the Chancellor'.

On becoming Secretary of State, Bennet vacated the post of Keeper of the Privy Purse, a vital 'above stairs' position which brought with it great influence as well as the power of administering large sums of money without the auditing and scrutiny obligatory in other departments of the Household. A friendly Keeper could do much to neutralize the prejudices of the Chancellor and the Lord Treasurer. It was therefore not surprising that the post was given to Sir Charles Berkeley who already rejoiced in the unofficial position of pimp to the King and Lady Castlemaine. Clarendon impolitely termed him 'a most vicious person', but he possessed the wit, charm and good looks which provided the best passport to the King's favour. Some years before, the Chancellor had dissuaded the Countess of Morton from marrying him, for he had already made the mistake of supporting his uncle, Lord Berkeley, who was one of Clarendon's most implacable enemies. He had fallen into further disfavour when he had joined other young men in the plot to discredit Anne Hyde, inventing the story that he had lain with her on several occasions.

There was little doubt that for the King and Lady Castlemaine, Sir Charles Berkeley was a key figure; although O'Neill told Ormonde that the appointment 'discontents the Bedchamber', the King, as Clarendon put it, was 'well pleased that he had gotten Sir Charles Berkeley into the other office about his person, whom he every day loved with more passion, for what reason no man knew nor could imagine'. At the same time there was some significance in the fact that William Morrice had been retained in office rather than Sir Edward Nicholas, his fellow Secretary of State. Morrice had originally been recommended by his kinsman, the Duke of Albemarle, who had been impressed by his ability to speak French and write shorthand. But of the two, Nicholas was undoubtedly the more able, in spite of his age. Morrice, however, was a Presbyterian, and so was more likely to support the cause of toleration; in particular he could be relied on to look kindly on the Declaration of Indulgence which had been drawn up after much talk and consultation in Lord Manchester's lodgings and elsewhere.

The Declaration was framed to nullify the intolerant policies enshrined in the Act of Uniformity. Its publication, coming as it did so soon after the appointment of Bennet, seemed to indicate that Lady Castlemaine and her friends were all-victorious and would stop at nothing. O'Neill even had a strong suspicion that they might be plotting to poison the Queen. The Lady had proved that she was capable of achieving her ends, though it sometimes meant resorting to rages or 'hectoring' when the King baulked at granting her requests. As O'Neill put it, 'the fatal victory this Lady has lately got makes her presume all her demands how unreasonable soever, will be granted, and I much fear, she takes not her measures ill, for I see nothing of her power nor his passion abated'. Sir Edward Nicholas had at first thought that his own dismissal could be laid at the door of his old enemy the Queen Mother. 'I am told, and have some reason to believe that this my remove was designed at Somerset

House', he wrote. Pepys heard that the Queen Mother and Lady Castlemaine together were responsible for laying the worthy Secretary aside. O'Neill observed that both ladies were 'very great, and both irreconcilable enemies of the Chancellor'.

There were rumours in the autumn that the Lady was with child again—'and has the impudence to be pleased with it', O'Neill angrily reported. She and her husband still met occasionally but 'never to eat or lie together', and nobody doubted that the King had fathered her child. There were hopes that Catherine too might be breeding, but the weeks went by and there was no confirmation of the news that so many wanted to hear. Sometimes the King tormented her, telling her she was with child, and when she said, 'You lie,' he laughed good-humouredly and vowed that he would have her taught to say in English, 'Confess and be hanged'.

If the Queen had showed signs of producing an heir the outlook for the Chancellor might have been more promising, but as it was everything seemed to be against him, and he was blamed for everything that went wrong—the usual penalty of power. Giavarina reported that there was a great deal of murmuring against the Chancellor 'who', as he told the Doge, 'tyrannizes over people, especially over their purses as all business passes through his hands because of the Great Seal'. Attempts to introduce cuts in the royal expenditure increased Clarendon's unpopularity, especially among those who were waiting for arrears of pay or who had been told that their jobs would be abolished in the interest of economy. He was forced to watch the King pursuing his pleasures in the public eye and with a complete lack of discretion. The much-criticized sale of Dunkirk had failed to solve any of his financial problems, and he was being made to feel that he was a relic of a past era due to make way for younger brains and a fresh approach. The situation was summed up succinctly by Pepys when he wrote that 'the young men get uppermost, and the old serious lords are out of favour'. Nobody, Pepys observed, and Clarendon had to accept, could claim the King's ear more than Sir Charles Berkeley, Sir Henry Bennet or Lady Castlemaine. The future now seemed to lie with 'the cabal that meet at Mistress Palmer's lodgings'.

The inevitable and final clash between King and Chancellor seemed to be imminent, and many people believed that Clarendon would fall before the end of the year. The King and his friends were full of confidence and did not doubt that now the monarch had pointed the way, Parliament would pass a Bill to make the articles of the Declaration law.

There had been rumours that as soon as Parliament met, 'some great man would be aimed at' and that Bennet would lose no time in bringing down the man Giavarina described as 'the cruel favourite'. But the furore over the Declaration distracted attention from the Chancellor who escaped the wrath of Parliament even though he offended the King by his lack of warmth in the nonconformist cause. His position was, however, still precarious, and although he allowed himself occasional bouts of cautious optimism his mood in general was one of deep despair. He was weary and in bad health, laid low by the gout which had assailed him with varying degrees of intensity ever since his first attack on the road to Bristol during the civil war. In the bitter weather which started well before Christmas 1662 he was often so ill that he was unable to leave his house. Meanwhile the Lady carried all before. The King loved her deeply and possessively; when Henry Jermyn, a little man with short legs and a head too big for his body, paid too much attention to her he was summarily banished from Court. If the King went to the theatre she was always at his side, and if he supped with the Queen he spent the rest of the evening in King Street. One evening, when the Lady was dining with the Gerards, she suffered the first symptoms of what could have been a miscarriage; the men were ordered to leave the room and women were called in to her. There were no such dramas for the Queen, and on December 23 the Duke of York's surgeon, Dr Pierce, told Pepys that Lady Castlemaine's interest at Court was still increasing and was far greater than the Queen's. The King was at the same time very kind to the Queen, as Pepys himself noticed, which made it all the stranger that he was still 'bewitched to this pretty Castlemaine'.

CHAPTER TEN

THE COMMITTEE

AS THE year drew to its close, the weather turned bitterly cold, with frost and snow, and thick ice on the Thames. Clarendon's gout was so bad that he found it hard to attend to business, but the King and his friends pursued their pleasures with even more energy than usual. The King and Queen watched the novel spectacle of skaters moving with 'strange and wonderful dexterity' on the ice which covered the new canal in St James's Park. This sport, recently imported from Holland, was one of the many foreign innovations which delighted the pleasure-seekers and caused the more staid to register their disapproval. The King had introduced to London the guitar player Francisco Corbetta who made his instrument so popular that many ladies were trying to master the difficult art, and a guitar was often to be seen on fashionable dressing-tables along with the rouge, powder and patches. The Comte de Gramont, banished by Louis XIV for certain indiscretions, arrived in England early in 1663 and discovered that he could not have found a more congenial place to spend his exile. His engagement diary was soon filled up a week ahead; he attended a succession of dinner parties where the ladies, with their fair complexions and far from demure glances, were as alluring as any he had come across in France. He wooed them with presents from Paris, perfumed gloves and pocket mirrors, apricot preserves and essences.

The year ended with a magnificent ball at Court, and everyone was interested to see that Lady Castlemaine had the honour of leading out in the *branle* the King's eldest illegitimate son, who had been brought over to England by his grandmother. The Duke of Monmouth was a well-favoured youth, and Henrietta Maria greatly preferred him to the Yorks' sickly children. Pepys was of the opinion that Lady Castlemaine was one of the three most accomplished dancers at Court, and she had plenty of opportunity during the festive season to show off her skill, for there was a ball every other evening, as well as country dancing, which the Queen particularly enjoyed. On one occasion the King left a ball as soon as it had begun, to sup with Lady Castlemaine, which caused something of a stir. There were plays, comedies and other entertainments almost every day. When the King suffered from an attack of persistent catarrh in the early spring, his trouble was attributed to the excesses of the carnival season, and Lent may have come as something of a relief.

Many people felt uneasy about the continuing example set by the King. Even if they themselves indulged in the fashionable pastimes of gaming, dancing or making music, they felt a residue of guilt left over from sterner times. Pepys was always making resolutions to refrain from visiting the theatre, and he felt apprehensive when his wife started taking dancing lessons, for he was sure no good would come of it. He noticed that the Earl of Sandwich's morals began to decline as soon as he became involved in the King's social life. One evening as they walked across the Privy Garden to attend a meeting of the Tangier Committee at the Duke of York's apartments, somebody called across to Sandwich from Lady Castlemaine's house. 'I see he is a servant of the King's pleasures too as well as business', Pepys observed, fearing that his kinsman was bound to lose large sums of money if the Lady started summoning him to play at cards. Sandwich told Pepys that 'he would be glad at any time to lose £50 for the King to send for him to play', but Pepys did not appreciate this kind of loyalty; although he was no saint himself he disapproved when Sandwich began to dabble with an impudent wench, indulging, as Pepys put it, in 'the liberty that he sees everybody else at Court takes', even flirting with the slut in the presence of his young daughter.

The King had by now set the fashion for adultery, and members of the smart set of pre-Restoration days felt that they could live without any of the restrictions which had hampered their activities during the interregnum. Anne Hamilton had managed to ensnare the Duke of York not long after she was married off to the proud and respectable Earl of Southesk. Thus she became the second of the two girls who had once lain abed together, plotting a rendezvous with Chesterfield on Ludgate Hill, to obtain for herself a royal lover. Later she became involved with a Frenchman and retired to France. Chesterfield himself had undergone some chastening experiences since the days when the girls had competed for his attention. He had married Elizabeth Butler, a daughter of the Duke of Ormonde, only to find that her enormous blue eyes also had a devastating effect on the Duke of York. He did not intend to let his wife follow his mistress's example, and so he removed her in mid-winter, although she was with child, to his Derbyshire stronghold, ignoring the bawdy jokes which circulated at Court about husbands who sent their wives to the Devil's Hole.

All such goings-on were, in Pepys's opinion, 'the effects of idleness and having nothing else to employ their great spirits upon'. Certainly during the carnival season it appeared that the King had given himself up completely to his pleasures. Even the sentries at the Palace remarked on the fact that he supped four or five times a week with Lady Castlemaine, staying with her until morning and returning through the Privy Garden alone, a habit which Pepys thought very unsuitable in a Prince of his standing.

With Clarendon well out of the way nursing his gout, the Lady's position improved dramatically. Pepys was shocked to hear that all the Christmas gifts presented to the King by the peers had found their way into her possession. The diarist was told that she and Sir Charles Berkeley were the greatest favourites at Court and were 'growing every day more and more'. Early in the year the King granted her lodgings in the Palace—'which I am sorry to hear, although I love her much', Pepys commented. She was set up in apartments which had been vacated the previous year when the Duke of Ormonde left for Ireland. One of the rooms was situated above the Holbein Gate, and it provided her with one of the best vantage points in the Palace. She could look out on one side over the river and the garden of statues, and on the other over the square where the guards always stood on sentry duty, and where everybody's comings and goings could be well observed. Sir Charles Berkeley, now that he controlled the strings of the Privy Purse, was able to see to it that the new apartments were lavishly provided with furniture and hangings.

In every way the Lady seemed to be in an unchallengeable position. There was no deterioration in her looks, as Pepys observed—'I up into the house among the courtiers, seeing the fine ladies, and above all, my Lady Castlemaine, who is above all that only she I can observe for true beauty'. When she attended a performance of Dryden's first play, *The Wild Gallant*, Pepys thought that she and her companion, the lovely Frances Stuart, were both well worth gazing upon, whereas the play he could have done without—he found the plot very confusing.

For Dryden, the only possible way of describing his ecstasy at seeing the favourite applaud his work, was to break into adulatory verses entitled 'Upon her Encouraging his first Play' which he addressed to Lady Castlemaine:

> But this long-growing debt to poetry
> You justly, Madam, have discharged to me,
> When your applause and favour did infuse,
> New life to my condemn'd and dying muse.
> These actions others do by chance
> Are, like your beauty, your inheritance.
> So great a soul, such sweetness joined in one,
> Could only spring from noble Grandison.

3*

>You, like the stars, not by reflection bright,
>Are born to your own heaven and your own light.

Dryden described the Lady up in her box 'Watching vain men below Contending for what only she could bestow', and this was the way most people saw her. As long as she was the King's favourite the best and quickest way to success was to study how to please her. To criticize her was suicide, as Lady Gerard found when she indiscreetly talked against her; although Lord Gerard was a man the King had always trusted and liked, his Lady found herself forbidden the Court, and nothing her husband could do would make the King change his mind.

Most people had come to realize that it was a waste of time cultivating the Queen's favour for she was now more left out than ever and it was said that from January to April the King did not sup with her once. He took her to Windsor for the Garter ceremony but her enjoyment was ruined by the fact that Lady Castlemaine was also there. Almost as humiliating was the King's attitude to the Duke of Monmouth, whom he treated as his legitimate heir, making him put on his hat when he danced with the Queen. O'Neill reported that the turn-out for the Garter celebrations had proved disappointing with 'a slender appearance of Knights of the Order and other Lords and indeed all sorts of people'. This was due, O'Neill thought, to the bitterness of those who felt they had not received their just reward for unswerving loyalty; at the same time the King's manner of living with Lady Castlemaine had rendered him 'odious to the people'.

As O'Neill realized, the long-standing grievances of unrewarded Royalists were now reaching a crescendo. Sir Robert Howard's popular play *The Committee*, first produced in the autumn of 1662, reminded the courtly audience at the Theatre Royal how the Royalists had kept the King's cause alive during the interregnum. Howard portrayed the Cavalier colonels very sympathetically, comparing them favourably with the over-serious and hypocritical members of the Committee of Sequestrations who had taken over their estates. The uncouth Abel 'driving the lint from his black clothes with his wet thumb' was typical of the Puritans whose main activity in their 'new-built Zion' was to force people into taking the Covenant against their will; there was a reminder for the King in the Cavalier's words:

>This is strange, and differs from your own principle,
>To impose on other men's consciences.

Had the King forgotten, as he championed the cause of the noncon-formists, that it was the Presbyterians who had proved far more in-tolerant than the Anglicans once they found themselves in a position of power? One of the songs in the play put the point even more clearly:

> The pulpits are crowded with tongues of their own,
> And preachers, spiritual committee-men grown.

It was the faithful Colonel Careless who gave vent to a loyalty typical of the old Royalists—the kind of loyalty that now all too often went unrewarded:

> Here, sing always
> For the King; I would have every man in his way do something
> For him; I would have fiddlers sing for him, parsons pray
> For him, men fight for him, women scold for him and
> Children cry for him.

The King may have enjoyed the play but he ignored its message. He still hoped that he could persuade the Parliament to accept his Declaration of Indulgence. 'Most of my time', he told his sister on 11 May 1663, 'is taken up with the business of Parliament, in getting them to do what is best for us all, and keeping them from doing what they ought not to do'. Although he reminded Members that he was by nature an enemy 'to all severity of religion and conscience', he was forced to concede too much in order to satisfy his financial needs. 'God knows', he told the Commons, 'I do not long more for any blessing in this world than that I may live to call a Parliament and not ask or receive money from them.' Such a time, as he well knew, had not yet come. The shortage of funds at Court was desperate; the subsidies voted to him at the Restoration which had once seemed so generous, now proved quite inadequate, and the hated Hearth Tax had not brought in anything like the original estimate. So the lack of money which had forced him to accept the Act of Uniformity now drove him to withdraw the Declaration of Indulgence. It was a heavy price to pay for the grudging sum which he received in exchange—'Parliament sitting and raising four subsidies for the King', Pepys wrote, 'which is but little considering his wants, and yet that parted withal with great hardness—they being offended to see so much money go, and no debts of the public paid, but all swallowed by a luxurious Court.'

The withdrawal of the Declaration was a shattering defeat for Bristol. Realizing that the tide was turning against him he tried to precipitate the removal of Clarendon. Articles of impeachment were drawn up, but they were ill-prepared and premature, reflecting as badly on the King as they did on the Chancellor. The judges ruled that the accusations did not amount to treason, and in any case the attempt of one peer to impeach another was irregular and without precedent. For all his eloquence Bristol was unable to carry Parliament with him; he lacked

Clarendon's sound political sense and succeeded only in making a fool of himself while the wily Chancellor wisely changed his ground and sided with the Anglicans.

Bristol was banished from the Court, and although Buckingham and Bennet had emerged unscathed, they had learnt some hard lessons. They realized that in future they must back up their campaign with a sustained effort to gain support in Parliament. And they also saw that they could never relax their attempts to control the King's policies. Their success in the summer of 1662, which had resulted in the appointment of Bennet, had not been followed by further changes; the King seemed disappointingly unready to part with Clarendon, and now that the Lady was ensconced in lodgings within the Palace walls it had become increasingly difficult to obtain his ear through her intervention. She had become, as Dryden put it in his adulatory verses, 'like the stars, not by reflection bright', and her hold over the King was apparently so strong that she had no need of anybody's help. Shining by virtue of her own luminance, she had become independent and selfish, and distressingly difficult to bribe. Nor was it possible to prophesy how long she would keep her hold over the King. Her reign had already lasted longer than any mistress could rightfully expect, and it had to be admitted that in the early summer of 1663 her looks had deteriorated; 'she begins to decay somewhat' was how Pepys put it. Although on June 1 a warrant was at last issued admitting her as a Lady of the Bedchamber, there was a strong feeling that the King had grown cold towards her, perhaps tired of her overbearing moods and sudden rages. O'Neill told Ormonde that Bristol had done himself little good by his 'great courtship' of the Countess. 'He has I believe lost his hold as well as she', O'Neill reported.

Sensing changes in the King's relationship with his fiery mistress, Buckingham and his friends had already begun to look around for a more malleable alternative. A group of men, labelled by Sandwich 'the Committee' made plans to sponsor a rival with beauty enough to ensnare the King. Led by Edward Montagu, the group decided to 'manage' the young and lovely Frances Stuart, an innocent girl in her early teens, who had been sent over by Minette to join the Queen's Household. The King's sister had parted with her reluctantly, describing her as 'the prettiest girl imaginable and the most fitted to adorn the Court'. She seemed the exact choice for the new cabal, which included Buckingham and also Bennet, who was always ready to enter any scheme provided it was to his own advantage.

La belle Stuart was a flawless beauty; she spoke perfect French, danced as well as Lady Castlemaine, and had a flair for dressing impeccably in the French fashion. She was the daughter of an exiled Royalist and had been brought up at the Court of Queen Henrietta Maria. At fifteen she was still unsophisticated enough to enjoy a game of blind man's buff, and her mental powers were hardly a match for the Lady's. Gramont said that it would have been difficult to imagine less brain combined with more beauty, but she was an inveterate gossip, and was delightfully ready to laugh at the King's jokes. At first Lady Castlemaine treated her as a friend, confident that she could outshine her; in February there were reports of a bizarre 'frolique' in the form of a marriage between the two beauties, celebrated with authentic accompaniments—a sack-posset in bed and 'flinging the stocking'. According to Pepys, 'my Lady Castlemaine, who was the bridegroom, rose, and the King came and took her place with pretty Mrs Stuart'. Some people said that the episode was a ruse to facilitate the King's 'coming to Stuart', who was unfashionably reluctant in such matters. It seems doubtful whether Lady Castlemaine would have been a party to such a plan, and although in the early months of the year the two women were often seen together, Lady Castlemaine detached herself when she realized that the King was becoming enamoured of her companion.

Buckingham managed to cultivate the delectable Frances with great success. He discovered that she enjoyed building card-castles and perfected the skill himself in order to please her. She was delighted with his impersonations, and when she met Bennet for the first time she immediately burst out laughing, recognizing him at once from Buckingham's mimicry. The Duke's hard but unexacting work was all part of the plot for 'the getting of Mrs Stuart for the King', who duly became infatuated with the girl's cold perfection. There were rumours in mid-May that she had already become the King's mistress. Not that Lady Castlemaine accepted the threat to her position without a fight; it was said that she was resorting to all the tricks of Aretin, a reference that needed no explanation for her contemporaries, since Giulio Romano's engraved *Postures*, with Aretin's pornographic text, was in common circulation at the time. But the Huguenot Marquis de Ruvigny, who had been sent over by Louis to further a union with the English, reported on June 15 'that no one doubted Miss Stuart had taken the Lady's place'. On June 30 Pepys recorded that the King was greatly taken up with both Castlemaine and Stuart. Pepys was not sorry to witness the mistress's fall from favour, but he was sad at the thought of another taking her place.

On July 3 Pepys heard the news that Lady Castlemaine had fallen from Court, and O'Neill had been able to tell Ormonde that she was on the brink of ruin—forced to concede victory to Miss Stuart. 'The Lady', he wrote, 'whose violence and spirit can ill endure a rival, is ready to leave the Court, and your lodgings much finer than you left them.' The Lady publicly announced that she would never again invite Frances Stuart to her apartments, and the King for his part declared that he would never set foot in them unless she was there. After some slighting words from the King, the Lady called for her coach and went off in a flurry to take refuge with her uncle at Richmond. Some said that the King pursued her on the pretext of going hunting, others reported that Frances persuaded Sir Charles Berkeley to accompany her to Richmond in an effort to placate the 'imperious' mistress.

There were rumours at the end of the month that Lady Castlemaine's tactics had succeeded and that the King had taken her back into favour. When Buckingham invited the King and Queen to his London home, Wallingford House, he of course omitted Lady Castlemaine from the list of guests; not that she minded. 'Well, much good may [it] do them', she commented to the Countess of Suffolk, 'and for all that I will be as merry as they.' She was right—once Buckingham's party was over, the King abandoned his wife and spent the rest of the night with the Lady. It was not going to be nearly as easy to dislodge her as everybody had hoped; Dr Pierce told Pepys that Sir Charles Berkeley still had such power over the King that he was 'able to fetch him from the Council table to my Lady Castlemaine' whenever he pleased.

The Committee was in every respect encountering more difficulties than it had originally foreseen. Miss Stuart's failure to meet all the King's demands was particularly vexing, and in August the Duchess of Richmond arranged a party where the King was to be given every chance to make Frances his mistress. The plan was frustrated by the unexpected appearance of Lady Castlemaine, followed by an equally uninvited guest in the shape of the Queen, who announced that she had come unaccompanied by Lady Suffolk because she was determined from now on that 'she would not always have a governess at her heels, especially in places where the King was'. Altogether the Queen had suddenly begun to show signs that she was a character to be reckoned with. O'Neill thought this could be due to the fact that her English had improved a great deal, so she was now able to understand what was going on and could also make herself understood. Lady Castlemaine herself experienced the Queen's new acerbity when she commented on Catherine's patience in submitting herself to a whole morning under the hairdresser's hands. 'I have so much reason to use patience that I can very well bear with it' was her tart comment—'one wipe' was how Pepys described the remark. Ironically, Catherine's looks had improved so much that some people thought this might indicate she was at last expecting a child. On July 13 when everybody was out in Hyde Park, Catherine looked so pretty in a white laced waistcoat and a crimson petticoat that the King was more than pleased to hand her down from the coach. Later that day there was a lively and glittering scene at the Palace when all the ladies amused themselves trying on each other's head-gear. In Pepys's opinion it was Frances Stuart who on this occa-sion stood out from all the others 'with her hat cocked and a red plume, with her sweet eye, little Roman nose, and excellent *taille*'.

Despite the appearance on the scene of yet another rival, the Queen's good humour continued throughout the summer. When the King went to fetch her from Tunbridge Wells where she had been hopefully imbibing the waters, she galloped out of the town to meet him and hugged him in an unexpectedly effusive manner. In September she went with him on his summer progress, secure in the knowledge that Lady Castlemaine would be unable to accompany them owing to the imminent birth of her child. The royal party visited Badminton, Ciren-cester and Cornbury, Clarendon's country home. They then proceeded to Oxford where they were greeted on their entrance to the city with speeches by Masters of Art, Doctors, physicians and lawyers. They stayed in St Giles's meadows until it was dark and entered the town by torchlight.

On September 20 Lady Castlemaine gave birth to a son, and such was her resilience that two days later she was on her way to Oxford to join the King. On September 24 the King went off on his own to view the works which were in progress in Christ Church meadow, and on his way back he called on Lady Castlemaine who had stationed herself strategic-ally at the house of Dr Richard Gardiner. Having spent the night with his mistress, he rose early, touched a number of people for the King's Evil and attended a convocation of the Schools, where he made many members of the nobility Masters of Art, including the Duke of Mon-mouth and Sir Charles Berkeley.

The royal party left Oxford amidst shouts and acclamations, having corrupted some of the more idle scholars who now went about whistling and singing in the frivolous manner of the Court. Soon after the royal pair returned to London, the Queen was despatched once again to Tunbridge Wells to ensure, as Comminges, the French Ambassador, told Louis XIV, that nothing was left undone which might help to provide an heir to the English throne. Catherine then went on to Bath, to see whether the waters there which, as Comminges put it *excitent le vomissement*, would promote fertility.

The Queen's absence gave the King an excuse to visit the Lady several evenings running. She had recovered well from the birth of her child and her beauty was as dazzling as ever. For a few days they were able to recapture the harmonious mood of the early times in King Street. Although Charles refused to accept paternity of the child she had just borne, he may have been able to forget his jealousy of the men she was said to encourage—Henry Jermyn, James Hamilton and Charles Berkeley among them. It was not perhaps fortuitous that Barbara had

named her new son Henry, for the rumours that Jermyn was her lover
had persisted; the previous summer she had complained to the King of
the little man's advances, although O'Neill believed that this had been
just a ruse to discredit Jermyn's uncle, the Earl of St Albans, who was
the Queen Mother's favourite—some even said he was her secret
husband. James Hamilton, whose sister Elizabeth was to marry Gramont
at the end of the year, was believed to be so in love with Castlemaine
that he had asked the experienced Chesterfield the best method of
wooing her. And Charles Berkeley, now created Lord Fitzharding, was
constantly with her, and had often been seen at the lighted window
of her room when she was on the point of undressing. But none of these
men could claim to be anything more than understudies to the King.
And although the King's eyes might stray in other directions, nobody
could completely oust the Lady, with her extravagant beauty, her
incorrigible wickedness, her sense of the dramatic and her irrepressible
humour. Sometimes the King would go across to King Street for supper
as he had done in the old days, and one evening when the cook came to
tell her that the kitchen was flooded and the chine of beef not yet cooked,
the Lady characteristically exclaimed with an oath, 'Zounds, she must
set the house on fire'. Fortunately Sandwich's housekeeper Sarah provided a less drastic solution and carried the joint next door, where she
obligingly looked after it until it was done.

A few days later the King set off to retrieve his dull but worthy Queen
from Bath. It was hoped that the cures so patiently and diligently undertaken would lead to the creation of a royal heir, although some people
murmured about the King, laying the sterility of the marriage at his door
and saying that it was he who needed to be cured—of his promiscuous
habits. In October, instead of showing the long-awaited signs of pregnancy, the Queen fell seriously ill with a high fever. As she grew delirious,
she talked only of her children, believing that she had been brought to
bed and wondering why her delivery had been so painless. The King
spent his days at her bedside, listening as she talked of her imaginary
family, and arguing with her when she said that her son was ugly. 'No,
it is a very pretty boy,' he told her, and she replied, 'Nay, if it be like you
it is a fine boy indeed.' At night he went for solace to the Lady, and
elaborate suppers were prepared in King Street for his entertainment.
Pepys with his own eyes saw Sarah's husband at the house next door
preparing a fine meal which Sarah told him was for the King and his
mistress; this Pepys found very strange.

At the same time the King's courtship of Frances Stuart continued.
He would take her into corners for half an hour at a time, kissing her in
full view of everybody. Frances would be waiting for him, expecting his
attentions—it was just like Barbara Palmer all over again, except that

Frances was firm in her refusal to do 'anything more than is safe to her'. With the Queen at the point of death, even Frances Stuart's sponsors could see the virtue of preserving her virginity in the hope that matrimony might later become a possibility. Comminges told Louis that there was much speculation at Court on the subject of another wife for the King and, he added, 'there are some who do not look beyond England to find one for him.'

The Queen's condition continued to deteriorate. The doctors tried every remedy they could think of, even applying pigeons to her feet, which not surprisingly did little to help her. The King went on his knees by her bedside, weeping, and his evident concern proved more effective than anything the doctors had prescribed. Her fever left her and she slowly regained her strength, although for a while her first thought on waking was always to ask, 'Where are the children?' For a time she was unable to walk and she had become so deaf that the envoys sent over by the French King had to shout their messages in her ear. But the new year saw her much restored, and the knowledgeable Pierce told Pepys that the King had lain with her the previous Saturday. She was able to attend a small ball in the Privy Chamber, as a spectator only, and the King told his sister that he and his wife were both off to have supper with Lady Castlemaine.

The King's genuine grief at her bedside had brought the Queen back to life, but his behaviour after her recovery showed her that even with her unshakeable devotion, her pious nature and pretty broken English, she would never command more than a fraction of his love. If old rivals faded, there would always be new beauties ready to take their place. As the King himself put it to his sister, known as Madame since her marriage to the French King's younger brother, Philippe Duc d'Orléans, 'we have a great many young women come up since you were here who are very handsome.' The King's obsession with Frances had become so well-known that anybody who had business with the King would enquire of the sentries, 'Is he above or below?' Lady Castlemaine too was still very much to the fore, in spite of the continuing rumours about her infidelity. Pierce told Pepys that 'my Lord Fitzharding and the Hamiltons, and sometimes my Lord Sandwich . . . have their snaps at her . . . [and] my Lord Sandwich will lead her from her lodgings in the darkest and obscurest manner, and leave at the entrance into the Queen's lodgings, that he might be the least observed'. The King took a lenient view, the degree of his involvement always fluctuating, but too deep to be easily abandoned. The company in King Street was too amusing, the suppers too delicious, and Lady Castlemaine herself too ravishing to be missed. Her children were established in her lodgings at the Palace and he felt for them too a great affection. He made a regular habit of going to the nursery at midnight, to take one of the children 'and dance it in his arms'.

The events of the year had proved to the Queen, to Lady Castlemaine and to the Committee that the King intended to continue exercising his unusual ability to play off different elements against one another without dispensing with any of them. He was capable of extracting the maximum enjoyment from his mistress, while at the same time flirting with a younger woman and treating his wife with such tenderness that she continued to love him dearly. In the same way he could introduce new men into the government without dispensing with old advisers, treating Clarendon, who many others found 'imperious and irascible', with amused tolerance. Not everyone admired him for his adroitness, but there was a growing awareness that thanks to the King's contradictory friendships and allegiances, life at Court was never going to be simple.

Realizing that Lady Castlemaine had survived the crisis of Frances Stuart's introduction in the King's orbit, the men who had suffered a setback at the time of Bristol's disgrace began to re-group and to frequent the King Street suppers more assiduously than ever. New recruits were forthcoming and the old mistress whose position had been threatened by a younger rival now consolidated her gains, allowing the King that satisfaction which Frances still withheld, frightening him with a show of well-calculated rage, or entertaining and amusing him if that seemed more apt, and in every way making each move with consummate skill.

'How loose the Court is', Pepys complained, 'nobody looking after business, but every man his lust and gain'. For the Lady lust and business were inextricably entwined. She harnessed beauty and brain in the game which she knew how to play better than anyone else. And when in December 1663 the news broke that she had become a convert to the Catholic church, it was not surprising that her decision was seen as yet another ploy intended to put her in better position for the next move in her political game.

CHAPTER ELEVEN

THE NEW MANAGERS

WHEN THE Queen heard about her Lady of the Bedchamber's conversion she said openly that she was sure Lady Castlemaine had not joined the Catholic church 'for conscience sake'. Bishop Stillingfleet commented that 'if the Church of Rome has got by her no more than the Church of England has lost, the matter is not much'. The French Ambassador, however, was glad to cultivate the notorious convert, and when he heard that she intended to worship at his chapel, he borrowed an orchestra of violins and told Louis that he intended to 'regale her as well as I can'. The King was kind enough to lend him the French musicians, who proved a great draw and attracted a large crowd of other well-known people.

Some thought that the Lady had taken the step to please her husband, in case she was forced to return to him, but Roger was at this time serving with the Venetian navy and was unlikely to be too concerned about the state of her soul. The more puritanical would not have put it past her to seek refuge in a Church which tended to take a comparatively lenient view of adultery. It was part of her duty as a Lady of the Bedchamber to attend the Queen in chapel, and there is a possibility that familiarity with the Mass may have persuaded her that the Catholic Church suited her better. But few of her contemporaries were ready to believe that she was motivated by a deep religious conviction.

Some members of Barbara's family were naturally distressed by the turn of events. Her mother, widowed for the second time in 1661, was still alive and it seems unlikely that she would have approved of her daughter's latest indiscretion; some members of the family were so outraged that they asked the King to intervene and persuade her to change her mind. He replied urbanely, and with characteristic good humour, that 'as for the souls of ladies, he never meddled with that'. As usual he kept well out of the controversy, remaining cool and detached when others grew heated. It was definitely true that as far as women were concerned, their religion was the least important thing about them; he was quite prepared to dispute with a Quaker girl provided she was pretty, but no doubt would have shown little interest in her arguments had she been plain. He remained loyal to his own principle that people should be allowed to worship as they pleased, provided they did not make trouble, but he himself was naturally drawn towards the Catholic church; he felt little personal affinity for the sects who proudly believed in their own power to fathom out for themselves the secrets of the Almighty. The doctrine of obedience appealed to him far more, and he found all rebels tiresome although, as he confided to Clarendon, 'for my part, rebel for rebel, I had rather trust a Papist rebel than a Presbyterian one'. As far as he was concerned, if a sermon was controversial or boring, he simply slept through it, 'which is a great ease' he told his sister.

The fact that many of the King's friends were thought to be secret members of the Catholic Church prompted a general suspicion that Barbara Castlemaine had turned Catholic to consolidate her position in the King's circle. Clarendon had come to believe that Charles's support of the nonconformists had passed beyond the bounds of prudence and could constitute a threat to the established Church. The Lady's conversion made him and other men of his generation look back to the days when Henrietta Maria's handsome papal nuncios had reaped a plentiful harvest of converts among the ladies of the Court. There was always the lurking fear that one day the King himself might follow his mistress's example and there was no doubt that his attitudes had undergone a subtle change in the four years since his Restoration. Although he had supported the Chancellor during the impeachment crisis, and had continued to visit Clarendon when he was confined to his house with gout, there was an underlying coldness impossible to ignore.

In February 1664 Pepys was told that the King was being 'led away' by half a dozen men. These included the Duke of Buckingham, James Hamilton, Edward Progers, the King's *valet de chambre* and 'confidant of his amours', as well as Lord Fitzharding, who, it was said, had been granted £12,000 per annum, a greater sum than the 1st Duke of Buckingham had managed to extract from the royal purse when he was at the height of favour. These men stayed so close to the King that it was impossible for his more serious servants to reach him. It was obvious that none of them would rest until they had dislodged the Chancellor. Unlike Clarendon and his minions, who decided what was best for the King and then told Parliament to agree, the new managers were hard-working enough to campaign for the support of individual Members, harnessing the opposition which had inevitably grown up against a man so long at the head of affairs. Henry Bennet, William Coventry and Thomas Clifford led the movement; they began to evolve a new method of parliamentary management, speaking often and at length during sessions, or whispering privately into many individual ears. Clarendon described them as 'busy and pragmatical'.

Impressed by Lady Castlemaine's hospitality and even more so by the important people he met at her house, the French Ambassador felt sure that she was associated with a strong cabal which was plotting to topple the Chancellor. It seemed that in the course of the daily debauches at Lady Castlemaine's, a political campaign was being worked out. Although there is no firm evidence to support Comminges' suspicions, it does seem clear that the conversation at the Lady's social evenings helped to influence the thinking of the men closest to the King throughout the year. If Frances Stuart had really gained the ascendancy and Lady Castlemaine's house had been abandoned by the King and by those who visited it regularly in the knowledge that he would be there, the course of events might have been different. As it was, the Lady herself, in her usual dramatic way, made it clear to everybody that she was still in the forefront of the King's life in spite of all the rumours that he only doted on Frances Stuart 'and that to leaving off all business iu the world'. On 1 February 1664, she pointedly left her box at the theatre and went to the King's, placing herself ostentatiously between him and the Duke of York. The playhouse was crowded for the popular play *The Indian Queen* written in collaboration by Sir Robert Howard and John Dryden, and put on with a magnificence of scenery and costume reminiscent of the Court masques of the previous reign. She could not have chosen a more public place to demonstrate to the world that she was still a force to be reckoned with. And if anybody remained unconvinced, there was further proof when the King celebrated his birthday and the anniversary of his Restoration in Lady Castlemaine's lodgings over the hither-gate, dancing with fiddlers throughout the night 'and all the world coming by taking notice of it'.

The King's three ladies, now that they had all learned to live with their rivals, managed to co-exist with a modicum of harmony and only occasional outbreaks of hostilities. There was one uncomfortable scene when a new calash arrived for the King from France and all three ladies vociferously disputed their right to be the first passenger in the enchanting open carriage. Since her illness the Queen had withdrawn more than ever into herself, spending her evenings in the company of her books of devotion, the pretty pious pictures that decorated the walls of her chamber and the bedside clock which had a lamp in it so that she could tell the time at any lonely hour of the night. It was said that nowadays she would always hesitate before going into her own dressing-room for fear of finding the King there with Frances. In February, Pepys was told that the King did not love his wife at all and in fact appeared to be in a sullen mood whenever he was with her; sometimes he at least made a pretence, and on May 19 he told his sister in a letter, 'I have been all this afternoon playing the good husband, having been abroad with my wife'. In July Catherine accompanied him when he went down to see the fleet put out of Chatham; it was a very hot day but the King managed to catch a bad cold. This was due to the fact that on account of the extreme heat he was unwise enough to remove the wig which he now always wore to hide his greying hair.

It seemed unlikely that the King would ever live to see Frances grow 'old and willing', but despite her reluctance the King continued to pay her as much attention as she allowed. When Pepys saw her in April he thought she had put on weight and was not as beautiful as before, and after visiting *The Labyrinth* at the King's Theatre—'the poorest play methinks I ever saw'—he admitted that Frances looked very pretty 'but not like my Lady Castlemaine for all that'. His admiration for the Lady showed no diminution; on the day Sir Arthur Slingsby's lottery was drawn he was delighted to find himself standing by her— 'whom I do heartily adore' he admitted.

During the long hot summer of 1664 all three ladies had their portraits painted. Catherine posed as a shepherdess and as Saint Catherine. Frances was painted in a buff soldier's doublet, and when Pepys saw her coming out of the chair-room after a sitting, he thought she looked very beautiful, with her hair all about her ears. Lady Castlemaine had already sat to Lely, and Pepys had been able to see, in the painter's studio in the Piazza at Covent Garden 'the so much by me desired picture of Lady Castlemaine'. Lely was inclined to be defeatist when it came to painting the King's mistress and his opinion was that 'it was beyond the compass of art to give this lady her due, as to her sweetness and exquisite beauty'. Her portrait, on this occasion, and perhaps significantly, was presented to the Earl of Sandwich.

Sandwich's cousin Edward Montagu, who must have incurred the Lady's displeasure by leading the campaign to procure Frances for the King, had made many other enemies at Court. He was proud, ambitious and sensitive to slights; he had quarrelled with Chesterfield over a question of precedence, and had incited Mr Cholmondeley to challenge him to a duel on account of the many affronts he had given. When Cholmondeley got the better of him and forced him into a ditch, Pepys was glad, 'in hopes', he wrote, 'that it will humble him'. Not above sponsoring Frances Stuart while still insuring against the future by paying excessive court to the Queen, Montagu would sometimes talk to Catherine for two or three hours at a stretch. His enemies soon informed the King that he had been known to squeeze and tickle her hand. Nobody could accuse the King of being uxorious, but when his innocent wife asked him what such favours could mean, he quickly assumed the rôle of a jealous husband and banished Montagu from the Court. He was used to joking grossly with his friends on this kind of subject, but he did not appreciate being told that 'he must have a care of his wife too, for she hath now the gallant'.

In August there were rumours that Lady Castlemaine had lately 'slunk a great belly away, for from very big she is come to be down again'. But as it turned out she had not made use of the King's Physician-in-Ordinary, Alexander Fraser, who was adept at helping the ladies of the Court 'slip their calves'. On September 5 she gave birth to a daughter, Charlotte, her fourth child and second daughter; the King immediately accepted her as his. Nine days after the birth, Lady Castlemaine entertained the French Ambassador's wife, and Comminges reported that the King 'did the honours of the house in a way befitting more a host than a guest'. A few days later, as she returned from an evening visit to the Duchess of York at St James's, the Lady was set upon suddenly by three masked noblemen who 'addressed to her the harshest and bitterest reprimand that can well be imagined', comparing her once again to Jane Shore, the mistress of Edward IV whose body had been thrown on a dunghill. Her maid and her page, the only attendants who were with her, helped her back to the Palace, and as soon as she reached her room she fainted. The King was informed at once, and he showed his concern by the speed with which he rushed to her apartments and his alacrity in ordering that all the Park gates should be closed and everyone inside arrested.

The incident proved that however great the Lady might become, she would always have her enemies. She was evidently affected by her fright for in October Pepys noted some deterioration in her appearance; his wife told him that she was 'so decayed that one would not know her'. But she soon recovered her full beauty and those who had so hopefully sponsored Frances were transferring their loyalty back to the Lady in the knowledge that it was at her evening gatherings they would spend their time most profitably. And as the autumn drew on the talk in King Street and at Court turned increasingly towards the possibility of war. The King's thoughts were now focused on foreign affairs, and the men who surrounded him expressed their loyalty in a fervent and patriotic urge to promote the supremacy of their country. There was a growing hatred of the Dutch whose rivalry thwarted English merchants in India, Africa and the Indies. The King's nature, and his experiences before the Restoration, made him value a quiet life above all else, but even he became influenced by the prevalent feelings of his circle, and by the enthusiasms of younger men who seemed to have inherited something of the Cavaliers' romantic and impractical view of war. Their belligerent attitude struck Clarendon as disturbing, for he and his Lord Treasurer understood too well that war was more likely to bring economic disaster than commercial expansion in its wake. But such considerations did not dim the ardour of the men whom the King had invited to serve on his unofficial committee of management. The lack of any real confidence between the King and his Lord Chancellor, and the general rift between older counsellors and younger men, made it possible for experienced voices to be muffled at a time when restraint was particularly desirable.

The King and Queen returned to London from Hampton Court in October. The King greeted his Parliament in an uncharacteristically aggressive vein. 'You have had leisure to attend your own conveniences in the country and the public service there,' he told Members, 'and I have been able to let our neighbours see that I can defend myself and my subjects against their insolence upon the stock of my own credit and reputation'. Such talk could easily be interpreted as the merest bravado. The 'stock of his credits', never too healthy, was at this time noticeably low. It was difficult to assess what the unpopular Hearth Tax had been able to yield, since the proceeds were being paid to the City to cover its loans, but one thing was certain—it would never produce the sum which had originally been calculated. All the same the work undertaken by the King's new managers was beginning to bear fruit. He had been well pleased with the good humour of both Houses earlier in the year, and on May 19 he had written to Madame that 'never any Parliament went away better pleased than this did'. Bennet and Coventry and their associates had been busy canvassing individual Members and putting the King's problems and needs in a favourable light. As a result the Commons proved far less niggardly than usual and the unprecedented sum of two and a half million pounds was voted to fit out the fleet.

As the two seafaring nations encouraged their ships to seize forts and territories in America, the Indies and in West Africa, the outbreak of war seemed inevitable, and the younger men at the Palace were now greedy for gallantry and renown. For a Court so dedicated to its pleasures the change in outlook was remarkable. The King and the Duke led the way, devoting much of their time to the consideration of naval affairs. The Duke spent most of November in Portsmouth, and on his return Pepys and his friends thought he looked in better health than before 'and a little more stern'. In the same month the English provocatively set on the Smyrna fleet off Cadiz and in distant waters each country attacked the other and indulged self-righteously in reprisals.

Clarendon still believed that war could be avoided. In his opinion the King had 'gotten into friendships which were most behoveful to him, and which could remove or reconcile all prejudices'. In taking a stand on behalf of the nonconformists, the King was not only acting disloyally towards the established Church, he was also encouraging the strongly Presbyterian elements in the City whose interests were threatened by Dutch aggression in foreign waters. It seemed to the Chancellor that the King was now by-passing the official Council, and that decisions were made at informal meetings of the new 'royal' party attended by Bennet, Coventry, Clifford and others. He disapproved strongly of the Commission of Prizes which was set up to allocate the money raised from the sale of goods seized on Dutch ships. But he found it impossible to explain to the King how mistaken he was in thinking he would be 'more rich in having one thousand pounds in his closet that nobody knew of' than in possessing a much larger sum granted to him by Parliament in the normal way. Now at last the King had found a means of by-passing the Chancellor and the Treasurer with their seals and warrants. Clarendon noted acidly that those appointed to the task of administering the Commission did not demur when offered generous salaries for their pains. Lord Ashley was appointed Treasurer, and although he was married to the Chancellor's niece, Clarendon had a low opinion of his ability. The immediate fear was that large sums would find their way into the Lady's pocket, and there certainly was a tell-tale note written against a Secret Service payment to Will Chiffinch, Keeper of the King's private closet, which read—'for Madam Palmer'. Most of the money, however, was rightfully paid to the Navy Treasurer, and only a small proportion saw its way into the Secret Service fund, which tended to cover a multitude of sins. The Chancellor probably overrated the Lady's ability to benefit from the Commission, but it was not surprising that his suspicions were aroused by the fact that as far as he could see, Ashley 'had got an entire trust with the Lady who very well understood the benefit such an officer would be to her'.

According to Comminges, the English talked of nothing but triumphs and victories, and there was none of the usual frivolity at carnival time. The masque which was staged at Court for Candlemas extolled in allegorical terms, like the old entertainments of the thirties, the glorious task of subduing the King's enemies. Wearing 'antique' costumes, the most beautiful ladies and the most handsome gentlemen of the Court took part, all representing the different nations. Needless to say, Lady Castlemaine was one of the principle dancers. Lady Sandwich talked sadly of 'the luxury and looseness of the times', and even Lady Castlemaine took it upon herself to tell some of her young friends that they were so frivolous no man would ever want to marry them; she jokingly prophesied that her four-month-old daughter Charlotte would be married before all the rest of them.

The King told his sister that he could not give his mind to the 'little masquerades' at Court. Although war had not yet been formally declared there was little doubt that hostilities would officially begin as soon as the winter was over. The Duke of York was working tirelessly to ensure that the fleet would be ready to sail when the better weather came. Both the English and the Dutch felt confident of success provided that their enemies did not manage to forge an alliance with France, in which case the contest could quickly become one-sided. Charles had always been careful to avoid offending his cousin Louis, and as he had told his sister the previous year, 'there is nobody that hates disputes as much as I do . . . especially with one whose friendship I desire as much as that of the King of France'. Using his sister as the channel of communication he now made it clear to Louis that his instincts led him towards an Anglo-French alliance, and he was only held back by the ignorant people who surrounded him. As a proof of his sincerity, he sent his closest friend, the charming Lord Fitzharding, as a special Ambassador to Paris, entrusted with the task of sounding out the French and ensuring that they would at least remain neutral in the war that was bound to come. Louis responded by sending to London his *Célèbre Ambassade*, which consisted of the Duc de Verneuil, a bastard son of Charles's grandfather Henri IV, and the diminutive Honoré de Courtin, himself a 'man of pleasure' picked for his ability to fit into the King's social circle.

Fitzharding returned from France, delighted by the friendly welcome he had received, and Charles found the *Ambassade* equally amicable. It was difficult, however, to persuade anyone to say anything very definite. Verneuil and Courtin thought that the English, for a nation virtually at war, seemed surprisingly dilatory, and they sometimes despaired of achieving a meeting with the people who mattered. One day the Chancellor would have an opportune attack of gout and on another an audience would be postponed just because it was Sunday —a very poor reason in the opinion of the French. The King for his part found that Courtin was subtly evasive, and the language too posed certain problems, especially as the King had forgotten most of his French; 'in truth', he confessed, 'the trouble I have in looking for my words allows the escape of my thoughts.'

The conflict between the English and the Dutch threatened to upset the delicate balance of European power and the French feared that if they supported either, the other would be bound to side with Spain. French fears and Spanish hopes accounted for an increasing diplomatic activity in London in April 1665. As usual both sides believed that the surest way of influencing the King was to gain the support of one of the women he loved. As soon as Courtin arrived in England he made it his duty to study the Court beauties and to decide which of them would best suit his purposes. He was impressed by Frances Stuart's qualifications; she seemed to him the prettiest girl on the English scene and she had grown taller and far more beautiful since he saw her in France. Lord Fitzharding promised to introduce him to Lady Castlemaine, but he was disappointed to find that the Spanish Ambassador, the Count de Molina, who arrived in England in April, had already won her favour with the help of bribery and flattery. According to Comminges the Spanish, who had always regarded the Lady as their particular ally, were redoubling their efforts to win her over; they were prepared to spend large sums of money, Madrid having provided them liberally with 'what to feed friendships with'. But Molina's attempt to woo the Lady by laying on a great feast for her benefit ended in disaster when all her coachmen and lacqueys indulged in too much liquor and had a fight with the Spanish servants—'the most amusing disturbance imaginable' in the opinion of the French. Comminges was confident that he was on better terms with Mademoiselle Stuart than Molina was with Madame de Castlemaine; all the same he had to admit that the ravishing but vacuous Frances was totally uninterested in politics and diplomacy; as a result he feared that all the 'incense' they were using to woo her over would bring them no advantage whatsoever.

War was officially declared between England and the Dutch on March 4, and on March 23 the Duke of York left to take up his naval command. After a preliminary cruise as far as the Dutch coast and back, the fleet set sail at the end of May carrying with it the King's brother, his cousin, Prince Rupert, and his best friend Charles Berkeley, Lord Fitzharding, who had been created Earl of Falmouth 'before he had one foot of land in the world' as Clarendon none too accurately put it. Falmouth had in fact acquired a plot of land in Piccadilly, just opposite the fine edifice Clarendon himself was building—on the proceeds of the sale of Dunkirk, some people were unkind enough to say. He had been married the previous autumn to Mary Bagot of Aston in Warwickshire, and she had been speedily introduced to the Queen's Bedchamber, or 'bad chamber' as she herself inadvertently but perhaps not inappropriately styled it.

Among those who had offered their services to the King was Roger Castlemaine, whom Pepys saw at St James's in March. It was rumoured that he had come with the intention of arranging a reconciliation with his wife; however the prospect of a nursery filled with royal children was too much for him, and he left for the fleet soon after. His service with the Venetian fleet made him better qualified than many of the other officers who, despite their distinctly amateur status, expected to be given posts of high command. The Duke of Buckingham, deeply hurt when the Duke of York explained to him that his peerage did not give him an automatic right to attend Councils of War or to command a ship on his very first voyage, remained ashore regarding this verdict as a 'personal disobligation'.

The Lady remained unmoved either by the arrival or by the departure of her husband. At about the time he left for the fleet, Pepys glimpsed her in the park 'impudently upon her back in her coach, asleep with her mouth open'. On March 14 she ordered the delivery of two rings worth £2,000, paid for out of money owed her by Mr Edward and John Fenne. For the ladies who remained at home while their husbands and lovers sought glory in the English Channel, life was certainly muted. Not all of them sat alone in a darkened room like the Duchess of York, saying prayers for her husband's safe return. Some played bowls, or went for sittings in Lely's studio. The Queen visited Tunbridge Wells as usual and the customary rota was drawn up for her Ladies of the Bedchamber. It was decided that Lady Castlemaine and Lady Falmouth should go down together when their turn came; both ladies were several months gone with child. But in early June the Lady was still in London, for when Pepys received a message from Sir William Batten on June 2, he knew exactly where to find the King. The message came from Harwich, and reported that the fleet had sailed from Sole Bay having sighted the Dutch fleet. Pepys was to tell the King that 'if the calm hinders not' the battle might well have already begun. He went straight to Court with the letter and was led up to Lady Castlemaine's lodgings, where she and the King and others were at supper.

CHAPTER TWELVE

A CATALOGUE OF DISASTERS

ON 3 JUNE 1665 the noise of gunfire could be clearly heard by Londoners as they went about their business on the river and in the City. For three days the King and his subjects listened with terrible apprehension, everyone praying for the safety of the Duke of York and his men. Soon there were rumours that the Dutch were retreating from an engagement off Lowestoft with the British in pursuit, but for several days there was no definite news, and when Pepys visited Lady Sandwich on June 6, she had still heard nothing from her husband; he found her 'neither confident nor troubled with fear'. In the relentless summer weather—Pepys said that June 7 was 'the hottest day that ever I felt in my life'—the waiting continued. As the noise of the gunfire gradually receded people allowed themselves to hope that the enemy was in flight. When the news finally came through that the Dutch had retreated in some disarray towards their own shores, there was universal rejoicing. Bonfires were lit and bells were rung in the City. It was only when the first heady excitement was over that there were doubts about whether the battle had been truly won, or whether the English had hung back, completely failing to follow up their advantage. 'While the English never cease to speak extravagantly, all their captains are showing remarkable faint-heartedness' was how they put it at the Hague, and John Evelyn was in agreement. 'Indeed', he wrote, 'the victory might have been a complete one, and at once ended the war, had it been pursued.'

Soon the ships were coming back into harbour, some of them damaged, and laden with their wounded, their trophies and prisoners of war. On June 16 the Duke of York arrived in London, and Pepys saw him at Court surrounded by his friends, 'returned from the sea, all fat and lusty and ruddy by being in the sun'. There were some who had not returned, most notably the Earl of Falmouth, whose handsome countenance had been blown to pieces by a cannon-ball. The death of a young and popular man with such a bright future before him brought home to everybody the less romantic side of war. He had been destined, it seemed, for the highest honours, growing daily 'more potent, opulent and . . . more formidable at Court'. When they told the King he wept uncontrollably, although the general grief was tempered by relief that the heir to the throne had been miraculously spared; the Duke of York had been standing so close to Falmouth that he had been spattered with his blood:

> His shatter'd head the fearless Duke disdains
> And gave the last first proof that he had brains.

There were misgivings now about the wisdom of allowing the Duke to see active service, and his mother was particularly anxious that he should never again risk his life with the fleet. His healthy looks proved that the sailor's life suited him, but the King felt under an obligation to tell him, to his great chagrin, that in future he must stay ashore.

The King had other worries on his mind, for the city of London to which the more or less conquering heroes had returned, was now facing 'another enemy, much more formidable than the Dutch'. As long ago as the previous September there had been cases of a deadly illness which started with a cold shuddering and led on to sickness and excruciating pain. Those who could remember the last great epidemics of the twenties recognized the symptoms all too well. Early in June Pepys saw two or three infected houses in Drury Lane marked with a red cross and 'Lord have mercy' written below. The sight filled him with fear, and he was forced to chew some roll tobacco to avoid infection. As always the disease spread rapidly through the overcrowded and foetid dwellings of the poor, and as the hot weather continued without a break cases were reported among members of the middle classes. When Pepys bought a new periwig he did not dare wear it for fear that the hair had been taken from an infected person. 'Lord', he wrote, 'how everybody's looks and discourse in the street is of death and nothing else.'

At Court there was strict security, nobody being allowed access unless they were in the royal employment. The Ambassadors had more difficulty than ever in finding out what was going on in the King's councils. In early July, along with an estimated 30,000 other people, the Court left London. Lady Castlemaine, having decided that the rooms assigned to her at Hampton Court were not fit for habitation, descended as was her habit on her uncle at Richmond. Courtin, probably not realizing how well such tactics had worked before, believed that she was unwise to leave the field to Frances Stuart. 'Madame de Castlemaine runs great risks', he wrote, 'and if her anger lasts she may well lose the finest rose on her hat.'

In London the streets were deserted, the shops shut up and 'all in mournful silence, as not knowing whose turn might be next'. There were no boats on the river and grass grew in the courtyards at Whitehall Palace. Parliament was to have met in London, but it was quickly adjourned and called to meet later in Oxford. Meanwhile it had been decided that the Court should move further away from the capital, and at the end of July arrangements were made for a general move to Salisbury. Pepys saw the cavalcade leaving Hampton Court, the ladies all dressed like men in riding habits, with velvet coats and hats with ribbons or a feather. He thought the fashion very becoming in most cases, even if it did make the Duchess of York look even more portly than usual.

The Duke and Duchess broke away from the main party and went off on their own to York. For Clarendon his son-in-law's decision was very understandable. 'The truth is', he wrote, 'the constitution of the Court at this time was such, the prevalence of the Lady so great, and the Queen's humour thereupon so inconstant, all together so discomposed the King, that there was no pleasure in being part of it; and therefore the advice was as soon embraced as given, by the Duke and his wife, who were well content to enjoy themselves in their own family apart.' Reresby reported that at York the Duke passed his time in 'shooting flying, and other exercising', the Duchess meanwhile receiving the ladies of the neighbourhood, 'which she did very obligingly'.

The King left his wife at Farnham, paying a visit to Portsmouth and rejoining her a few days later at Salisbury where the influx of courtiers, ambassadors and hangers-on had already caused an acute shortage of accommodation. Everybody was complaining about their lodgings. 'The sojourn in this place does not please their Britannic Majesties', one of the French contingent wrote, 'it is situated very low, streams of water run along the middle of the streets, the winds are continual and reign here with tyranny.' There were plans afoot for the King and Queen and their immediate entourage to move out to Wilton, but the Pembrokes were spared the inconvenience of a royal invasion thanks to the intransigence of the Lady who firmly opposed the scheme. In Salisbury, Frances Stuart had been quartered in the royal lodgings while the other ladies were boarded out in houses nearby. It was said that the King visited either Frances or the Lady every morning before breakfast, and it is possible that the mistress was afraid she might not fare so well if the King removed himself to Wilton.

There was a tight security ring round the town and those outside found it hard to discover what was going on; many suspected that the processes of government had come to a halt, 'nobody setting to heart the business of the kingdom, but everybody minding their particular profit or pleasures; the King himself minding nothing but his ease, and so we let things go to wrack'. Although the key men in the administration had followed the King to Salisbury, it was difficult to tell what they were doing. Outside the town there were rumours that the plague had struck and that a number of important people had died, including the Duke of Buckingham.

Back in London those who had been left behind to look after what remained of the government machinery walked through streets empty except for the occasional corpse or coffin. There was an uncanny silence except for the spasmodic tolling of the bell. Few shops were open, no boats plied on the river and all places of entertainment had been closed. Pepys, however, was able to enjoy one pleasure which was unaffected by the current restrictions; he was lucky enough to dream that he had Lady Castlemaine in his arms, and that she allowed him to use 'all the dalliance' he desired. He could think of no greater bliss. 'What a happy thing it would be', he mused, 'if when we are in our graves (as Shakespeare resembles it), we could dream, and dream but such dreams as this—that then we should not need to be so fearful of death as we are this plague time.'

In early September there was some alarm when the King himself fell sick and was forced to spend three nights in his own bedchamber. His illness was finally diagnosed as colic, 'which after a fortnight's much grumblings did at last grievously torment him'. On his recovery he left Salisbury with 'some select persons' to visit Lord Ashley. The ladies meanwhile amused themselves, playing bowls or hunting, and the Ambassadors intensified their efforts to win support by giving supper parties in honour of the King's favourites. The French Ambassadors were so successful that Frances Stuart dreamt she was in bed with both of them.

As soon as the King returned the Court packed up and thankfully left Salisbury for Oxford. The problem of finding lodgings began all over again, but at least the Colleges were made available, many scholars giving up their rooms. The Queen was able to stay at Merton in the same apartments as her mother-in-law had occupied during the civil war. The Duke of York lodged with Dr Richard Allestree, a Canon of Christ Church, the Spanish Ambassador Molina at New College, while Verneuil, Comminges and Courtin went to Magdalen. The King arrived on September 25 and the next day greeted the Queen at the gate of Merton College. On September 27 Lady Castlemaine followed with her two children Charles and Henry Fitzroy, settling herself with Anthony Wood and his family. Henry Jermyn also lodged with the Woods, and his frivolity caused some disapproval, especially when he 'pretended to joke and play the rogue at Mass'. Wood found that the courtiers in general were 'high, proud and insolent', and although they were neat and bright in their apparel, they were at the same time 'very nasty and beastly, leaving at their departure their excrement in every corner'.

Once Parliament assembled at Oxford, the King made his appeal for more money to help meet the heavy expenses incurred by the navy. 'I told you when I entered upon this war', he reminded Members, 'that I had not such a brutal appetite as to make war for war-sake.' All the same, as no decisive victory had been won, the need to maintain a navy remained, a fact that many Members would have preferred to forget. After several peaceful weeks visiting their estates in the shires, the country Members' thoughts were running on such questions as a ban on the import of fat cattle from Ireland, rather than on the progress of a war designed to protect the interests of the merchants. They had been angered by reports that nonconformist preachers had taken the liberty of preaching in the churches abandoned by Anglican clergy in plague-stricken London. For them such preachers constituted a greater threat to the nation than the Dutch, and they quickly introduced a Bill to ban preachers within a five-mile radius of the capital.

Since the naval battle off Lowestoft the political sands had been shifting again. The Earl of Sandwich returned from the fleet to find the Court seething with reports of mismanagement and lost opportunities. In spite of all that Clarendon could do to support him he was removed from his post. He greeted his dismissal with a touch of relief, knowing that his command would become impossible if while he was at sea his enemies ashore were continually plotting his downfall. He was offered, and accepted, an embassy in Spain, 'out of reach of noise or clamour', and meanwhile he found what solace he could in playing the guitar in his cabin aboard the *Royal James*—he commended the instrument above all other music in the world, because he found it 'so portable and manageable without much trouble'. Clarendon had an uneasy feeling that his son-in-law was falling under the influence of Sir William Coventry, who had a habit of busily taking notes at meetings of the sea-captains; Clarendon suspected that he only recorded what suited him, twisting the evidence in order to put the Duke of York 'in mind of what he had to do'. The Chancellor also feared that trouble-makers were out to make a rift between the royal brothers, and a coldness between them had already become apparent.

When Pepys saw Sandwich he was impressed by his melancholy face and unshaven look; the sight of the fallen man made him realize that he himself would have to practise some 'courtship', if he were not to suffer the same fate. 'Lord, to see in what difficulty I stand', he wrote, 'that I dare not walk with Sir W. Coventry, for fear my Lord [Sandwich] or Sir G. Carteret should see me, nor with either of them, for fear

4

Sir W. Coventry should.' The delicate situation he found himself in was all too typical, and many other people were walking warily as they struggled to remain in the ascendant. 'Courtship' was the quality most needed to ensure success. Clarendon realized that Bennet, inscrutable and devious, and a great deal cleverer than he liked to admit, had forged an alliance in the inner councils with Sir William Coventry; he foresaw that as a result there would be 'an alteration in the whole carriage and debate of all manner of business'. And with Sandwich out of the way, Coventry had 'full sea-room to give vent to all his passions, and to incense the Duke'.

Although the pattern of power seemed to be changing, Lady Castlemaine remained in as commanding a position as ever. As the chosen tool of the Spanish Ambassador, she was helped by the fact that the French had become increasingly unpopular throughout the autumn; by the end of 1665 it was evident that a rupture between the two countries was not far off. In the streets Englishmen no longer took off their hats to the French envoys. The King was still so concerned for the Lady's welfare that when her child was due he allowed her to move into Merton where on December 28 she gave birth to a son who was christened George on New Year's Day. Anthony Wood, in recording the occasion, described George as Roger Castlemaine's son, which was improbable, but not impossible, as Roger had been in London nine months before. Nobody seriously doubted that the King had fathered the child. It was commonly believed that although the plague had died down in London, he was not able to leave Oxford because Lady Castlemaine had been 'lately put to bed'; even the boys in the streets were openly spreading it about that the King would delay his departure 'until my Lady Castlemaine be ready to come along with him'.

When the King finally left Oxford at the end of January the Queen stayed behind. She needed a little time, the King told his sister, to 'fancy all clear' in London. As always everyone was hoping that Catherine was with child; she had only to stay in her room for a couple of days for the whole world to be convinced that she was showing signs of pregnancy. Just before her return in February there were further rumours that she had miscarried, and this time there did seem more reason than usual to believe that she might still bear a child and that in future the King would not have to 'endeavour for a thing impossible'.

The Queen Regent of Portugal had recently died, which put all the ladies of the Court into mourning. Pepys thought that Frances Stuart looked very pretty *au naturel*, while Lady Castlemaine was quite disappointing without the help of colourful clothes and beauty spots. Not that the King seemed to notice any deterioration in her charms, and Lady Carteret expressed a common opinion when she cried out 'against my Lady Castlemaine that makes the King neglect his business'. A notice which had been attached to her door at Oxford crudely delivered the message that had it not been for the King's protection she might well have found herself on the ducking-stool suffering the punishment reserved for scolds:

> *Hanc Caesare pressam a fluctu defendit onus*
> The reason why she is not duck'd?
> Because by Caesar she is ——.

The truth was that the Lady had so far survived every challenge. Frances Stuart had proved ornamental rather than influential, the Queen Mother remained a peripheral figure and the death of the Earl of Falmouth had not proved as disastrous as might at first have been expected. Although nobody would ever match Falmouth's charm, or fill his place in the King's affection, the Lady had seen to it that she was on the best of terms with Baptist May, his successor as Keeper of the Privy Purse. May had inherited the unofficial office of pimp along with the Privy Purse, and he carried on the work in both departments as efficiently as Falmouth had done before him. He ensured that the Lady continued to benefit from the fund which he had in his care; in March elaborate work was in progress at Hampton Court to improve the Lady's lodgings there. She was buying jewels on the King's account —diamond rings worth £2,000 had been delivered to her, and the jeweller John Leroy petitioned the King soon after his return from Oxford for payment of £357, the balance of £850 due for a ring delivered to the Countess of Castlemaine 'which she said was for his Majesty'.

The friendly Earl of Falmouth had managed to keep on good terms with both the King and the Duke, even when there was coldness between the brothers. The Lady too made great efforts to ensure that she was on a favourable footing with the heir to the throne. Pepys believed that it was 'to fortify herself with the Duke' that she helped Henry Brouncker, James's Gentleman of the Bedchamber, to procure for him the reluctant Lady Denham. The Duke had fallen in love with Denham, described by some as a strumpet, although she herself maintained that she would never join the ranks of the royal mistresses who were condemned 'to go up and down the Privy Stairs'. In spite of all the efforts of Brouncker and the Lady she insisted that the Duke must visit her own lodgings in Scotland Yard, and in the middle of the morning only.

The Lady's machinations extended into any field where she might expect to reap some profit for herself. Everybody knew that through her they could gain favours and perquisites, and they acknowledged her expertise when it came to assessing the amount any honour was worth to the buyer. When she estimated that an Irish viscountcy should not be valued at more than £1,000, few people would have quarrelled with her. She calculated that a £40 bribe would be enough to make a man risk his life when her lodgings caught fire and she wanted somebody to bring out her favourite cabinet. She was right of course—one of the onlookers duly went back into the flames and retrieved her precious furniture.

Now that Charles had finally broken with France, an alliance with Spain had become more than a possibility, and the Spaniards intensified their efforts to use the Lady's influence. The King himself hoped that the Spaniards would be encouraged by the fact that his only ally, the bellicose Bishop of Munster, had mounted an attack in the Netherlands. Pepys was probably not alone when he felt apprehensive on hearing that war had been declared on France; 'God knows how little fit we are for it', he wrote. The King, as always, allowed himself to feel optimistic, but others were less sanguine and in general nerves were stretched when the better weather came and the fleet put out to sea. On June 1 John Evelyn, as he was walking in his garden, heard 'the great guns go thick off', and on June 5 news reached London of a bitter battle lasting for four days with heavy losses on both sides. At Sheerness on June 16 Evelyn saw the sad spectacle of the damaged ships limping home—'more than half that gallant bulwark of the kingdom miserably shattered, hardly a vessel entire, but appearing rather so many wracks and hulls, so cruelly had the Dutch mangled us'. There was criticism of the way the fleet had been handled by the Duke of Albemarle, and some were of the opinion that it would have been better managed if 'my Lord Sandwich had had the ordering of it'. At Court the Duke of York chafed at being forced to stay ashore, and sought his distractions elsewhere—notably with Lady Denham.

When Pepys visited the Court on July 22 he found an atmosphere of gloom and did not see a single smiling face. The King, understandably on edge, picked a quarrel with the Lady. The fracas began when the Queen pointedly told her in front of other ladies that the King risked catching a cold by staying so late at her house. Lady Castlemaine, never at a loss for a telling riposte, replied that in fact the King never stayed late with her, but left in the early hours of the morning and spent the rest of the night somewhere else. The King, entering at this moment, overheard what she had said and told her angrily that she was a bold impertinent woman and must leave the Court at once, staying away until he sent for her. This she did, but not before she had threatened to publish every love-letter he had ever written her. Establishing herself in lodgings in Pall Mall, she managed to keep quiet for several days before demanding to collect her belongings from Whitehall. The King gave her permission and stipulated that she should come in person.

By now his rage had cooled, and as soon as they met there was the usual reconciliation, Lady Castlemaine having stage-managed the affair to perfection with her own particular mixture of passion and calculation.

One day in late July the King and the Duke heard the sound of gunfire as they played bowls on the leads at Whitehall. News of a successful engagement was brought to the Palace in the early hours of July 29, and this did something to dispel the general air of depression. The ladies of the Court left for Tunbridge Wells, and meanwhile at the Savoy hospital, John Evelyn saw with pity the plight of the wounded, many of whom were hideously dismembered.

It had been a hot dry summer, and when fire broke out in the City in a street so narrow that 'the engines could not play'—the conduits and pumps in any case soon ran dry—the flames, fanned by strong winds, soon spread and threatened to engulf the entire capital. The population fled, piling belongings into carts and boats, and camping out in the surrounding countryside in miserable huts and hovels. Those who owned wagons were able to profiteer at the expense of the less fortunate, charging exorbitant rates for carrying precious possessions out of reach of the blaze. At one time it seemed that the Palace itself would be consumed, although at least some fire-fighting equipment had been installed after the fire at Lady Castlemaine's lodgings in January 1664. The King and the Duke actively helped to stay the blaze; they directed fire-fighting operations, supervised the blowing up of houses, organized the distribution of bread and cheese to the poor, and worked until they were exhausted. Finally, on the fourth day, the blaze died down, leaving acres of devastation.

Many saw the holocaust as God's judgment on a depraved nation—'What we highly deserved' as Evelyn put it. The Court, however, did not seem in the least chastened by the experiences of the summer, and the Duke of York in particular 'looked too gay and too little concerned'. He had turned his back on business and given himself up to his pleasures —'what with his woman', as Pepys put it, 'and his hunting three times a week'. In the summer the ladies, dressed in riding habits, periwigs and hats, had been scarcely distinguishable from the men except for 'a long petticoat dragging under their men's coats'. Now this fashion had given place to another equally scandalous style with skirts so short that they only just reached the ankle. It was said that the Queen very much liked her feet to be seen. For men the King had introduced the Persian tunic, made in black cloth, pinked with white and far less expensive than tailored clothes made in Paris. The Queen's birthday ball was a black-and-white occasion, the courtiers looking like a flock of magpies. Pepys recorded that Frances Stuart was a glorious sight in a black dress trimmed with white lace, her head and shoulders dressed with diamonds. Lady Castlemaine, 'without whom all is nothing,' Pepys wrote, was also present, but she kept in the background, leaving the floor to her rival, who excelled at the new French dances.

Black clothes symbolized the mood of an uneasy autumn season. After the dry summer there had been late rains which brought with them the fear of flooding and famine which would have completed the catalogue of disasters. Dislike of papists was vocal and widespread, and scaremongers were even ready to blame a French Catholic for deliberately starting the fire of London. A rising of Covenanters in Scotland gave further cause for alarm. In the cities the continuing fear of impressment kept many men off the streets. The Parliament which reassembled in September was in a vindictive mood, and Pepys noted apprehensively that it threatened to be 'mighty severe' in examining the naval accounts. Sir Henry Bennet now Lord Arlington, Coventry, Carteret and Sandwich all had much to fear from Parliamentary probing, while Albemarle, whom Pepys was pleased to call 'that block-headed Duke', was also under a cloud for his conduct at sea during the summer. Now it was the Duke of Buckingham, whose enthusiasm had been so cruelly dampened by the Duke of York in 1665, who could turn on his former friends, secure in the knowledge that he himself was immune from criticism since he had not been allowed to satisfy his ambition to become a naval commander.

There was no doubt that Buckingham's star was in the ascendant. His protégée Frances Stuart seemed at last to be on the verge of becoming the King's mistress. Even Pepys had to admit that she exceeded Lady Castlemaine, and he recorded in his diary that she was 'the beautifullest creature that ever I saw in my life'. In December he was told that the younger woman claimed the King's attention almost entirely, while the Lady had to be content with one visit a week. Lady Castlemaine in fact seemed to be strangely subdued. She had hardly been seen all the autumn, and when Pepys had a sighting early in October he thought she had never looked so ill. It seemed as if the year might end with a major political upheaval as well as a startling change in the pattern of favour at Court, and when it became known that the King had settled all the Lady's debts which were said to mount up to £30,000, many people thought that this was the first step towards removing her completely from his life.

CHAPTER THIRTEEN

THE FALL OF THE CHANCELLOR

IN THE important parliamentary debates of December 1666 the Duke of Buckingham dominated the scene. He was witty, amusing and compelling; young Members saw him as the leader of the future, the territorial loyalties of Yorkshire Members guaranteed him a nucleus of support and to these were added the nonconformists whose cause he had championed, as well as anyone with a grudge against the current administration. The serious-minded Clarendon despised his methods, acidly describing how he 'assumed a liberty of speaking when and what he would in a dialect unusual and ungrave, his similes and other expressions giving occasion of much mirth and laughter'. Outside the Parliament House his handsome figure acted as a magnet, and wherever he went the crowds would follow him. In the world of the theatre he was well-known and influential, numbering among his friends the Howard brothers, Robert and James, who were both by now successful dramatists. But perhaps most disconcerting of all for the government was the alliance he had forged with men whose interests and assets lay in the land, for they were the first to lose their enthusiasm for a war which had so far proved expensive and unfruitful.

The massive sums voted in previous sessions had vanished in the smoke of an inconclusive naval battle and some lesser engagements of an inglorious nature. The country was by now severely in debt, and the fire of London, so damaging to trade, had reduced the amount of money the King could expect to raise by means of the customs and excise duties. With thousands of homes destroyed by fire, the Hearth Tax was unlikely to yield anything like the original estimate. To clear his debts, pay his seamen and fit out his fleet for another summer, the King needed money, and everybody guessed that in the end it would be raised by means of taxation based on the possession of land. This the landowners were unlikely to grant without a close enquiry into past expenditure and into the general conduct of the war. Since he had played so small a part in hostilities himself, Buckingham had little to fear, and he welcomed the prospect of castigating those who had rejected his enthusiastic offers of participation. In December his astute and influential friend Sir Robert Howard brought in a 'proviso' which was tacked on to the Poll Bill, and which stipulated that a committee of nine should be set up, empowered to examine the naval accounts. The Bill was passed by a large majority although the King did all he could to defeat it, even scouring the playhouses and bawdy houses to find his supporters—or so it was said. There was no last-minute panic for Sir Robert and the Duke; their victory was the result of months of hard work and careful organization. On every possible occasion they had spoken out, making themselves 'remarkable by opposing all things which were proposed in that House for the King's service, or which were likely to be grateful to him', as Clarendon put it. They had supported the Irish Cattle Bill, thus currying favour with the landed interest, while at the same time encouraging the nonconformist merchants in the City. Their efforts had resulted in a massive and well-disciplined opposition, which was causing the government much concern.

Arlington, perhaps more than anybody else, had good reason to fear an enquiry into the management of the war. He had been directly responsible for a delay in sending vital information to Prince Rupert concerning the Dutch deployment of their navy, and this had resulted in a disastrous division of the English fleet. He knew well that this lapse, if it came under investigation, could put his whole career in jeopardy. Since the days when, in the summer of 1662, he had joined the movement to bring about the Chancellor's downfall he had moved away from his alliance with Buckingham and was now associated once more with the hated Clarendon. His recent marriage to Isabella van Beverwaert, a daughter of Louis of Nassau, had given him a new family loyalty which made it impossible for him to support the Irish Cattle Bill. Isabella's sister was married to the Duke of Ormonde's son, the Earl of Ossory, and as a family they were all bound to oppose a measure which was likely to bring grievous hardship on the Irish cattle drovers. Clarendon too felt impelled to support his old friend Ormonde and he was not unmindful of Irish interests. Meanwhile Buckingham threw himself in on the side of the English landed gentry; normally never up before eleven o'clock he was to be seen first thing in the morning and he stayed all day to hear the debates which sometimes went on until after the candles had been brought in.

Clarendon and Arlington were all too aware of the dangers that confronted them—the opposition drawn in by Buckingham, the threats of investigation, the rumours of nonconformist plots. It was even reported that the Earl of Bristol might soon be putting in a reappearance. The Duke of York broke off his relationship with Lady Denham; it was said that she was one of Bristol's supporters, and that she had been talking to him about business, a habit he disliked in a mistress. She died soon afterwards, the gossips finding it hard to discover whether her demise was due to poison or a broken heart. Since the Duke of Buckingham seemed to be the focus of discontent and trouble-making, Clarendon and his friends felt it vital to remove him before he could do them any more harm. The Duke's temper was notoriously fiery. On December 19 he became involved in an altercation with Lord Dorchester whose hat and periwig he knocked off. Both men were sent to the Tower but were soon released. A duel between Ossory and Buckingham was arranged but failed to take place when the Duke mistook the meeting place— on purpose in Clarendon's opinion. Since neither of these episodes had proved serious enough to bring about Buckingham's downfall, Arlington busied himself bribing informers and producing treasonable correspondence including a letter in which the Duke commissioned an astrologer to draw up a horoscope of the King's nativity. There were dangers inherent in a prediction of the King's death, and there appeared to be enough evidence to justify Buckingham's arrest on a charge of treason. He evaded his captors and went into hiding; meanwhile he was deprived of all his offices. The King made no strenuous attempts to find him, although he was said to be in hiding with friends in London, for his trial might have proved something of an embarrassment seeing that his friends in Parliament already regarded him as a martyr.

In December, Roger Castlemaine was in London. Encouraged perhaps by Buckingham's support of the nonconformists, he published a pamphlet entitled *The Catholique Apology* in which he lamented the severity of Parliament's attitude towards the papists, and pointed out how lenient some Catholic princes were, by contrast, towards the Protestants. The moment for such frank propaganda had not yet come, and the pamphlet was rapidly seized by order of the House of Commons. And if he had hoped that the King might, after all these years, be about to end his illicit relationship with Barbara, in this too he was disappointed. In December the King proved that he still cared for her by banishing Henry Killigrew from Court for spreading rumours that she had revealed her lascivious tendencies at a very early age. Realizing that he was to gain no satisfaction from his wife, and no encouragement for his Catholicism, Roger left once again for the Continent. Pepys reported that the Castlemaines parted on good terms, intending 'never to trouble one another more'.

One evening in January 1667 Lord Conway supped with the King at Lady Castlemaine's. They were, he wrote, 'very merry, and not sensible of the troubles and dangers which I fear are drawing in fast upon us'. The Queen was lying ill with a fever, and the Lady had at last seen a chance to rid herself of Frances Stuart's rivalry. For three years Frances had contrived to encourage the King while still keeping him at bay, but recently he had become so importunate that she doubted

4*

her ability to maintain this delicate balance. Her only escape seemed to lie in matrimony, and she had expressed herself ready to accept any man with an income of £1,500 a year, providing he would make an honest woman of her. It is hard to say how serious she was in this intention, but she discreetly reciprocated when the Duke of Richmond began to pay his court to her. He had recently become a widower for the second time, and being a fourth cousin to the King he could consider himself eligible. At the age of twenty-seven he had already become addicted to alcohol, and he was so deeply in debt that he would hardly have satisfied the modest financial requirements stipulated by Frances herself. Such considerations did not however, deter the Lady, who had seen in this nascent romance her long-awaited opportunity to remove her rival for ever.

The plan was carefully laid. One evening when the King was visiting Frances Stuart's apartments, the Lady watched outside, and the moment she saw him emerge she took a short cut to his apartments through Will Chiffinch's lodgings, 'a route', as Gramont put it, 'with which she was not unacquainted'. The King was in a bad humour because Frances had sent him away early with the excuse that she felt unwell. The Lady, who sat waiting for him as if she had been there for some time, registered surprise. Baptist May, whom she had detailed off to watch for the moment when the Duke of Richmond entered Stuart's apartments, now gave her the secret sign, and she was able to intimate to the King that his precious friend, far from suffering from a 'little ailment' was probably sitting up in bed with the Duke of Richmond at her side. 'Don't accept my word for it,' she said. 'I might be saying this from motives of spite or jealousy.' Curiosity overcame the King; he returned and found the Duke and Frances together. He was not at all pleased; in fact his eyes reflected a fury of which the Duke had never imagined they were capable. The flawless Frances was in disgrace. On April 3 the Duke married her in secret and the King declared that he would never see her again. 'Now the Countess of Castlemaine does carry all before her', Evelyn told Pepys.

Once again the Lady had shown the resilience which people had come to expect of her. Now, after six years, she was just as much in favour as she had been at the King's first coming over. When she wanted money, she dictated her demands to her woman, Wilson; 'Wilson,' she would say, 'make a note for this or that to the Privy Purse for money'. Never for one moment did she contemplate the thought that her demands might be refused. According to Clarendon, she 'procured round sums of money out of the Privy Purse (where she had placed Mr May) and other assignations in other names, and so the less taken notice of, though in greater proportions'. She outwitted the Chancellor by obtaining grants of land in Ireland; these did not come under his scrutiny and he was powerless to obstruct them. No doubt under severe pressure the King had agreed to bestow on her the gift of Phoenix Lodge in Dublin, with all its extensive parkland. Not that the Duke of Ormonde was prepared to surrender it without a fight. He explained to the King that it was the only summer residence available to the Lord-Lieutenant, and it was all the more valuable since Dublin Castle was in bad repair and had no open space around it or summer grazing for the animals. The Lady resented his opposition and 'fell upon him' when he was injudicious enough to put in an appearance at the Palace. She treated him to a torrent of abuse and ended by saying that she hoped to see him hanged. Ormonde replied coolly that he was not in so much haste to put an end to her days, for his only ambition was that he might live to see her grow old.

The Lady had always found another useful source of income in the 'incense' offered by the diplomats, and now the French as well as the Spanish were more than ready to use her as their source of information. Charles was hoping for a rapprochement with his cousin Louis as a preliminary to the ending of the war with the Dutch, and he was using his sister as an intermediary. The French Ambassadors had never found Frances Stuart anything but vapid and uninteresting; the Lady on the other hand was highly intelligent, extremely open to bribery, and alert to current trends. Almost as soon as Frances was married they sounded the Lady out, with satisfactory results for both parties. She told them in a 'point-blank' way very pleasing to the French that King Charles had told her Lord Arlington would not hear of an alliance with France. 'His Majesty [Louis XIV] hopes you will profit by this good beginning', Lionne, the French diplomat and Secretary of State, told the new French Ambassador, Colbert de Croissy, 'and he authorizes you, if you judge well, to let her know that you have reported what she said to his Majesty, who charges you to offer her his warmest thanks. In this order of ideas, the King has directed your brother, the Treasurer, to send her a handsome present, which you can give her as if from yourself. Ladies are fond of such keepsakes, whatever may be their breeding or disposition, and a nice little present can in any case do no harm.'

There had been rumours that Lady Castlemaine had misdirected some of the Queen's dowry in favour of the Earl of Falmouth, but there is little evidence to show that she ever made any efforts to enrich anybody except herself, her children and, later, her lovers. Clarendon thought that even her closest relations had not greatly benefited from her endeavours, though some of them were very 'clamorous'; he thought she had made little attempt even to pay off her father's debts. If she had been able to help her aunt and uncle, the Suffolks, to solve their financial problems, they might not have felt the need to sell their great country mansion to the King. As it was, although both the Earl and the Countess had important posts in the King's and Queen's Bedchambers, they were quite unable to keep Audley End up and at the same time maintain the expense of life at Court. The house, a fine monument to the power and prosperity enjoyed by the Howards in earlier reigns, was conveniently situated within easy reach of Newmarket. As the King increasingly spent his leisure time at the races, it became important to provide him with a permanent base. The deal helped to pay off Suffolk's debts, and since he himself was appointed to the post of Keeper at Audley End, he was spared the expense of entertaining the Court as he had done the year before, while at the same time enjoying the privilege of remaining close to the King throughout the summer season.

The arrangement was undoubtedly as convenient for Lady Suffolk's niece as it was for the Suffolks themselves. She had every excuse for joining the royal party on its increasingly frequent visits to Newmarket and she could also keep even with Lord Arlington who, since his marriage, had become disconcertingly independent of the King Street set. His wife Isabella was an excellent hostess and he was building himself a mansion, Goring House, on the site of the present Buckingham Palace. Having sold Holdenby Hall which he had acquired from the King, he too was making sure that his out-of-town house was strategically placed in the vicinity of Newmarket. He had bought and was doing up a big house at Euston in Suffolk.

While his subjects busied themselves with plans to capture his undivided favour, the King himself quietly pursued his own schemes, in particular doing all he could to bring about a much needed armistice. But to the outside world it seemed that he was more concerned to settle the quarrels among the women around him than to work for a peace with his foreign enemies. The French King found much to laugh about in his English cousin who made his bastards into princes and his mistresses into masters, but the English were far from amused when they saw him walking idly in the Park with the Duke of Monmouth or with Lady Castlemaine as if he did not have a care in the world. He himself brushed criticism aside; his private life was his own, and when Bishop Crewe had the temerity to point out to him 'the inconsistency of some practices with the receiving of the Holy Sacrament', he received a very cold answer. Pepys might complain, as he did in a letter to Lady Sandwich in February 1667 that 'the ladies lie longest in bed, and govern all when they are up', but the King had no intention of removing from his life the woman who had been his companion for so long and whose children he loved. Without her exotic presence Whitehall might have been a better place, but it would also have been duller and certainly less stylish. She attracted to her side people as good-looking as herself—her waiting-woman Wilson was outstandingly beautiful, and the little black boy who always accompanied her possessed a precocious arrogance which Pepys's prim cousin Roger found extremely shocking. 'A pox on this dog!' Pepys heard the boy exclaim on one occasion to a hound which stood in his way, and Roger who also witnessed the incident, remarked that had the child been his he would have given it a good hiding.

The disappearance of Buckingham from the scene had done little to sweeten the attitude of Parliament and in February it was prorogued until the following October without voting adequate supplies for the continuation of the war. The King's only hope therefore was to do all he could to conclude the peace. Since he could not afford to equip the fleet most of his ships lay out of commission at Chatham, with a chain stretched across the river as its only protection. By-passing the Ambassadors as well as Arlington, whose Dutch marriage made him somewhat suspect, the King carried on negotiations through his own family—his sister and his mother's close friend the Earl of St Albans. It was arranged that a meeting of plenipotentiaries should take place at Breda in the summer with the hope that the Dutch, who had not yet agreed to an armistice, would soon join the negotiations. Optimistic out of necessity, the King allowed himself to believe that the Dutch were as eager to bring about a cessation as he was and would not jeopardize the outcome by prolonging hostilities.

For Clarendon and Arlington the prorogation came as a relief. As long as Parliament was sitting they knew they must face the dangers of an enquiry into the conduct of the war. It was useless now for the Chancellor to protest that he had at the outset expressed his opposition to the very idea of a war with its wastage of life and resources. In spite of all the efforts of his enemies to remove him, he had remained in power, and must shoulder the responsibility for a campaign he had never wished to see. He was old now, and tired, and always in the background was the uneasy fear that he had not heard the last of the Duke of Buckingham. Some thought the Duke had avoided arrest out of fear, but those who knew him better suspected that he had gone to ground in order to give his supporters more time to organize his defence.

In May the Chancellor lost a friend and colleague when Lord Treasurer Southampton died, much mourned by his associates—Pepys even saw the porter weeping at the door of his house. He had seemed ready to die, 'bidding Adieu with the greatest content and freedom in the world'. But for Clarendon there was no release as he faced mounting unpopularity and organized opposition. New accusations were being invented, and old ones revived. Some said Lady Castlemaine herself had suggested to the King that it was Clarendon who had organized Frances Stuart's marriage to ensure that she would never bear the King an heir who might supplant his own grandchildren—'or wipe their noses of the Crown', as Pepys succinctly put it. Clarendon had at last moved into his great house in Piccadilly, but his enjoyment of his new abode was spoilt by the slogan which appeared at the gate, raking up old grievances —'Dunkirk, Tangier and a barren Queen'. Stoically he faced up to pain, to criticism and to personal sorrow. His two frail grandsons died within a month of each other and shortly afterwards he lost the wife who had stood by him through all the difficulties of exile and high office.

When the Dutch fleet left harbour in June it was the general hope that nothing more was planned than a pleasant summer outing. Disillusionment came swiftly, for with unbelievable audacity, the enemy sailed up the Medway and attacked the English fleet as it lay helpless at Chatham. The chain across the river was easily broken, several ships were set on fire, and that most noble vessel, the *Royal Charles*, was ignominiously towed away. In London there was panic, and 'wild despair' spread into the galleries and privy lodgings at the Palace. Many people started to pack up in a hurry, 'ready to leave their houses and estates to the mercy of the enemy, whom they believed already at their backs'. Convinced that she would be the first to be slaughtered when the Dutch reached London, Lady Castlemaine succumbed to an attack of the vapours. The King, however, kept his composure; he let the Duke of Albemarle go down to Chatham to inspect the damage, while he himself spent a cheerful evening with Lady Castlemaine at Monmouth's house; they all went mad 'hunting of a poor moth', or so it was said.

The King's calmness helped to prevent the spread of panic, and although he was compared to Nero fiddling while Rome burned, as usual he was doing more business than everyone gave him credit for. The Council met every day, and Pepys saw that at the Palace most people were overcome with trouble and care—'and with good reason', he added. Attempts were made to raise the militia in the eastern counties; Pepys cynically noted that young Hectors like the Earl of Chesterfield were unlikely to achieve much besides debauching the countrywomen in those areas where they decided to carry out their military operations. Everyone knew that action of some kind was needed, and the most obvious step was to call a Parliament without delay, but there were many people who dreaded the thought of the enquiry which would inevitably follow. Clarendon reminded the King that Queen Elizabeth had defeated the Armada without recourse to a Parliament. He still sincerely believed that real sovereignty lay with the King and his Council backed up by a Parliament called spasmodically to vote supplies. His analysis was too simple, for the government was in fact carried on with an ill-defined mixture of King and cabal, family blocks and faction, old counsellors and younger men eager for power, not to mention a cunning mistress and in addition a highly vocal Parliament which had no intention of limiting its powers to the voting of money.

The King sat through the long Council sessions, apparently detached, fondling his dogs and listening to everyone in turn. At last, after days of uncertainty, he decided to recall Parliament at the end of July, contrary to the advice of his brother who suggested that he should raise money without asking anybody's permission. Although Pepys knew that he, like many others, would be under scrutiny if Parliament instituted an enquiry, he thought that the news of its recall was the best he had heard for some time. 'Pray God it may hold,' he wrote, 'though some of us must surely go to the pot.'

The news that Parliament was to meet brought Buckingham out of hiding. He sent Sir Robert Howard to the King with a message requesting an audience, but when this was refused he gave himself up to Secretary Morrice, secure in the knowledge that his friends in Parliament would come to his aid. Having dined openly in a tavern with some of his cronies, he went straight to the Tower. Arlington witnessed these developments with some apprehension. He had been forced to stand by while Sir Robert Howard interceded with the King; Howard was so sure of himself that he had declared he would have his head cut off if he could not prove that the witnesses called by Arlington had been suborned and bribed. On July 1 Buckingham was examined by Arlington, Morrice, Coventry and Clifford. He was a match for all of them, and he made it clear, by his witty and irreverent answers, that there was no case against him. This made his enemies more determined than ever that he should stay in the Tower indefinitely.

Lady Castlemaine now saw fit to enter the fray. With Frances still banished from the Court, the Duke of Buckingham could find no other female advocate, and she could forgive him for sponsoring her rival knowing that he was likely to support the cause of tolerance if he were allowed to rejoin his friends in Parliament. She told the King that Buckingham should be released at once and restored to all his places. The King replied that she was a whore and a jade who meddled in matters that were nothing to do with her. She then called the King a fool who suffered his business to be carried on 'by fellows that did not understand them' while his best subjects languished in prison.

On July 8 Buckingham appeared before the Privy Council which was presided over by the King. Several Members of Parliament, headed by Sir Robert Howard, attended the meeting to give the Duke encouragement and to see fair play. Little evidence was produced and what there

was Buckingham demolished with his usual brilliance. To the King he
spoke submissively, but he directed some sharp and slighting remarks
at Arlington. He had little difficulty in proving that the letter he had
allegedly written to the astrologer was in fact in his sister's hand; she
had invented it as a 'frolic'. As for the charge that he had courted popularity, he remarked that 'anyone committed to prison by my Lord Chancellor or my Lord Arlington could not want being popular'. On July 17
he was released and he left the Tower escorted by a large crowd of
jubilant supporters. It was at the lodgings of his cousin Lady Castlemaine that he made his peace with the King and was allowed to kiss
the royal hand. Many people believed that it was primarily due to her
intervention that the Duke had regained his liberty, and it certainly
appeared that the Villiers charm had once again wrought a miracle.

Nobody could say with any certainty just how secure Lady Castlemaine's position was. As always, rumours that she had fallen from power
were quickly followed by the news that she was more in favour than
ever. One of the Clarendon group's informers, John Finch, wrote from
Florence to report a visit from the Catholic 'Mr Howard of Norfolk'.
His most recent information had been that Lady Castlemaine was dis-
carded, but Mr Howard now refuted this news as 'impossible'. The
reappearance of Buckingham and the imminence of an end to the war,
together with the summoning of a Parliament gave all nonconformists
and enemies of Clarendon the courage to make some strenuous and
united effort. Like an omen of doom the Earl of Bristol reappeared
on the scene. He even went so far as to take his place in the House of
Lords, although he at least had the grace to withdraw as soon as the
King arrived in the Chamber. Buckingham too put in an audacious
appearance, fully robed and 'as brisk as ever'. John Finch reported that
his Catholic visitor 'was in high discontent and much embittered against
the Lord Chancellor'. There was no doubt that dislike of the old adviser
was reaching fever-pitch, and he had become more than ever vulnerable
to attack since the death of the Lord Treasurer. A temporary reprieve
was given when the King prorogued Parliament after a short session,
since the 'snarling peace' had by now been signed, and there was no
immediate need for a money grant to fit out the fleet. But the threat of
an enquiry into the miscarriages of the war still remained, and Clarendon's enemies were intent on making good use of the time that remained
before the autumn session of Parliament.

Few summers had gone by without a major row developing between
the King and his mistress, and this year was no exception. So far every
quarrel had ended in reconciliation, with the King apparently more
enslaved than ever. It is probable, therefore, that in the summer of
1667 the Lady staged an imbroglio with the King in order to consolidate

her position rather than to risk a rupture. The controversy blew up over the question of the paternity of the child she told him she was expecting. The gossip-mongers had been busy spreading rumours that she had spent most of her time recently with Henry Jermyn, and it was convenient for the King to attribute the child to somebody other than himself. Lady Castlemaine's nursery was already well stocked, and he can hardly have relished the expense of another bastard at a time when he had barely enough money to pay the Palace servants. He told her bluntly that he would not be prepared to own the child in view of the fact that he could not remember having lain with her once during the previous six months. 'God damn me, you shall own it' was her characteristically impious reply; she added that if he refused to have it christened at Whitehall she would carry it to the Palace, dash out its brains before his very eyes on the Gallery wall and, for good measure, would bring all his bastards to his apartments and parade them outside the closet door.

Somebody had said that the Countess of Castlemaine in one of her rages was less like Medea than one of Medea's dragons. But the King, no doubt keeping well to the fore the thought that he could not pay his servants a 'farding' towards their wages, or even supply them with bread, remained firm and refused to accept responsibility for another child. Realizing that she was making no progress, the Lady made 'a slighting puh with her mouth' and left the Palace, some said for ever. There were rumours that she had withdrawn to the country, although she had in fact travelled no farther than Covent Garden, where she took refuge with Lady Harvey. On previous occasions when she had fallen into one of her temperamental moods she had made straight for her uncle at Richmond, but at this crucial moment, when the Court was still in town and momentous changes were in the air, it would have been unwise to remove herself too far from the scene of action. Lady Harvey, one of the ambitious Montagus, was more than ready to meddle in a royal dispute. Although she lacked beauty, she was clever and amusing; one of her contemporaries described her as 'a witty and intriguing wench'. Her family was still strong enough at Court to be of use in any move to rid the opposition of the tenacious Chancellor, and as Presbyterian nonconformists they were likely to benefit by his disappearance. After the death of Edward Montagu in the naval battle of 1665 his younger brother Ralph had managed, not without some murmurings at Court, to switch from his post of Master of the Horse to the Duchess of York to the more important post, left vacant by Edward's death, of Master of the Horse to the Queen. Less quarrelsome than his brother, but equally greedy for power, Ralph Montagu had played his part in keeping the family to the fore, while Elizabeth Harvey saw to it that she had a hand in every court intrigue. The Lady's strategic withdrawal to Covent Garden was in all probability part of a carefully prepared plan. The King certainly visited Lady Castlemaine there several times, and the quarrel was spun out until she finally persuaded him to go on his knees and beg forgiveness. Nothing more was heard of her child.

Bearing in mind Lady Castlemaine's tempestuous behaviour, it is not surprising that when a medal was struck to commemorate the Peace which was concluded that August at Breda it was the more pacific Frances who was chosen as the model for Britannia. It was a peace which brought little satisfaction to anybody. Thanks to the shaming disaster at Chatham, and the general impoverishment of the nation, the English plenipotentiaries had found themselves unable to drive a hard bargain, and had been forced to accept the best terms that were offered. Few people mentioned the subject at Court, and even less so in the City. When the news came through a few bonfires were lit, but no guns were fired because of the expense. The King was not in a happy position. He had been 'hectored out of his wits' by his mistress, and he knew that he now faced one of the most dangerous attacks ever mounted by the House of Commons. The removal of Clarendon was his one means of pacifying an alien Parliament. As the Chancellor was later to put it, he realized that 'the disgracing of a public minister would cover himself and the rest of his Court'. The continual criticism levelled by Lady Castlemaine and others had, in Burnet's opinion, finally infected the King, who 'without giving himself the trouble of thinking went along with the rest'. As it happened, the King was genuinely weary of his Chancellor's 'imposing way' and felt that the moment had come at last to break the long association which had now lost its usefulness. Many people believed that the King would have liked to free himself from Lady Castlemaine as well, but that he remained 'so weak in his passion that he dare not do it'.

In comparison with the Lady, Clarendon seemed helpless. He could not resort to emotional blackmail, or threaten to publish love letters, parade bastards at the door or batter babies as yet unborn. In Sir William Coventry's opinion no man was fit to serve a prince 'that did not know how to retire and live a country life'. The King's way of putting it was to suggest that his old counsellor would be better out of reach of Parliament. The Chancellor appreciated the King's thoughtfulness, but his own wish was to be given a chance to face his accusers so that it could be proved whether or not he deserved to be put out of office. He said that he would be willing 'to lose that and his head both together'.

On August 26 Clarendon visited the King at ten o'clock in the morning. The interview lasted for two hours, and when he left the King's apartments everybody could see that there was a look of sadness on his face. Despite the lateness of the hour, Lady Castlemaine was only just out of bed; she ran out in her smock into the aviary which overlooked the Whitehall garden, her woman pursuing her with a dressing-gown. Lord Arlington stood looking out at the departing Chancellor from a window in her lodgings with an expression of 'great gaiety and triumph' unusual in a normally solemn man. Seeing that Clarendon, as he crossed the garden, no longer held the mace and purse of his office, Lady Castlemaine clapped her hands and stood there 'joying herself at the old man's going away'. Clarendon looked up and saw her. 'Oh, Madam, is it you?' he enquired, and said nothing more, except to remind her that one day she would grow old.

Clarendon then went on his sad and elderly way, and after he had gone past, the young men who had been watching crowded round Lady Castlemaine, talking to her in the bird-cage and telling her she was the bird of paradise.

CHAPTER FOURTEEN

THE RIVALS

NEWS OF the Chancellor's fall spread rapidly through the Palace. In the King's closet Baptist May fell on his knees and told his master that now, for the first time, he could call himself King indeed. It was Bab May, the indefatigable go-between, who had brought the Lady back to the Palace from Covent Garden, effecting a reunion with the King below the window of the Treasury Chamber. Many people believed that she had come back just in time to organize her old enemy's removal; there was also a general feeling that although she had returned to the Palace, all was not well between her and the King, and it was rumoured that he had offered her a pension of £4,000 a year provided she agreed to live in France and trouble him no more. All the same on September 10 Pepys heard that she was 'as high as ever she was'; when he visited Bartholomew Fair he was surprised to see a crowd of people in the street all waiting for her to emerge from a puppet show. He thought that had he been in her shoes he would probably have stayed at home for fear of meeting abuse on account of the part she had played in Clarendon's dismissal, but as it was the crowd greeted her enthusiastically and she 'went away without any trouble at all'.

The removal of Clarendon was a triumph for those who had worked so long for his downfall, but it did not solve any immediate problems. The more cynical saw it as just another random stroke of chance in a world where all changes were 'accidental and laid upon no principles of doing good'. There seemed little sign of the strong and united opposition which had threatened the Chancellor before Bristol's inept attempt at impeachment and nobody was concerned now to formulate policies but only to work for personal gain. 'I find by all hands', Pepys wrote on August 29, 'that the Court is at this day all to pieces, every man of a faction of one sort or another.' Every day new changes were expected, and speculation was rife on the subject of successors for the Lord Chancellor and the Lord Treasurer. The King, wisely avoiding the necessity of an immediate and ill-digested decision, had put the Treasury in Commission. He appointed Sir Orlando Bridgeman as Lord Keeper, leaving the Chancellorship vacant. Bridgeman was not attached to any group or faction; he was a much respected man of integrity who frankly felt out of his element in the scheming atmosphere of the Court. Meanwhile Buckingham and Arlington did all they could to gain the ascendancy—Buckingham seeking revenge on Arlington for attempting to bring about his ruin, and Arlington still struggling to eradicate his dangerously popular rival from the political scene.

There was little doubt that Buckingham had found his way back into the King's good graces. 'The truth is', Sir John Reresby wrote of the Duke, 'his temper was so suitable to the King's he had much to do to be angry with him long, which made him dispense with many insolences.' The Marquis de Ruvigny, in England again with proposals for an alliance, noticed that *la cabale du duc de Bouquinquan* was troubling Milord Arlington and Sir William Coventry a good deal. Even the most clear-sighted found it hard to make out just how the new alignments would work out. The fact that Lord Arlington had been seen at the Lady's window as the Chancellor took his leave across the garden made people wonder whether he had not changed his allegiance with a rapidity surprising even in a man who was not noted for lasting loyalty. On the other hand Lady Castlemaine's intervention on the Duke of Buckingham's behalf most certainly had to be weighed in the balance. There were reports that Sir William Coventry had joined Lady Castlemaine's faction, although this he strenuously denied, telling Pepys that he would never as long as he lived 'truckle under anybody or any faction, but do just as his own reason and judgment directs'. He protested that he had 'never had any discourse with Lady Castlemaine or any of those about her on the subject of public business and had never visited her or at least not this twelvemonth, or been at her lodgings but when called on any business to attend the King there, nor had anything to do in knowing her mind in this business'. All the same, in spite of his protestations, his reason and judgment had directed him towards men whose fortunes were improving.

Henry Brouncker, who had been dismissed from his post as Groom of the Bedchamber to the Duke of York for daring to suggest that Clarendon would 'hector' the King into allowing him to retain the Seal, had also aligned himself with the opposition; Pepys recorded that he was now 'great with Bab May, my Lady Castlemaine and that wicked crew'. As a result he had quickly gained the King's favour, and 'was likely to be cherished there'. He had always been known to act as the Duke's go-between and it was now thought that he would be able to act as pimp to the whole family.

The Duke of York's relationship with Clarendon had put him into an uncomfortable position. His open disapproval of the attitude taken to his father-in-law by both Coventry and Brouncker had lost him two of his closest associates, and his relationship with the King had suffered too. The royal brothers took time off for a few days' hunting in October, and at one party everyone was in such a 'maudlin pickle' that they all ended up by kissing one another—the King kissed the Duke and the Duke kissed the King. However in their more sober moments they showed rather less affection, and it was thought that the dismissal of Clarendon had created 'a kind of inward distance' between them. The Duke of York was a natural target for the ex-Chancellor's enemies, and it was feared that they might clamour for his impeachment especially as he was thought to favour the retention of an army in times of peace, a measure which many saw as a threat to parliamentary government.

Altogether the removal of the Chancellor had produced nothing so much as a feeling of apprehension and instability. While the men manœuvred for position, the women also did what they could to insure against the future, although it was rumoured that they too were likely to 'have a rout'. The Queen had been on view rather more than usual in September 1667, dining three times a week in public to the sound of violins. This did not prevent rumours spreading that she was likely to enter a nunnery at any moment—there certainly must have been times when she was tempted to do so. The Duke of Buckingham toyed with plans to replace her with a more malleable consort well schooled in advance to further his own schemes. Lady Castlemaine, however, resented the idea of a fertile Protestant substitute for a Queen who at least had the merit of employing a number of Catholics in her Household. The return to favour of the Duke of Buckingham and the reappearance of the Catholic Earl of Bristol augured well for the Lady and her fellow Catholics, but all the same it was no time to relax. The Parliament due to meet in October included in its programme an investigation into the activities of the papists, and it was essential that its attention should be focused instead on the enquiry into 'the several miscarriages of war'. When Lady Castlemaine went down to visit the Earl and Countess of Sunderland at Althorp in September, she was in all probability motivated by more than a simple urge to breathe the Northamptonshire air. The Countess was a daughter of the Earl of Bristol; a charming but ambitious bride, who was later to be described by Princess Anne as flattering, dissembling and false. She was already making her mark at Court and inviting the great to partake of her hospitality in the house which her extravagant husband was altering and extending. The presence of the Lady at one of her house parties in the autumn of 1667 signified that she was doing what she could to promote her father's cause as well as her own.

The current atmosphere of uncertainty still prevailed when Parliament met. Pepys gloomily predicted that Clarendon would have his head cut off, the Duke of York would lose his title as heir presumptive, the Duke of Monmouth would be declared legitimate and the King would divorce his Queen—on grounds that had yet to be decided. It was hard for anyone to prophesy the final outcome of the struggle for supremacy which had developed between Arlington on the one hand and Buckingham on the other. At the end of October Ruvigny picked up rumours that Arlington was to be dismissed, and Pepys noted on November 15 that Buckingham and Bristol were 'the only counsel the King follows, so as Arlington and Coventry are come to signify little'. At a party in the Whitehall music room on November 16, it was observed that nobody looked more cheerful than the Duchess of Buckingham, 'her Lord being once more a great man'. The King, always a good judge of a man's worth, had come to appreciate the Duke of Buckingham's influence in Parliament, and he looked to him now to use his persuasive powers in the cause of producing a generous grant of money. With this end in view he was perfectly prepared to let the world believe that, as Pepys put it, Buckingham and Bristol were his only 'cabinet council', even though he had few illusions about Bristol, and saw him as a man who could 'in three years . . . get himself a fortune . . . and lose all again in three months'.

The Duke of Buckingham somewhat rashly boasted that the Commons would be wax in his hands, but his limitations soon became evident. A brilliant leader in opposition, he lacked the application to carry out the details of a positive policy. Many of his earlier supporters felt unready to follow him once he had identified himself with a Court which, to gentlemen up from the country, seemed to be the source of corruption, extravagance and vice. The King relied on his eloquence to obtain £500,000 in subsidies, but neither he nor his supporters were able to persuade Members to vote more than a meagre £310,000. The Duke's large promises to look into all grievances and to be what Burnet described as 'a patron of liberty of all sects' had at the outset brought him strong guarantees of support. 'It is pretty', Pepys had written, 'to hear how people do speak kindly of the Duke of Buckingham as one that will enquire into faults.' But such support has a tendency to fade at the first sight of disappointment.

Buckingham's desire to have his revenge on Arlington at first seemed almost obsessive and his feelings were so strong that he even took the extraordinary step of inviting Clarendon to join him in annihilating the rival. Clarendon characteristically refused to countenance such a ruse, even to save himself. Offended by this snub the Duke suddenly changed his tune and decided to appease Arlington with the offer of a place in the new administration as Lord Treasurer. The able and loquacious Sir Robert Howard was to become one of the Secretaries of State and

Sir William Coventry the other. In an attempt to restore his popularity with the Commons, Buckingham proceeded with plans to impeach Clarendon, leaving Sir Robert Howard and Sir Thomas Osborne, later Lord Danby, to deal with the details. In mid-November it seemed certain that Clarendon would be brought to trial, but the prospect caused some alarm to other ministers who felt that once a precedent had been created they might well find themselves facing more convincing charges than any raked up against the ex-Chancellor. The King too shirked the prospect of an impeachment. He was too humane a man to relish the thought of consigning his old governor to the block, and he had no wish to face the dilemma his father had found himself in when forced to sign away the Earl of Strafford's life. As always he avoided a collision by finding a way round the problem. He persuaded Clarendon to leave the country, and on December 3, abandoning the great house he had lived in for such a short time, Clarendon took a boat at Westminster and later sailed for Calais.

The departure of the King's most sober and experienced counsellor solved no problems for those who now struggled to take his place. The King had still failed to nominate a successor; he preferred to hold the balance between opposing advisers rather than risk coming under the domination of any one man. Buckingham's hopes of gaining the ascendancy were less bright in the new year of 1668 than they had been the previous autumn, largely as a result of his own indiscretions. His association with young lords notorious for their debauchery, his familiarity with actors and actresses at the theatre, and his blatantly adulterous affair with the Countess of Shrewsbury all helped to alienate his more puritanical supporters. In January he became involved in a duel with the Earl of Shrewsbury who was wounded in the fight and afterwards died. One of Shrewsbury's seconds was also killed, and yet pardons were issued for all those involved, and this fact, coupled with Buckingham's open and continuing association with Lord Shrewsbury's widow contributed to his growing unpopularity.

So in place of Clarendon, Southampton and Sir Edward Nicholas, the King had to rely on men such as the Duke of Buckingham—'a man' as Pepys put it, 'of no more sobriety than to fight about a whore'. Thanks to the Duke's waning popularity the Court had been singularly unsuccessful in organizing parliamentary support. Most of the session was spent in going over old ground rather than in planning for the future. 'The House is in a most broken condition', Pepys recorded, 'nobody adhering to anything, but reviling and finding fault, and now quite mad at the "Undertakers", as they are commonly called—Littleton, Lord Vaughan, Sir R. Howard, and others that are brought over to the Court and did undertake to get the King money; but they despise and will not hear them in the House, and the Court doth do as much, seeing that they cannot be useful to them as was expected.'

With Parliament in an uncompromising mood the King's financial problems were more acute than ever, while fear about possible enquiries into past mismanagement tended to produce a general stultification. Pepys was probably not the only person who experienced nightmares about the defence he felt sure he would be called upon to make in Parliament concerning the naval accounts. While the machinery of government appeared to be almost at a standstill, the European nations looked on, delighted to see England fall into a state of unreadiness. 'So we are all poor and in pieces, God help us', wrote Pepys; 'while the peace is like to go on between Spain and France, and then the French may be apprehended able to attack us.' Scarcity of funds, a lack of any underlying motivation other than personal ambition, threats from the Continent and above all the lack of sympathy between King and Parliament put people in mind of the days leading up to the civil war. King Charles I had suffered under continual financial difficulties, but he had at least remained faithful to his wife, loving her if anything to excess. His son's indulgence in extra-marital relationships gave the Restoration Parliament an added excuse for limiting money grants, particularly now that Clarendon's restraining hand had been removed.

Without the watchful presence of his childhood governor, the King had little curb on his natural instincts, while the Duke of Buckingham actively encouraged him by making beautiful women available. The Duke's plan to bring about a royal divorce had predictably failed to meet with success, which made him turn his thoughts to other possibilities. The Lady was in many ways as influential as ever, and her looks showed no signs of waning—Pepys remarked on her prettiness when he saw her at the Mass on Christmas Eve 1667. She was still on good terms with Buckingham even though they disagreed on the question of a royal divorce. It was said that he owed his pardon after the duel at least in part to her intervention. All the same she was too selfish and too involved in affairs of state on her own account and on behalf of her fellow Catholics to provide him with the subservient instrument he required.

At Christmas time Frances, Duchess of Richmond, came back to London with her husband and there were soon rumours that she had been reinstated in the King's affections. Whispers even reached Madame in Paris, but the King quickly reassured his sister; 'if you were as well acquainted with a little fantastical gentleman called Cupid as I am you would neither wonder nor take ill any sudden changes which do happen in the affairs of his conducting, but in this matter there is nothing done in it.' Thanks to the Duke of Buckingham the King had already been introduced to a more fertile source of beauty and he had no need to pursue his old inamorata. He had, on the whole, been content to view theatrical ladies from the auditorium, but he now made no strenuous attempt to resist the tempting opportunity of entering the back stage world of the playhouses.

When Pepys first visited his actress friend Mrs Knipp in the dressing-room at the theatre he was shocked and disillusioned. The women players were so made-up he felt a loathing for them, 'and what base company of men comes among them, and how lewdly they talk', he complained. Those who had from the outset predicted that nothing but trouble would result from the introduction of women players into the theatre could feel vindicated as they saw the actresses 'inflaming' young noblemen and becoming their whores or even their wives. Evelyn listed several prominent men who had become involved with such 'impudent wenches', including Sir Robert Howard and the Earl of Oxford, Lady Castlemaine's uncle. The Howards were by now deeply involved in theatrical affairs of every kind; Sir Robert had collaborated with Dryden in writing *The Indian Queen*, while James's *All Mistaken, or the Mad Couple* had already played successfully with Charles Hart and Nell Gwynn in the main parts. The brothers whose sister Elizabeth was married to Dryden had introduced into the Duke's Company a well-favoured girl by the name of Moll Davies, who was said to be the illegitimate daughter of their brother Colonel Howard, although there was also a theory that she had been sired by a blacksmith who lived near the Howard estate in Wiltshire.

Moll Davies had first appeared on the stage when she was little more than a child and she had become famous for her pleasant singing voice and even more so for the ethereal lightness of her dancing. As Richard Flecknoe put it in his poem *To Miss Davies*:

> Who would not think to see thee dance so light,
> Thou wert all air? Or else all soul and spirit? . . .
> Thou miracle! Whom all men must admire
> To see thee move like air, and mount like fire,
> Whoe'er would follow thee or come but nigh,
> To thy perfection, must not dance but fly.

In the autumn of 1667 Moll was appropriately cast as Ariel in a somewhat free version of *The Tempest*, but it was her touching performance of the song 'My lodging it is on the cold ground' which won the King's heart and made him resolve to take her 'off the ground and put her into his bed'. By the beginning of 1668 reports were circulating that he had been ensnared by Moll, the Howard brothers having acted as pimps and 'got her for him'. People did not fail to note that on one

occasion the Queen pointedly left the theatre just before Moll was due
to sing 'My lodging'. On January 11 Mrs Knipp came and sat by Pepys
at the theatre and imparted the news that Miss Davies was leaving the
Company, 'the King being in love with her; and a house is taken for her
and furnishing and she hath a ring given her already, worth £600.'
Two days later, when *The Indian Emperor* was performed at Court by
an amateur cast, several of the players came to watch. Pepys thought
that most of the performers looked like fools or sticks, but this did not
worry the King, for he hardly looked at the stage at all but sat gazing
at Moll, while Lady Castlemaine seemed 'melancholy and out of humour
all the play, not smiling once'.

Three weeks later Corneille's *Horace* was acted at Whitehall in a
translation by Katherine Philips, 'virtuous Mrs. Philips' as Evelyn
approvingly called her. It was one of the most glittering occasions ever
seen at Court, with magnificent costumes and a masque with antique
dances between each act. The part of Horace was played by James
Hamilton, and Lady Castlemaine played a leading role as Camilla.
Although no comments have come down concerning her histrionic
ability, there was little doubt that she far outshone all the other ladies,
including the Queen, even though everyone was smothered in jewels.
Nobody could match her in the splendour of her attire, or in the value
of her jewellery which was variously estimated at £40,000 or £200,000.
It was said that the King had removed some of the Crown jewels from
the Tower for her use.

Pepys had undoubtedly been right when he had noted only a fortnight before 'Lady Castlemaine doth rule all at this time as much as
ever she did'. All the same she evidently felt some uneasiness when
she saw the King's eyes resting on the actress. There were soon reports
that Moll had been granted her own separate establishment and that
she was already showing off the ring costing £600 which the King had
given her. There was always the hope that the King would tire of her
as soon as she began to put on airs and graces, but Lady Castlemaine,
like everybody else, must have guessed that this would not be the end
of it, for in the background was the enchanting Nell Gwynn whom the
King had already sent for several times.

Lady Castlemaine had herself struck up a friendship with the Cockney
comedian in 1667, but Nell had abandoned her when she left the stage
and took on as her lover the rakish Lord Buckhurst who was one of
Buckingham's wilder companions. Nell's absence from the stage was
short-lived and she returned in the autumn of 1667, as lively, as pretty
and as irrepressible as ever. Pepys thought that she outshone Moll
Davies in everything except her dancing, and although she could be
disappointing in a serious role, her comic genius was undeniable. She

was also remarkable when she played the part of a boy; in Pepys's opinion she had all 'the motions and carriage of a spark', and a breeches role also gave her a chance to show off her fine legs. When Pepys saw her take the part of Florimel in Dryden's *The Maiden Queen* he believed that it 'could not be better done in nature'.

The actor Charles Hart had been the first to recognize Nell Gwynn's talents, removing her from her bawdy-house background and finding her an occupation more suited to her talents than orange-selling. He had put her on the stage and made her his mistress; later she was to call him her Charles the first. When she proved unfaithful to him he came to hate her, and it may have been a mutual dislike of the little Cockney that first brought Charles Hart and Lady Castlemaine together. When Pepys was indiscreet enough to take Mrs Knipp for a drive in the Park in April, she was able to impart the news of the latest scandal; 'my Lady Castlemaine,' she revealed, 'is mightily in love with Hart of their House and he is much with her in private and she goes to him and doth give him many presents; . . . and by this means she is even with the King's love to Mrs Davies'. Certainly Hart provided her with a very satisfactory King-substitute if looks were anything to go by. He had such a fine carriage that he would have been able to teach 'any king on earth how to comport himself'. He was one of the most popular actors of his day, always playing to full houses, and unlike Nell he excelled in noble and tragic roles. Pepys was disappointed when he saw some of the actors in their ordinary clothes in broad daylight, but Hart was as magnificent off the stage as he was on it by candlelight, with a dazzling presence, a tall figure and a charming manner. In every way he lived up to his reputation as Shakespeare's great-nephew, and it was not surprising that Lady Castlemaine found him the next best thing to the monarch, using Hart to show the King that he did not hold the monopoly in infidelity.

As many people had prophesied, Moll Davies soon lost her enchantment. Ariel became earthy, as inane as the Duchess of Richmond and as demanding as Lady Castlemaine. Nelly was different; her impishness and humour were qualities not so easily tarnished. The King showed his appreciation of her gifts by setting her up first in a house in Lincoln's Inn Fields and later in Pall Mall, probably spending more on her than on all the other mistresses combined—£60,000 in three years was the common estimate. But according to Burnet he never treated her 'with the decencies of a mistress, rather with lewdness of a prostitute'. At the Palace she would have been out of her element and she remained an extra-mural attraction, the Duke of Buckingham and Sir Robert Howard hoping to lure the King from Whitehall so that they could feed him with their propaganda well away from the listening ears of their rivals. Nell was greedy enough for riches, and the King was never to tire of her charms, but she could not match the senior mistress in the high game of politics and diplomacy. In a characteristic *coup de théâtre* at the end of Dryden's *Tyrannic Love*, she had put the point herself. She had just killed herself on account of an unreciprocated passion for a character played by Charles Hart, but as she was being carried out on the bier, she sat up suddenly and remarked:

> Sweet ladies, be not frighted, I'll be civil,
> I'm what I was, a little harmless devil.

Lady Castlemaine was not 'frighted' by her new rival. As always, once she had come to terms with the situation, she accepted the fact that she must share the King's affection and remained calm. She saw to it that in spite of the new threat from the world of the theatre she still extracted the full measure of reward for the trouble she took in bearing the King's children. Although no doubt Buckingham would have wished it otherwise, gossamer Moll and Cockney Nell would never usurp the position that the shrewd and discerning Barbara had made for herself in the inner circles of government and power.

CHAPTER FIFTEEN

THE WHORES' PETITION

WHEN GILBERT SHELDON, the worthy bachelor Bishop of London, was told that stories suggesting he had homosexual tendencies were being spread about by the Duke of Buckingham and Lady Castlemaine, he said with some acerbity, 'Sir, I wish you would put away this woman that you keep.' The slander campaign mounted by the cousins seemed to be part of a more general attack on the ecclesiastical bench, and the bishops felt disturbed and offended by the King's attempts to gain a greater measure of toleration for the dissenters. Clarendon had always supported the bishops, and since his dismissal they had become more vulnerable; it was no coincidence that, ignoring their animosity, the King made a second attempt in the new year of 1668 to bring in a Bill for Comprehension and Indulgence.

In the face of what appeared to be a threat to the established Church, the Anglicans in Parliament became strongly united. As their ranks closed, the uneasy alliance between the Protestant and Catholic nonconformists began to disintegrate. When the possibility of a new Bill was discussed on February 10 the attitude of the House was hostile, and Pepys recorded that Members 'did mightily and generally inveigh against it'. Instead of supporting the cause of toleration they resolved to send a message asking the King to put into execution the existing laws against all those who deviated from the Act of Uniformity. Their opposition was motivated by a genuine fear that the sectaries were abusing the freedom they had been allowed to enjoy since the Restoration. It was never difficult to start a scare about Catholic infiltration, and now the return of the Earl of Bristol to the political arena was painted in ominous colours; one of Pepys's friends remarked that 'this nation could not be safe while that man was alive'. Nobody was allowed to forget that the King himself had a Catholic mother, that he had married a Catholic Queen, had kept a Catholic mistress for years and now seemed disturbingly eager to plead the Catholic cause.

A deep and inbred fear of papist plots was matched, in most Anglican minds, with apprehension concerning the activities of the more extreme

Protestant sects. Such fears seemed to be justified when in the early weeks of 1668 reports started to come in from the provinces of unruly behaviour by the fanatical sects. It was said that they had been turning lawful congregations out of churches, and showing their disapproval of clerical vestments by pulling the surplices over clergymen's heads. The Duke of Buckingham, with his usual indiscretion, added tinder to the fire with crack-brained schemes to solve the King's financial problems by the appropriation of funds belonging to the Anglican Church. So the King found himself under pressure to act with great severity against those whose cause he had always championed. Pepys believed that if he had been a man 'of any stomach or heat' he would have stood firm and adhered to his beliefs, but if there was one thing the King disliked more than religious intolerance it was civil disobedience. In March, alarmed by exaggerated reports of religious turmoil, he issued a proclamation urging the enforcement of the Act of Uniformity.

Bitterness at the King's sudden abandonment of their cause provoked an upsurge of anger among the Protestant dissenters in the City. On Easter Monday a crowd of apprentices rioted, setting fire to houses of ill-repute. For several days there were outbreaks of violence. 'Lord, to see the apprehensions which this did give to all people at Court' Pepys exclaimed. The soldiers were put in arms, and alarms were beaten by drum and trumpet throughout Westminster—Pepys commented that it was as if the French were coming to town.

Further shock was caused at Court by the appearance of a pamphlet entitled *The Poor-Whores' Petition* which was freely circulating in the City, addressed to the Countess of Castlemaine—'the most splendid, illustrious, serene, and eminent lady of pleasure'. It was written on behalf of all the inmates of the bawdy-houses, and the whores appealed to their most famous fellow practitioner in the hope that she would plead their cause and give them protection in the name of Venus, described as 'the great Goddess whom we all adore'. Pepys managed to acquire a copy, and although he did not consider the style particularly witty, he found the pamphlet 'devilish severe' against the Lady and the King, and he reported that Lady Castlemaine was 'horribly vexed' at its appearance. He was surprised that such a document had ever come to be published, and he saw it as yet another indication of the looseness of the times and the 'great disregard of the King or Court or Government'. Dining at George Montagu's house in Cannon Row, Pepys was told in the greatest secrecy that the King, the Duke and Duchess of York and Lady Castlemaine were 'now all agreed in a strict league'. The breach caused by the dismissal of Clarendon had finally been healed, a fact that had not gone unobserved in dissenting circles. In spite of the secrecy surrounding this league, it was generally agreed that the King and his Catholic mistress as well as the Yorks—who were known to be attracted to the Catholic Church—were all on unusually good terms at this time. The knowledge that this alliance, extremely unholy in the eyes of Protestant dissenters, was in existence, may have helped to shake the insecure foundations of their association with the papists. It may also have prompted a far more searing libel than the relatively innocuous *Whores' Petition* which appeared towards the end of April 1668.

The new pamphlet came out in the form of an answer to the petition. It was entitled *The gracious Answer of the most illustrious Lady of Pleasure the Countess of Castlem* . . . and it was evidently written by somebody well acquainted with the Lady's recent activities. Reference was made to her appearance on 'the theatre at W.H., being to amazement wonderfully decked with jewels and diamonds, which the (abhorred and to be undone) subjects of this kingdom have paid for'. With much flaunting of the royal 'we', the Countess was made to recall how her single-minded devotion to the goddess Venus had accounted for her rise to fame.

> We have *cum privilegio* always (without our husband) satisfied ourself with the delights of Venus; and in our husband's absence have had numerous offspring (who are bountifully and nobly provided for).

The Gracious Answer was, however, more than a personal attack on the Lady's morals. As her husband's quickly suppressed pamphlet, *The Catholique Apology* had put the view that Catholics were just as obedient as the rest of the King's subjects, so now *The Gracious Answer* turned out to be a full-blooded attack on the Catholic Church, on high church Anglicans and dangerous foreign influences. In it the Lady was made to promise that under her approving eye a Bill would be drawn up framed to punish the rebellious apprentices and to give full licence to all 'bawdy-houses, playhouses, whorehouses &c'. A close committee, including among its members the Earl of Lauderdale, Henry Brouncker and Bab May would 'consult the grievances of the sisterhood and remove all things that may hinder their happy restoration with all freedom, safety and honour'. The Bill, while giving full freedom to the whorehouses, would also suppress all private meetings of the Protestant sects and would forbid the printing of subversive material while curtailing the activities of nonconformist preachers. Meanwhile the Catholic Church would be allowed to flourish under the Countess's patronage because, unlike the Protestants, its exponents declared that 'venereal pleasure, accompanied with looseness, debauchery, and prophaneness are not such heinous crimes and crying sins', but lesser transgressions, which confessors of the meanest order were able to forgive. Bearing

William Villiers, 2nd Viscount Grandison
Photograph Courtauld Institute of Art

George Villiers, 2nd Duke of Buckingham
Photograph Courtauld Institute of Art

Barbara Villiers,
later Duchess of Cleveland

Philip Stanhope, 2nd Earl of Chesterfield
Photograph Courtauld Institute of Art

Roger Palmer, 1st Earl of Castlemaine,
with his secretary
Photograph Courtauld Institute of Art

King Charles II

Baptist May in 1662

Edward Hyde, 1st Earl of Clarendon

Barbara Villiers, Duchess of Cleveland

Sir Henry Bennet, 1st Earl of Arlington

Queen Catherine
Photograph A. C. Cooper

Barbara Villiers, Duchess of Cleveland
Photograph A. C. Cooper

King Charles II
Photograph A. C. Cooper

Frances Stuart, Duchess of Richmond
Photograph A. C. Cooper

Louise de Kéroualle

Nell Gwynn

Moll Davies
Photograph Courtauld Institute of Art

Jacob Hall

William Wycherley

Isabella Bennet, 1st Duchess of Grafton
Photograph Jarman, Bury St. Edmunds

Lady Anne Palmer in 1663,
later Countess of Sussex
Photograph A. C. Cooper

Henry Fitzroy, 1st Duke of Grafton
Photograph Jarman, Bury St. Edmunds

Lady Charlotte Fitzroy,
later Countess of Lichfield

James II when Duke of York

Anne Hyde, Duchess of York

Ralph, 1st Duke of Montagu
Photograph Tom Scott

Thomas, 1st Baron Clifford of Chudleigh
Photograph Courtauld Institute of Art

The royal progress by water from Hampton Court to Whitehall in August 1662

Bridgewater House, formerly known as Berkshire House and
Cleveland House, south front
Photograph John Freeman

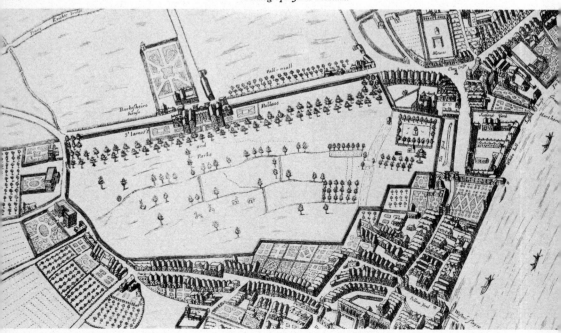

Map of London 1658. Berkshire house is on the top left, opposite St. James's Palace

in mind that the city of London had been burnt by 'good Roman Catholics', the rebellious apprentices were warned that the time would come when the French would be ready to take over the whole nation; as yet they were arriving in small parties only, lying incognito with the other Catholics.

The Petition and *The Answer*, together with all the events that had occurred in the six months following Clarendon's fall, had taught the King several lessons which he was not slow to learn. The Undertakers had failed to provide him with an amenable Parliament, and even the industrious Sir Robert Howard, efficient when it came to the examining of accounts and 'the rolling out of officers', was helpless when it was a question of putting through policies favoured by the King. Open attempts to improve the lot of the dissenters had led to riots in the City and a bitter libel directed against the Lady and the Catholics. From now on discretion would be the King's watchword. He was determined to formulate his policies in secret, finding his own methods of implementation, and playing off his Ministers against each other so that nobody was in a position to dictate to him. And by way of a reply to *The Gracious Answer* he blatantly bestowed on his Catholic mistress a settled pension of £4,700 a year to be paid for out of Post Office funds in the names of her uncles, Viscount Grandison and Colonel Villiers. He also bought for her a fine property, Berkshire House at the bottom of St James's Street, with extensive grounds backing onto the Park and a pleasant outlook over the as yet undeveloped St James's Fields. The grant of £4,000 for the purchase was borrowed from a City goldsmith, and the loan was repaid the following January out of customs duties.

Lady Castlemaine moved into her new abode in May 1668 with her three youngest children, Henry, Charlotte and George. The two eldest, Anne and Charles, now aged seven and six, were for the time being in Paris. The King did not fail to visit her every day, although Ruvigny reported that it was as 'a good friend' only. It was said that she had recently acquired 'a most stately rich pleasure boat' and that 'somebody' had supped with her on board. There was a pleasant irony in the fact that Berkshire House had been built in 1628 by Thomas Howard, Earl of Berkshire, the father of the two play-writing Howard brothers; in addition her enemy the Earl of Clarendon had occupied the house for some time after the fire of London and before his mansion in Piccadilly was fit for habitation. But perhaps its most considerable advantage was the fact that it was situated just across the road from St James's Palace where the Yorks spent their summers, thus enabling the 'strict league' to continue without calling too much attention to itself. Certainly the Lady's friendship with the Duchess continued to flourish, and

5

it is probable that by now Anne had become a confirmed Catholic and was intensifying her efforts to convince her husband that in Rome he would find the one true Church, founded by Christ himself.

Although Lady Castlemaine kept her lodgings at the Palace, her move to St James's caused considerable speculation, and the common theory was that the King had at last decided to pension her off. On May 31 Pepys heard that she was 'mightily out of request, the King coming little to her, and she mighty melancholy and discontented'. On May 7 the Queen was said to have miscarried 'of a perfect child' and the King was solicitous, visiting her every night and supping with her 'with great pleasure'. It was rumoured that Moll Davies, now well set up in richly furnished apartments in Suffolk Street with a coach and footmen in attendance, was with child by 'somebody'; on the King's birthday she took part in a play at Court and the Queen pointedly left the room just before she was due to dance her jig. The Duchess of Richmond too was much in evidence. Although one of her eyes had been affected by her attack of smallpox, she was otherwise unmarked and as beautiful as ever. The King paid her several public visits and even went so far as to row himself down to Somerset House in a small boat, clambering over a wall when he got there as a locked garden gate stood between him and his former love. One day he was so taken up with Frances that he forgot it was post day and failed to write his usual letter to Madame. The Duke of Richmond was allocated lodgings at the Palace, some fine rooms in a little building near the bowling-green, and before long Frances was sworn in as a member of the Queen's Bedchamber, the Countess of Suffolk surrendering her place to the newcomer. Great changes were reported at Court, with disputes developing between the 'two factions of women, my Lady Castlemaine and Mrs Stuart'; there were rumours that the number of Bedchamber women was to be reduced to six. Such developments were less than pleasing to the Lady, who retired to bed 'ill more in mind than body'.

In May the King adjourned Parliament with what Pepys described as 'a short, silly speech', and he spent the summer hunting at Windsor, at Bagshot and in the New Forest. In October he stayed at Audley End to be near Newmarket for the racing. The two main contenders in the battle for power, the Earl of Arlington and the Duke of Buckingham, did what they could to cultivate the King's favour, and Buckingham in particular kept close to the royal party. He had become insufferably arrogant, aping the King by setting up his mistress with establishments in King Street and Pall Mall; it was said that at Bagshot he had turned Prince Rupert's horses out of the inn and stabled his own there instead, just as if he were a Prince himself. Judging by the way he acted, some people were afraid that he had a mind to overthrow the King and bring

in a Commonwealth with himself at the head. 'Some people have got
the bit into their mouths . . . and would likely run away with all', Sir
William Coventry told Pepys, who understood the reference all too well.

But the King had no intention of allowing the Duke of Buckingham
to dominate the scene. He might carouse with the Duke's debauched
companions until he became so drunk that he was unable to grant the
Earl of Arlington an audience, but in the sober light of day he gave
Buckingham no more encouragement than was necessary. He prevari-
cated, listened to advice, and went his own ways. 'Whatsoever opinion
my Ministers have been of, I . . . always follow my own judgment', he
told his sister. As far as appointments were concerned he carefully kept
a balance between the two factions, allowing each to bring a limited
number of supporters into the vacant places. When, for example, two
Commissioners were appointed for the Navy, one of them, Sir Thomas
Lyttelton, was a protégé of Arlington's, while the other, Sir Thomas
Osborne, was a Yorkshireman who owed allegiance to the Duke of
Buckingham. After the two men had been brought in to kiss the King's
hand, Pepys carefully avoided talking to either of them for fear of
being thought 'to look either way'. The Earl of Arlington would have
liked to acquire the lucrative and enviable position of Master of the
Horse for his brother-in-law the Earl of Ossory, but Buckingham outwitted him, taking the post for himself in exchange for a large sum of
money. On the other hand when Buckingham tried to make Sir Robert
Howard Secretary of State, Arlington was 'too hard for him' and
arranged for a deal between the retiring Secretary William Morrice, and
his own candidate Sir John Trevor.

Lady Castlemaine played no part in the manœuvring that went on in
the autumn of 1668. Pepys found it hard to believe Dr Pierce when he
said that Lady Castlemaine had become the Duke of Buckingham's
mortal enemy; 'it seems', he wrote, 'she doth disgust his greatness and
his ill usage of her'. Some people, the more perceptive, had an inkling
of her new allegiance to the Yorks, and this even, with supreme irony,
made some suspect that she might be plotting with the Duchess to bring
back the Earl of Clarendon. In the summer of 1668 Lady Chaworth
reported to Lord Roos that Lady Mordaunt had arrived in England
from Montpellier where she had been seen a great deal in the Earl of
Clarendon's company, and everyone was whispering that Lady Castlemaine, 'one of the cabal', had brought her over. On the whole, however, perhaps chastened by *The Whores' Petition*, Lady Castlemaine
lay low. She spent part of the summer perfecting the furnishings in her
new house and she was at Hampton Court for a few weeks, leaving other
ladies to join in the struggle for supremacy.

Realizing that Moll's attraction was not to be of lasting duration,

Buckingham quickly transferred his patronage to Nell Gwynn, but
Arlington was prepared to trust in the efficacy of his wife's entertainments at Goring House and Euston to cultivate the necessary support
of diplomats and politicians. It was said that he allowed his wife to
accept a present of 10,000 crowns from the French Ambassador. He
was also on good terms with Lady Harvey who was making her name
as a manipulator of appointments and emoluments. She had succeeded
in securing for her brother Ralph Montagu the important post of
Ambassador to France, and her husband Sir Daniel had been despatched, thanks to her influence, on a mission to Constantinople with
Roger Castlemaine as a member of his staff. She herself certainly liked
to claim most of the credit for easing Sir John Trevor into the Secretary's place, and it was her proud boast that she had made one Secretary
of State and could control another. The Duke of York believed that when
Robartes was appointed in the Duke of Ormonde's place as Lord-
Lieutenant of Ireland, 'the ladies Harvey and Trevor bullied Arlington to give up the Duke of Ormonde'. The French Ambassador, Colbert
de Croissy, even thought that Lady Harvey was capable of manipulating
the mercurial Buckingham and he believed it was at her soirées that
occasional truces between the rivals were engineered.

    The King, the Duke of York and Lady Castlemaine managed to keep
clear of the controversies that centred round Buckingham and Arlington. The Duke of York, in fact, seemed strangely passive, and Pepys
was horrified to see how many 'creatures' were given naval appointments without the Duke's knowledge. There were rumours that his
regiment was to be disbanded and that before long he would lose his
naval command—'which doth shake me mightily', Pepys admitted.
There were fears that Sir William Coventry, one of the Duke of York's
few remaining supporters, was likely to be singled out for attack. He
was an outspoken man, able and efficient—he had designed for himself
a highly practical circular desk 'with papers round him to which he can
easily turn himself round on his chair as he pleases'. He believed that
he would survive any attack, since he had made himself useful to everybody. But he was not so indispensable as he thought; ranged against
him were the Duke of Buckingham and Sir Robert Howard who had by
now become adept at their 'rolling out' technique. They rightly guessed
that the one kind of attack the serious-minded Coventry would not
tolerate was ridicule. Howard had written a play called *The Country
Gentleman*, and Buckingham concocted a scene, which was to be added,
in which Coventry, thinly disguised as a character called Sir Cautious
Trouble-All, would be seen sitting in the centre of his unmistakable
circular desk. The projected ruse came to Coventry's ears, and he did
not relish the thought of being lampooned in public. He threatened to

cut off the nose of any actor who dared to impersonate him, and later, when plans still went ahead in spite of his threat, he wrote Buckingham a letter which could only be taken as a challenge to a duel. Arlington, who was in the plot, artlessly betrayed the secret to the King, who looked unfavourably on duelling. A charge was drawn up and Coventry found himself in the Tower, his career apparently at an end.

The King caused the offending scene to be deleted from *The Country Gentleman*, but he made no attempt to pardon Coventry for his understandable response to extreme provocation. Charles told his sister that Coventry was a troublesome man, and he was glad to be rid of him. Coventry himself told Pepys that he was in any case weary and overworked and felt glad to retire. He disliked his fellow Treasury Commissioner Sir Thomas Clifford who had recently been appointed Treasurer of the Household. His only regret was that for all his conscientiousness his services were so little valued that he could be deprived of all his offices on the slightest pretext. It seemed that there was no place in the present system for a man who simply wanted to do his job honestly and diligently without paying out money corruptly or using up his energies in flattering the people who mattered.

Pepys and others found it all very difficult to understand. Everyone was perplexed, for nobody knew the secret of the King's thoughts. Only the French King and his sister realized that he had quietly made up his mind to negotiate, ignoring all the normal channels and official diplomats, choosing as his mediator his much-loved Henriette. While his Ministers argued about the merits of calling a new Parliament or of making do with the old, he had resolved to manage without a Parliament at all. Since affairs on the Continent were just as precariously balanced as they were at home, the King had decided to sell his support to the highest bidder, and he guessed that France would be prepared to pay him the best price. The rest of the world saw him bound to the Protestant powers, Holland and Sweden, by the Triple Alliance negotiated by Arlington in January 1668, but he had few scruples about breaking one *entente* in favour of another that might prove more profitable.

It would have been difficult for anybody to guess, at the beginning of 1669, just what the English King had in mind. Even those who respected him least would hardly have thought him capable of such a *volte face*, even less would they have believed that he did not flinch from putting his own soul down on the negotiating table. Little though he had in the way of bargaining power, he could pay for the French King's money grants with the promise that he would turn Catholic, even, in the fullness of time, announcing his conversion publicly as a prelude to bringing his country back to Rome.

The King confided his intentions, in deepest secrecy, to a chosen few at his brother's lodgings. It was at this time, if we are to believe James's own account in J. S. Clarke's *Life of James II*, that the Duke was 'more sensibly touched in conscience and began to think seriously of his salvation'—he had in fact resolved to follow his wife and the other member of the 'strict league', Lady Castlemaine, into the Catholic Church. The King himself was described by the same biographer as announcing his own conversion with the tears flowing down his face. The witnesses of this inflammable disclosure were the Catholic Lord Arundel, who had stepped into Ralph Montagu's place as Master of the Horse to the Queen, Sir Thomas Clifford, known to have Catholic leanings, and the Earl of Arlington. The Duke of Buckingham was significantly absent, for the King had a low opinion of his discretion and knew that he was a strong supporter of those very dissenters whose opinion of the Catholic Church had been enshrined in *The Gracious Answer*.

The secret of the January meeting was closely guarded. The fact that it took place at all is noted only in James II's memoirs, and this has led some historians to doubt whether it ever happened. Had any of the King's contemporaries known about the meeting, they would hardly have credited it. As it was they were left guessing, groping their way, almost totally perplexed.

CHAPTER SIXTEEN

A PARTY AT DEPTFORD

'I HAVE HEARD read with great pleasure', Louis XIV wrote to Colbert de Croissy in February 1669, 'the curious details you have written to M. de Lionne about the intrigues of the English Court, and the broils of the ladies who are the chief personages there'. The French King had provided his Ambassador with a generous fund to be used for bribing the ladies who appeared to be so influential at the English Court. 'I shall take more pains than ever', de Croissy assured Lionne, 'to ascertain what goes on among the ladies, since you do not think it beneath you to show an interest in their quarrels, and the King himself deigns to wish for information in those little affairs, on which great events so often hinge.' But the Ambassador's enthusiasm soon began to wane when he realized how quickly the money slipped away and with what meagre results. It seemed pointless to make gifts indiscriminately 'just to satisfy the greed of the women here for rich keepsakes'. By the middle of February he had given away all the presents he had brought from France, including some clothes which had been made up specially for his wife. 'I have not money enough to go on at this rate', he complained.

In spite of the efforts of Lady Harvey and Lady Arlington, the French Ambassador still came back to the old conclusion that the Countess of Castlemaine was the most influential of them all. Lord Ashley had tried to introduce a new element by bringing to the King's notice an attractive girl called Jane Roberts, but she had proved as unrewarding as Frances—she was a clergyman's daughter and had scruples. Colbert de Croissy thought that the King at times looked gloomy and attributed his mood to the fact that Lady Castlemaine had turned her handsome serving-maid Wilson out onto the streets at midnight on discovering that she was with child. Wilson had waited on the King when he visited Berkshire House, and her grace and beauty, as de Croissy put it, had made the impression that might be expected on 'a prince who is fond of change'. All the same, he added, 'this amour does not prevent Madam Castlemaine from being as powerful as ever', although it was essential that the King should not think that they believed she ruled him, as he might well take that in bad part. 'I should therefore advise giving her only such trifling tokens as a pair of French gloves, ribands, a Parisian undress gown, or some little object of finery.' The Ambassador's advice was warmly welcomed. 'His Majesty attaches great importance to all you say about Lady Castlemaine', de Lionne told him, adding, 'you can if you think fit, agree with your brother touching the present the King intends to make this lady.' Naively, the French believed that a few French ribands would be enough to persuade the Lady that she could feed suitable doctrines into the King's ear. 'His Majesty', wrote de Lionne, 'warmly approves your idea of getting her to put into the King of England's head that the Presbyterians and nonconformists are ill affected towards monarchy.'

It is unlikely that the Lady needed to remind the King of a fact that had been in the forefront of his mind for some time—fostered by the apprentices' riots of the previous year, and by the rumours that Buckingham intended to put himself at the head of the nonconformist sects and set up a Commonwealth. She was clever enough to let the French feel that it was worth their while cultivating her friendship and plying her with presents, but she gave away no secrets, and Colbert de Croissy was left as confused as ever as he tried to trace the pattern of Court favour and ministerial power. Everyone spent so much time 'turning about' that it was hard to detect any settled loyalties, and even if he did succeed in winning any of the ladies over to his side there was no guarantee that they would proffer the right advice to the King, nor was there any certainty that the King would listen to them if they did.

The French Ambassador's perplexity, like everybody else's, largely sprang from the fact that the King was using his sister, rather than any of the ladies at the English Court, as his chosen instrument. In February de Croissy said he had heard the King say the only woman he trusted was Madame, and Ralph Montagu in Paris had begun to wonder just what part the King's sister was playing in the diplomatic game. He found the French Court much like its English counterpart—'full of cabals and stories'—and as far as he could tell, Madame was more influential than most people realized. Like many others at the French Court she regarded Buckingham as a natural ally, but distrusted Arlington for the part he had played as prime mover of the Triple Alliance, suspecting that thanks to his wife's origins he would always be a friend of the Dutch. Montagu informed Arlington that Madame had told Louis that 'no good was to be expected of me, for I was sent hither to do just as you pleased and directed'. Lady Castlemaine, after giving Colbert de Croissy 'a piece of her mind' on many subjects, told him that she had recently received a letter from Madame urging her to make up her quarrel with Buckingham. She was puzzled to know why Madame was so keen for a reconciliation, and it was de Croissy's wife who advanced the theory that 'union with France depended on the agreement of all the favourites with each other'.

It was now the King's task to disillusion his sister, warning her of Buckingham's indiscretion, and persuading her that Arlington was more trustworthy than she realized. There was a great danger that if Buckingham were to hear of the King's promised conversion and in general to be let into the secret of the negotiations between Britain and France, he might betray the plans to 'the people of the late times', that is to the Presbyterians. For this reason Charles suggested that his sister would be wise to refrain from communicating with Buckingham too often 'for fear that something may slip from your pen which may make him jealous that there is something more than what he knows of'. On the other hand Charles did all he could to reassure her about Arlington's character. 'Nobody is more your servant than he', the King wrote in one letter, and in another he told her, 'I will answer for Arlington'. As a result of his efforts, Montagu noticed a distinct change in Madame's attitude, and in May he was able to write to Arlington, 'I have had several *éclaircissements* with Madame about you, and I believe shortly you will be upon as good terms as you care to be.' Madame actually showed Montagu some of the King's letters which proved that her brother wrote to her about private matters, speaking his mind 'of all things very freely to her'. For this reason Montagu believed it essential for Arlington to make sure he was on good terms with her—only that way would he consolidate his position and confirm his ascendancy over the Duke of Buckingham.

In the early months of 1669 it looked as if Buckingham would carry all before him. Everything, in Pepys's view, augured ill for the Duke of York. When he heard that Sir William Coventry had been sent to the Tower, and the Duke of Ormonde had been dismissed, he felt that the end had come for the Duke of York and probably for himself as well. 'This news of Sir W. Coventry did strike me to the heart and with reason, for by this and my Lord of Ormonde's business, I doubt that the Duke of Buckingham will be so fleshed, that he will not stop at anything . . . and Sir W. Coventry being gone, the King will have never a good counsellor, nor the Duke of York any sure friend to stick to him—nor any good man will be left to advise what is good.' The King might be secretly warning his sister to be wary of Buckingham, but he let the rest of the world believe that his childhood friend was still in favour. At Newmarket in March, Buckingham entertained the King very nobly every night, and it was thought that when they both returned to London there would be great alterations at Court—all in Buckingham's favour.

5*

Encouraged by his success in bringing about the fall of Sir William Coventry, Buckingham decided to aim another dart at his enemies with the help of his friends in the theatre. Knowing that the Montagu clan was putting all its weight behind Lord Arlington's cause, he set about discrediting the 'busy and officious' Lady Harvey. As Madame provided a convenient cover for her brother's dealings with the French, so Ralph Montagu was able to camouflage his correspondence with Arlington by directing his letters to his sister's house in Covent Garden. It was no problem for the Duke to persuade Mrs Corey, an actress with the King's company, to take the part of Sempronia in Ben Jonson's *Cataline*. Everybody knew at once who was being aimed at, for Sempronia was an ageing courtesan with an ambition to become 'a great stateswoman'. Had Lady Harvey been a man, she would doubtless have issued a challenge, but she revenged herself by persuading her cousin, the Lord Chamberlain, to imprison the actress. Mrs Corey answered the Chamberlain's questions boldly and saucily, confident that she had the backing of powerful personages. Thanks to Lady Castlemaine's intervention she was soon released from prison, no doubt to the satisfaction of the King who immediately ordered a repeat performance so that he could enjoy seeing it for himself. Lady Harvey was incensed and organized a crowd of supporters who hissed and threw oranges when the play was staged again. 'It seems the heat is come to a great height, and real troubles at Court about it', Pepys reported, expressing the opinion that it was all nothing more than 'foolish women's business', and wishing that the King would refrain from becoming involved in such matters.

The message for Lady Harvey was that she entered the maelstrom of Court politics at her peril. For others the *Cataline* episode proved that Lady Castlemaine was as powerful as ever. As rumours of the King's intended alliance with France began to leak out many people were prepared to believe that it was the Catholic mistress who had persuaded the King to betray his country. In the spring the Earl of St Albans arrived in England and it was the common belief that he had come well furnished with French money 'to buy a breach with the Dutch'. This only served to prove how wise the King had been to choose a less obvious method of conducting his nefarious negotiations. 'You cannot imagine what a noise Lord St Albans' coming has made here', he told his sister. Pepys was probably not the only person to prophesy that an alliance with the French would make the Parliament mad and spell ruin for the whole country, for once he was furnished with French money the King would more than ever be able to 'wanton away his time in pleasures'.

Pepys had good cause to feel depressed when he saw his friends dismissed, with Sir William Coventry in the Tower and Henry Savile also in detention. He had every reason to believe that his protector, the Duke of York, was on the verge of political ruin. On the evening of March 4 he met another of the Duke's protégés, Sir Jeremiah Smith, who told him that the treatment of Savile, who was confined in the Gate-house, had caused some controversy between the royal brothers; the Duke of York was, in fact, 'mightily incensed'. That same evening Pepys and Sir Jeremiah paid Sir William Coventry a visit in the Tower, and then took a boat down river and went straight to the Navy Treasurer's official residence at Deptford where they found a large crowd of people including the Duke and Duchess of York, Lady Castlemaine's uncle, Edward Villiers, and Lady Castlemaine herself. Pepys was invited to sit down with some of the Maids of Honour—'which did me good to have the honour to dine with and look on' he recorded. He was plied with a variety of excellent wines—'more than I have drank at once these seven years'—and he soon began to realize that the people there were 'all of a gang' and were in fact all supporters of the Duke and Duchess. A health was drunk to the union of the two royal brothers, and it was evident that there was a great deal more to the occasion than a good dinner. From the conversation it was possible to tell who were con-sidered the Duke of York's friends and enemies, and much of the talk centred round the iniquitous treatment of Henry Savile.

After the meal Pepys went upstairs and found the Yorks surrounded by a distinguished crowd of ladies and gentlemen. The Treasurer's house was in the process of being refurbished; there were no hangings on the walls and no chairs to sit on. The royal heir and his huge wife, like everybody else, had settled themselves on the floor and a parlour game was in progress. Everybody in turn had to choose a letter of the alphabet and then decide which qualities beginning with that letter they most liked and disliked in the person they loved—'I love my love with an A, I hate my love with an A'. Pepys noted that the Duchess of York and Lady Castlemaine were particularly witty when it came to their turn, but unfortunately he made no record of what they actually said. It was in any case an evening of great conviviality, which served to bring together the Duke's supporters—an unofficial preparation for the campaign to rid Buckingham of his strength. When it was all over everyone went home by barge, and Pepys returned to his wife who thought he had been away far too long; she was in fact 'mighty angry and suspicious'.

At first it had seemed that the Duke of Buckingham's plan to discredit Coventry and drive a wedge between the royal brothers had been nothing but a success. But the healths drunk to fraternal unity in the course of the party at Deptford signalled an unexpected reversal in the Duke of Buckingham's fortunes. Although everyone had feared that during the spring season at Newmarket Buckingham would consolidate his position with the King, and would return to find that great changes at Court were to be made in his favour, the exact opposite proved to be the case. The previous autumn James had reproved Bab May for allowing the King to consort with Buckingham's cronies, and in particular with Lord Buckhurst and Sir Charles Sedley who were notorious for their debauchery—it was even said that on one occasion they had been seen running naked through the streets of London. It may be that Bab May had taken the reproof seriously and had been more circumspect of late in his choice of companions for the King's leisure hours. In any case, when the King returned to London the favours everyone had expected to see lavished on the Duke of Buckingham now quite failed to materialize.

For a start the King withdrew the candidate put forward by the Duke of Buckingham for a place vacated by Sir William Penn on the Navy Board. He recommended instead Sir Jeremiah Smith; this was an unexpected blow for Sir Robert Howard, who had diligently conducted the enquiry leading up to Penn's dismissal. Howard himself, and other members of his family, suffered a setback when the King and the Treasury Lords called in the patent of the Green Wax. Howard or his agents had now been discovered bargaining with those sentenced to pay fines and releasing them, at a price, 'to the obstruction of public justice'. Motivated by the promise of good compensation if the patent was willingly surrendered, and probably also by the fear of further investigation, Howard entered into negotiations with the King, as always driving a hard bargain. Astute and superbly self-confident though he was, Sir Robert had to learn that he could not count himself immune from the kind of enquiry he was all too ready to conduct into the behaviour of others.

As the days went by it became evident that the disgracing of Sir William Coventry was less of a coup than Buckingham and Howard had hoped. He was visited by crowds of loyal supporters and a queue of coaches built up outside the Tower. A petition for his release was handed to the King on his return from Newmarket, and Lord Arlington hardly waited for the reply before he sent the warrant for his discharge 'which', as Pepys put it, 'looks a little like kindness or a desire of it'. Coventry was pardoned and released, but his failure to get on with the Catholic-minded Lord Clifford precluded his return to office. The Buckingham group had hoped to replace Sir William with one of its own candidates, Sir Thomas Osborne, but the King even denied the Duke this satisfaction; he failed to appoint anybody new and resorted to the simple ruse of reducing the number of Treasury Commissioners.

The Dukes of Buckingham and York were predictably at odds when the House of Lords was asked to dissolve the marriage of Lord Roos who wished to be free of an unfaithful wife so that he could beget legitimate heirs. Buckingham hoped, and York feared, that the case would create a precedent, enabling the King to be rid of his Queen. The Bill went through, but the King set everybody's mind at rest by instructing Bab May to spread it abroad that he would never consider divorce a feasible proposition. He insisted that 'it was a wicked thing to make a poor lady miserable, only because she was his wife, and had no children by him which was no fault of hers'. In May 1669 there were hopes, as there had been the year before, that Catherine was with child, and Pepys saw her at dinner with the King 'in her white pinner and apron, like a woman with child'—he thought she looked more handsome in that simple garb than she did when decked out with all the trappings of a Queen. But on June 7 the King told his sister that after all their hopes Catherine had miscarried again without any visible accident, the physicians still divided as to whether it had been 'a false conception or a good one'.

The Duke of York was by now in an optimistic mood. He told Pepys on May 10 that 'he did now think he should master our adversaries'. The Duke of Buckingham's schemes to abduct the Queen and send her to the plantations, with a view to obtaining a divorce on grounds of wilful desertion, no more endeared him to the King than his equally quixotic schemes of pillaging the Church. Every day the Buckingham faction seemed to be losing ground while the Duke of York's fortunes improved, and with them Lady Castlemaine's. Pepys had been told as early as January that she was 'mighty great' with the Yorks, and also 'in higher command over the King than ever, not as a mistress, for she scorns him now, but as a tyrant to command him'. There could be little doubt that she was on the winning side, and the French celebrated her success with bribes of increasing value; on May 3 Ralph Montagu visited Martiall's, one of the smartest shops in Paris, and saw them packing up a present worth at least £1,000. 'I find since', he told Arlington, 'that it is for my Lady Castlemaine, which you will quickly know there.'

In May, Lady Shrewsbury's men set on Harry Killigrew, wounding him seriously and killing one of his men. The attack was said to be provoked by Killigrew's accusation that he had once slept with the lady in question. The Duke of York hoped that Buckingham might be implicated in his mistress's troubles, and was 'mightily pleased' to hear about the episode, but Buckingham escaped prosecution and made it clear that he was by no means beaten. Throughout the summer and autumn of 1669 Buckingham and Arlington went on 'pecking one at the other', and the fear was still very real that when Buckingham gave it out he was with his wenches, he was in fact attending secret meetings with former Commonwealth men. His waning influence and suspect activities helped to increase the severity meted out to Protestant nonconformists. It was said in March 1669 that the King had been 'hot of late against Conventicles', and the lenient treatment dissenters had enjoyed when Buckingham was in the ascendant gradually gave way to a form of persecution. Attempts were made to control meetings of the fanatical sects, but the Quakers often proved more than a match for their persecutors. On one occasion, for example, as fast as the soldiers restrained one speaker, another stood up and began to hold forth.

Early in 1670 the Duke of Buckingham fell ill, which allowed the negotiations with France to proceed more quickly and with less fear of discovery. Long conferences were held at Whitehall in the lodgings of the Queen's almoner Father Patrick. The 'Grand Design' which at the outset had seemed no more than an impractical dream, was now likely to become a reality. Impatient to bolster his campaign against the Dutch with English naval support, Louis seemed ready to meet his cousin's demands, many of which verged on the impudent. When it came to naming a date for his conversion to the Catholic Church, Charles tended to be vague, but his demands for money were much more specific; he named £800,000 as a modest reward for the involvement of the English fleet and he insisted that all naval forces must be under the command of an English admiral.

Many of the details were still undecided when Madame set out for the French coast in May 1670 with over 200 attendants. In England it became known that Lady Castlemaine had been granted the honour of going over to fetch her. The royal family decided not to go to Windsor for the Garter celebrations which were to be held instead at Canterbury. Madame set sail before the welcoming party had time to start out, and the King went down by water to Gravesend and then on by road to Dover where the reunion took place. There was a great deal of gaiety to camouflage the fact that negotiations were in progress and Lady Castlemaine, it was reported, 'far exceeded the French ladies both in bravery and beauty too'. She was well furnished with new jewellery having bought on April 20 'a table diamond ring' worth £300. On May 7 she spent £1,800 on '2 large diamonds in bodkins'. All the same, some thought that there would be family counsels only, others suspected that plans might be made to find a French Queen for Charles, and there was always the lurking fear that the Duke of York and Lord Arlington might be endeavouring to bring about a league with France 'for a sum of money'. Even some of the King's most trusted advisers were left in the dark about the Treaty of Dover which was signed on

May 22. The only thing that seemed clear to everybody was that the King was speaking the truth when he said his sister was the one woman who had ever had any real hold over him. 'She has much more power over the King her brother than any other person in the world', the French Ambassador told Louis, 'not only by the eagerness the other ministers have shown to implore her favour and support with the King and by the favours he has accorded simply at her request . . . but also by the King's own confession and the tears he shed on bidding her farewell.' The admiration was mutual; 'she [Madame] is truly and passionately concerned for the King her brother' Montagu told Arlington.

All the same the affection the King felt for his sister was a brotherly kind of love and it did not prevent him letting his eye dwell on other feminine objects. When he told Madame that he would accept one of her jewels as a keepsake, the casket was brought to him by a young girl from Brittany, Louise de Kéroualle, whose childish beauty immediately caught the King's eye. He ignored the casket and suggested that the girl who carried it would make a better present than any of the jewels. Madame ignored the hint and firmly took the girl back to her parents.

Only a month after returning to France Madame died an excruciating death and the two Kings were left without the slender and delicate go-between they had both used to such good effect. The French King's instinct was to find a replacement as soon as possible; recalling that his cousin had taken notice of Louise de Kéroualle, he made arrangements for her to be sent over to the English court at once. Even before she left, the Savoyard Ambassador in France had guessed what was intended. 'She is a beautiful girl', he told the Duke Charles Emmanuel II, 'and it is thought that the plan is to make her mistress to the King of Great Britain. He [Buckingham] would like to dethrone Lady Castlemaine, who is his enemy, and His Most Christian Majesty will not be sorry to see the position filled by one of his subjects, for it is said the ladies have great influence over the mind of the said English King.'

For the time being the English King had other matters on his mind. His task now was to reveal gradually, and particularly to those ministers who had not already been let into the secret, the significance of the agreement signed at Dover. Clifford and Arlington had been entrusted with the details, but Buckingham also had to be enlightened, for although his power was on the wane, he was too deeply entrenched in the King's life to be cast out altogether; and in opposition he was inclined to be at his most dangerous. He was still capable of working his way back into the King's good graces with brilliant imitations of his adversaries—Arlington in particular. 'In France they treat Secretaries rather differently' was Ralph Montagu's acid comment on the subject. It was

Buckingham and not Arlington who went over to France to offer official condolences on the death of Madame, returning with the *traité simulé*, a doctored version of the Treaty of Dover. He set off in charge of Louise de Kéroualle but he absent-mindedly left her languishing at Dieppe while he pressed on to meet his pregnant mistress who was awaiting him at Dover. It was Ralph Montagu who finally came to her rescue and asked Arlington to send a yacht to bring her over, thus giving his patron a good start with the young lady whose potentialities he was not slow to appreciate.

While Buckingham and Arlington kept up their old rivalry Lord Clifford unobtrusively overtook them both in the King's favour. If there was an inner circle of friendship, it probably enclosed the Yorks and Lady Castlemaine, whom Charles continued to visit frequently at Berkshire House. In July 1670 when the Court was still 'shaked' by the death of Madame, he created her Baroness Nonsuch, Countess of Southampton and Duchess of Cleveland 'in consideration of her noble descent, her father's death in the service of the Crown, and by reason of her own personal virtues'. Not everybody was as sensible of the new Duchess's virtues as the King himself, but his action in ennobling her still further seemed to prove that in spite of rivals, in spite of the onset of age and the changing pattern of political power she still could not be ignored. And yet the King, sphinx-like as ever, continued to keep everybody guessing. Did she rule him as a tyrant, was he tired of her, or did he love her just as much as ever?—nobody knew. To confide in few and to keep his own counsels was now the King's policy. If he seriously wished to prepare the ground for a public announcement of his conversion, he would do it silently, introducing into his immediate entourage and without calling attention to the fact, as many people as possible who were either Catholic or had Catholic leanings. And if for months he had succeeded in adroitly balancing two faction against each other, he now played the balancing game even more skilfully, ruling with the help of an unofficial committee of men whose initials conveniently spelt out the word cabal—Clifford, Arlington, Buckingham, Ashley, Lauderdale. They were not drawn together by any common principles or zeal to further the common good, for in varying degrees they were all men who were motivated by ambition and who tolerated each other's presence only because the King made it plain that they could enjoy his favour on the one condition that they were prepared to share it.

The *traité simulé* of necessity omitted the Catholic clauses of the Secret Treaty, and debates concerning the payment of subsidies due either before or after the King's declaration of his conversion could never be revealed to Buckingham and others. But for both Charles and Louis the Catholic question was a lesser consideration; uppermost in the French King's mind was his struggle to eradicate the Dutch as a power to be reckoned with in Europe, while for his cousin the most pressing need was to raise money at any price. Having irrevocably sold his soul to the French on the mere promise of funds which were never to materialize in full, the King now entered a world of secrecy where he was to remain for the rest of his life. The strain of living with a succession of lies, of fearing the revelation that might come at any time, the humiliation of knowing that the French King had the power to blackmail him with the threat of telling the country what he had promised at Dover— all this might have destroyed the nerve of a different kind of man. As it was he had sentenced himself to playing the game that was most suited to his talents—remaining in the chair, ready to gather up the threads when the argument was over; while others were ready to risk their lives and their careers for their beliefs, he was prepared to leave his own faith in abeyance, calmly aware that even the soul of a King had a less inflated value than some would have set on it. Relaxed and cool, he trod the brittle surface of his country's stability as if unaware of the seething unrest that lay beneath, when a sudden unwise move or a hint of panic might have cracked the thin crust which his own tolerant and kindly attitudes had done much to create. And so in spite of all his weaknesses, his subjects came to love him, knowing him as an ordinary man who walked in the Park and fed the ducks, who visited his mistresses one after the other in the course of a single afternoon and who loved his children with a normal father's love, even though none of them were the children of his Queen.

CHAPTER SEVENTEEN

SONS AND LOVERS

I N JUNE 1670, soon after the King's sister had returned to France, Nell Gwynn presented him with a son. 'Nell Gwynn the player is brought to bed of a brave black boy' was how one report put it, thus pointing to the paternity of the child, for the King had always been noted for his swarthy complexion—'he is so dark I am ashamed of him' his mother had written when he was only four months old. The child was christened Charles, and his godparents all came from the same faction—they were the Duke of Buckingham, Lord Buckhurst and 'a lady of quality', presumably Lady Shrewsbury.

The new Duchess had learned to tolerate rivals although not always without a show of jealousy. The observant Pepys, noticing Moll Davies look down and smile at the King from the box where she was sitting at the theatre, had seen Lady Castlemaine blush like fire, and she had hit back at the King, treating him as he had treated her, by showing him that she could be unfaithful too. Now that he had turned his attentions to Nell she took to herself a lover in her turn, and while the King walked the tight-rope of international intrigue, she introduced into her life one of the King's three official acrobats, Jacob Hall, who had delighted not only the Court but all London with his dancing. He was magnificently handsome with a fine figure and legs that compared very favourably with Henry Jermyn's—in fact the King in his jocular way had once suggested that if he had to have a rival he would recommend Hall as a far more worthy object of her affections than the diminutive Jermyn. Hall excelled at dancing and vaulting on the ropes, and his act included somersaults and flip flaps, flying over rapiers and leaping through hoops and over men's heads. Pepys was more than impressed when he went to his performance at Southwark, 'I saw such action as I never saw before,' he recorded.

Rope-dancing was popular with all kinds of people—Anthony Wood paid out sixpence to see a performance at Oxford—and Hall, taking advantage of the vogue, set up his own booth at Charing Cross, without, however, acquiring the necessary permission to do so. He was committed to prison for continuing to build when the local authority had ordered him to stop. Thanks to Lady Castlemaine's intervention he secured his release and, as Gramont put it, 'out of gratitude he did not disappoint the Lady's expectations in any way'. The liaison was celebrated in a great many rhyming couplets, most of them far more complimentary to the acrobat than they were to the Countess, but she remained impervious, only growing more radiantly beautiful as a result of the association. She was as generous to Hall as she had been to Hart, using her influence to ensure that his income was augmented by a regular salary, and allowing herself to be painted playing the violin in an ermine robe, her head adorned with a plume of feathers, while Jacob leant over her with a guitar.

The Duchess was happy to share her favours between the King and the acrobat, and the King made no scenes when he learnt about his rival. One day he arrived at Berkshire House with love letters somebody had intercepted and brought to him, but he gave them back to her with the one stipulation that in future she should try to be more discreet. 'Madam all I ask of you, for your own sake is, live so for the future as to make the least noise you can, and I care not who you love.' Discretion was not in her nature, but she did her best, and took advantage of his leniency, allowing herself to love and be loved by others. Unavoidably all her activities were noted and her exploits magnified; there are a variety of anecdotes to show that however hard she tried, she could never live a colourless life. It was said that she boxed Lord Rochester's ears when he attempted to kiss her as she alighted from her carriage:

> By heavens! Twas bravely done!
> First to attempt the Chariot of the Sun,
> And then to fall like Phaeton

as the Earl put it himself. Rochester, who employed a footman whose specific duty it was to keep watch at ladies' doors, was never short of gossip; he credited the Duchess, to whom he was related, with a fine variety of lovers including the Duke of Monmouth, Cavendish, Hennington and Scrope—'Scabby Ned' and 'sturdy Frank'. John Ellis, a lewd young man, educated at Westminster School and Christ Church, was said to have boasted indiscreetly of succeeding the King in the Duchess's affections, with the result that she hired men to castrate him, an incident referred to by Alexander Pope in *A Sermon against Adultery*:

> What push'd poor Ellis on th'imperial whore?
> 'Twas but to be where Charles had been before.
> The fatal steel unjustly was applied,
> When not his lust offended, but his pride.

The playwright William Wycherley had a rather less unsavoury association with the Duchess after she had leant out of her chariot in Pall Mall and called into his, 'You, Wycherley, are the son of a whore' —perhaps not such an offensive remark as it sounds since she was referring to the lines:

> Great wits and braves
> Have always a punk to their mother.

Wycherley made his coachman pursue her, and he delivered a reply lewd enough to make even the Lady blush. That night she was in the front row of the King's box at the theatre in Drury Lane, and Wycherley was in the pit below her, entertaining her wittily throughout. She enjoyed his play, *Love in a Wood* with Charles Hart in the leading part, so much that she visited it twice running, and he dedicated the printed edition to her, after she had asked him to send her a copy. There was a legend that she used to creep out to see the handsome Wycherley, disguised as a country girl in a straw hat, pattens and a basket. 'He who will be constant to your Ladyship till he can find a finer woman', he told her, 'is sure to die your captive.'

Andrew Marvell was less complimentary. To him, the Lady seemed so obsessed with sex that she was reduced to seducing her lackey, whose 'brazen calves and brawny thighs' had aroused her desire. In his *Last Instructions to a Painter* he wrote:

> Stripp'd to her skin, see how she stooping stands,
> Nor scorns to rub him down with those fair hands,
> And washing (lest the scent her crime disclose)
> His sweaty hooves, tickles him 'twixt the toes.
> But envious Fame, too soon, began to note
> More gold in's fob, more lace upon his coat
> And he, unwary and of tongue too fleet,
> No longer could conceal his fortune sweet.
> Justly the rogue was whipped in porter's den;
> And Jermyn straight has leave to come again.

All the Lady's lovers tended to be handsome, and John Churchill, whose mistress she became in 1671, was no exception. Their liaison has been painted as an unwholesome relationship between an ageing courtesan and an innocent boy, but the Duchess was still only just the wrong side of thirty while Churchill was twenty-seven, matured by his army service and deeply tanned by the sun. The Duchess and John Churchill were second cousins, and since he was, besides an Ensign in the Guards, a Page of Honour to the Duke of York, it was not surprising that their paths crossed. His sister Arabella had become the Duke's mistress, only withdrawing from the Court when she had 'a burthen she was not long able to bear', and his aunt was in charge of the Duchess of Cleveland's plentiful nursery. Since boyhood he had been in the habit of visiting the nursery and filling 'his belly with sweetmeats with his aunt'. Legend had it that the Duchess had seen him when she came upon him suddenly on the backstairs and had immediately taken a fancy to him, much to the delight of his aunt who arranged for him to take a bath in the Duchess's bathing room, scenting his linen with the richest perfume for good measure.

The young Ensign had returned from service in Africa 'tempered by discipline and danger' to quote his famous descendant Winston Churchill. He was in great need of money, for he was as impecunious now as he had been when his father Winston had run into debt when buying the necessary equipment for his service. The Duchess of Cleveland's generosity to her lovers was well known, and it may be, goodlooking as he was, that he was deliberately out to try his luck when he crossed the road to Berkshire House from St James's. Inevitably a liaison between two brilliantly attractive people became what Gramont described as the gossip of the town, and everybody was soon giving way to the exquisite enjoyment of airing their views; 'some', according to Gramont, 'asserting that she had given him Jermyn's pension, coupled with Jacob Hall's emoluments, because he combined the advantages of both in his single person, others maintaining that he seemed too indolent and was too slightly built to support her favour for very long, but all agreeing, that a man, who was favourite to the King's mistress and brother to the Duke's, had made a very good start in life and could scarcely fail to rise to greatness.'

There were many estimates of the price the Duchess was prepared to pay in order to acquire a place for her lover at Court; it is certainly true that Churchill was able to buy an annuity with the sum of £5,000 which she gave him, perhaps with the proviso that he invested it wisely so that it could become, as in fact it did, the foundation of his later fortune. Churchill was not immune to the charge of avarice, which was to be levelled at him frequently when he became Duke of Marlborough, and he was certainly careful with the money she provided for him, investing it with Lord Halifax who as Winston Churchill has put it 'in the intervals of statecraft conducted a rudimentary form of life insurance'. It was said that the Duchess obtained 140,000 crowns from the Privy Purse for his use, and settled him into the post of Groom of the Bedchamber to the Duke of York; the more unpleasant gossip was that she earned the £5,000 she gave him by selling herself to the elderly Sir Edward Hungerford for £10,000, although with her usual astuteness she managed to pocket the money while tricking the ancient rake out of his pleasure. As Alexander Pope was to put it:

> Who of ten thousand gull'd her knight,
> Then asked ten thousand for another night.

In spite of all her peccadillos, the King was true to his word and he made no fuss, continuing his visits to Berkshire House, openly and in the afternoons. On 2 March 1671 John Evelyn, who had been taking a stroll through St James's Park, 'both saw and heard a very familiar discourse between [the King] and Mrs Nellie, as they called an impudent comedian, she looking out of her garden on a terrace at the top of the wall and he standing on the green walk under it. I was heartily sorry at this scene', wrote the diarist and added, 'Thence the King walked to the Duchess of Cleveland's, another Lady of Pleasure and curse of our nation.' Only a few weeks before, the Duchess of Cleveland had shone as brightly as ever at the grand ballet in the Palace, dressed in a rich petticoat and a short man's coat, a periwig and cravat with a fine hat and mask. The fact that she could still outshine everybody else was galling for those who had hoped to eradicate her with the introduction of rivals. The Duke of Buckingham, who had expected so much from Nell Gwynn, could only feel put out by the King's new habit of visiting both his mistresses, the new and the old, in the course of his daily stroll. Making one last effort to bring his cousin down with the ruse she had used so effectively on Frances Stuart, he bribed a waiting-woman to tell the King when Churchill was at Berkshire House. Built on a larger scale Churchill was unable to hide under the bed as Jermyn had done in a similar crisis; instead the Duchess locked him into a cupboard where she more normally stored drinks and sweetmeats. Ignoring her excuse that she had lost the key, the King insisted on having a drink. When Churchill was revealed, the King said genially but with a touch of cynicism, 'I forgive you, for you do it for your bread'. An even more famous story had the athletic Churchill precipitating himself from the Duchess's window into a courtyard below on hearing of the King's imminent arrival. But the King preferred to be amused rather than angry, and the affair continued until by the beginning of 1672 it became evident that the Duchess was expecting Churchill's child.

While pursuing a course of action which was to result in another inmate for the Berkshire House nursery, the Duchess had been working hard to ensure the future of the children already under the care of Churchill's aunt. The arrival of a son for Nell Gwynn made her intensify her efforts to find suitable heiresses and titles for Charles, Henry and George. For Charles, now elevated to the peerage as Earl of Southampton, she had selected Mary, the seven-year-old daughter of Sir

Henry Wood. As Clerk of the Spicery under Charles I and Clerk of the Green Cloth under Charles II, Sir Henry had kept a rigorous control over other people's expenditure while he himself made his money illegally by the jobbing or 'brokage' of Court places. There were plenty of stories which described him condemning the extravagance of Court employees—he had even been heard 'damning the parsons for so much spending the wine at the sacrament'. It was now his turn, as Andrew Marvell put it, to find out how 'he commands that pays'. Hearing that the King had chosen his daughter as a suitable spouse for the simple-minded Earl of Southampton, Sir Henry remarked urbanely that as he had acquired his fortune under the King he must dispense it according to the royal wishes; he only regretted that his fortune was not greater, for the young Lord's sake. At the age of seventy-three Sir Henry could be relied on to expire in the not too distant future, which was an added attraction. He was so bent and deformed that Marvell compared him to St Denis—a beheaded martyr who was usually depicted carrying his head in his hands. The eight-year-old Earl was himself no great beauty, for his teeth stuck out like tusks, one theory being that his simple-mindedness had been caused by his cruel mother's ruthless attempt to pull out the offending teeth herself. A meeting was arranged between the boy and his future father-in-law, who obediently settled all his estates on the heirs of his daughter Mary and her young husband. He did, however, have the wisdom to postpone the marriage until Mary had reached the age of sixteen, granting her the right to refuse, but the Duchess saw to it that handsome compensation would have to be paid if the royal bastard should finally find himself rejected.

Mary Wood was not the only child heiress to be sacrificed on the altar of the Duchess's avariciousness. The Earl of Arlington, benefiting from the Duke of Buckingham's carelessness in leaving Louise de Kéroualle behind in France, had become the main sponsor of the Duchess's new rival. All the same he was never averse to making the best of all worlds. He had one daughter to dispose of and since he was now in his fifties and his wife was not young it seemed unlikely that he would ever be gifted with an heir. His daughter Isabella was just three years old, a singularly sweet-natured child, and much as he loved her, he did not flinch from using her as a pawn in the complex political game to which he had devoted his life. Since he had become one of those who had been let into all the secrets of the treaty with France, he had felt unable to accept any bribes from the French, or to countenance their attempt to wean his wife away from her Dutch affiliations. For fear that suspicion might be aroused by any marked favours, the King had discouraged Madame from giving Lady Arlington a diamond ring while she was at Dover; instead Madame had encouraged her brother to allow a marriage between Isabella and one of his sons, a sure way of guaranteeing Arlington's future favour with the King and the ever-influential Duchess of Cleveland. That Madame had the matter very much at heart was proved by the fact that she gave Montagu a message for the King shortly before her death, reminding him of his promise to promote the match; '. . . tell the King my brother I hope he will for my sake, do for him what he promised, *car c'est un homme qui l'aime, et qui le sert bien*'. The King found it hard to ignore his sister's dying wish, and he assigned to Isabella the most attractive of the Duchess's sons whom he had at first felt reluctant to acknowledge, but whom he now referred to as 'our dear natural son Henry Fitzroy'. Henry was well-favoured and full of charm, and Arlington pressed on with plans for the marriage fearing all the time that the Duchess might bestow her son on an even more eligible heiress, the five-year-old Lady Betty Percy who had inherited from her father all the Northumberland wealth. She was said to be the richest girl in England.

Although ready to spite his cousin in every other connection, the Duke of Buckingham was prepared to support the idea of acquiring Lady Betty Percy for Henry Fitzroy—he was always happy to seize any chance of outwitting Lord Arlington. In fact the Duchess was secretly reserving Lady Betty for her youngest son George, and she saw to it that Henry and Isabella were united at the earliest possible moment. She persuaded the King to grant Arlington an earldom, and to admit him into the select circle of Knights of the Garter. Arlington, for his part, agreed that all the property granted to him by the King should descend to Henry's heirs. The inheritance included Euston Hall, with its picture gallery, chapel and orangery, its stables for thirty horses and its 2,000-acre deer park 'a very noble pile', according to John Evelyn '. . . not only capable and roomsome, but very magnificent and commodious, as well within as without, nor less splendidly furnished'.

The wedding took place at the beginning of August 1672, after a fortnight's postponement which gave the bridegroom's mother time to recover from the birth of a daughter whom she named Barbara. The situation was somewhat bizarre and it gave no pleasure to John Evelyn, who thought that Isabella was 'worth for her beauty and virtue the greatest Prince in christendom'. The diarist wrote on August 1, 'I was at the marriage of my Lord Arlington's only daughter, a sweet child, if ever there was any, to the Duke of Grafton, natural son of the King by the Duchess of Cleveland, the Archbishop of Canterbury officiating, the King and all the grandees present; I had a favour given me by my lady, but took no great joy at the thing for many reasons'. The two fathers, on the other hand, apparently felt no qualms when they saw their young children at the altar. Arlington was devoted to his

daughter, who was the only human being known to make him unbend.
As the Duke of Buckingham put it:

> For tho' to us he's stately like a king,
> He'll joke and droll with her like anything.

As far as Arlington was concerned there was no sin in allying Isabella
with the offspring of one of those ladies John Evelyn referred to uncompromisingly as whores and concubines, and since the crowned heads of
Europe disposed of their children at an early age, he was content to
follow their example:

> His age with only one mild heiress blest,
> In all the bloom of smiling nature dressed;
> And blessed again to see his flower allied
> To David's stock, and made young Othniel's bride.

So Henry, passed over in the first share-out of titles which the King
had bestowed on his children in 1670, became Viscount Norwich and
Baron Sudbury, and later Earl of Euston and Duke of Grafton. In his
case there was no marriage settlement cloyed with delaying clauses.
Lord Arlington had intended to bring up his son-in-law at Euston so
that he could be trained in the management of the estates which would
one day be his. The Duchess, however, refused to part with her son,
insisting that he needed no other guidance than the education that nature
and his mother could provide—this she considered 'sufficient accom-
plishment for a married man'. Henry remained in the Berkshire House
nursery along with his new half-sister Barbara and another new addition
in the shape of Mary Wood who had been abducted by the Duchess on
the death of Sir Henry. Although the marriage settlement had included
a clause which stipulated that Mary should be put in the care of her aunt,
who was to be paid £450 a year to bring her up 'firmly instructed in the
true Protestant religion', the Duchess had removed her a fortnight
after she was orphaned. Mary's aunt was forced to forfeit both the
girl and her annual income. The King had promised to contribute
a dowry of £2,000, but this he conveniently forgot to pay, even when
Mary went through a form of marriage with the young Charles. The
Wood family initiated proceedings in Parliament, pleading that this
was 'a case of an extraordinary nature'—and nobody could quibble with
such an analysis. They found it hard to touch the King, and even
harder to tie down the Duchess, who was protected by the privileges
of a peer, and as a 'feme covert' was also shielded by the rights of a
husband who was opportunely out of the country. Her only concession
to the infuriated relations was to arrange for Dr Wood, the Dean of
Coventry and Lichfield, to become a Bishop—not the first time she

had been successful in the ecclesiastical sphere, for she had previously helped her uncle Henry Glemham, 'a drunken swearing rascal', to become Bishop of St Asaph. It was to Dr Wood that the bulk of Mary's fortune would have passed had she refused to marry Charles at the age of sixteen, but he preferred the prospect of rapid promotion. Although suspended at one time by his Archbishop for gross neglect of duty, he enjoyed his see for eight years, dying just about the time when Mary should have reached the moment of decision on her sixteenth birthday.

While the Duchess kept Mary Wood under her eye she decided that Charles and George should be granted the benefits of an Oxford education. She travelled down in person and summoned to her lodgings Dr Fell, the Dean of Christ Church. She treated him with great civility and asked him to care for her son George who had been born at Oxford among the scholars and was more inclined to receive instruction than Charles who, she had to confess, was 'a very cockish idle boy'. The academics did not relish their task and they knew there was little they could expect from the Earl of Southampton. 'It is the general desire among us that he come not', one of them admitted. However he behaved in an orderly manner, even though he could never attain the reputation of 'not being a fool'.

The Duchess's daughters were just as sought-after as her sons. When John Evelyn travelled to Norwich from Euston Hall with Lord Henry Howard—'my Lord and I alone in his flying chariot with six horses'—the Baron could not keep to himself the fact that he hoped to marry his eldest son to one of the King's natural daughters by the Duchess of Cleveland, 'by which he reckoned', Evelyn wrote, 'he shall come into mighty favour'. Lord Clifford had been busily trying to arrange a marriage between the infant son of Sir Francis Radcliffe and eight-year-old Charlotte Fitzroy. A special yacht had brought the Duchess's eldest daughter Anne back from France, and in August 1674 she was married to Thomas Lennard, 15th Lord Dacre. Anne's husband was related to the Duchess through her aunt, Elizabeth Bayning, who had married the 14th Lord Dacre. The Palmers still liked to think of Anne as Roger's child, and they had presented her with a genealogical tree tracing the family back to the fourteenth century. But on this occasion the King treated her as if she was his own child, arriving from Windsor at noon and staying in the Duchess's lodgings at Hampton Court for a while before he led the bride through to his own chamber, the Duchess following on the Duke of York's arm. Prince Rupert, the Duke of Monmouth, as well as the King's natural son by Catherine Pegge, the Earl of Suffolk, the Lords Arlington and Danby and Lord Keeper Finch all attended the ceremony which was carried out by the Bishop of Oxford according to the rites of the

Anglican Church. After the service the King kissed the bride, and bride-cake was ceremoniously broken over her head. Dinner was served in the Presence Chamber with the Duchess presiding over a glittering and distinguished company.

Before long Lord Dacre was created Earl of Sussex, and rooms were assigned to the young couple over the Gatehouse at Whitehall —the same lodgings the Duchess herself had occupied. In spite of her tender years Anne moved into her husband's home in Warwick Street. Her younger sister Charlotte, however, remained in the nursery for some years after she had gone through a form of ceremony with Sir Edward Lee when she was still only nine years old. Her dowry of £18,000 was only £2,000 less than her sister's, and the King had to pay off the expenses of both weddings in instalments, mostly from secret service money. The Duchess as usual was none too meticulous about paying the bills, and she herself spent over £1,000 on wedding clothes, which included 'several parcels of gold and silver lace'. In 1684 many of the bills were still outstanding.

Louise de Kéroualle had presented the King with a son shortly after the birth of Barbara Churchill, but as yet he refused to acknowledge it, and continued to heap honours on the Duchess's children. In the general share-out of favours following the death of the Duke of Albemarle, the Earl of Southampton had acquired, mainly thanks to his mother's intervention, the Keepership of Hampton Court. In 1673 he was invested with the Order of the Garter. Arms were granted to Anne and Charlotte, who were made Lady Companions of the Order of the Garter, and all three sons were granted arms, crests and supporters. Henry, who had been created Earl of Euston, was appointed Receiver-General and Comptroller of the Seals of the Court of the King's Bench and Common Pleas. When the Duke of Richmond died in 1672 greedy eyes were at once focused on his vacant titles. To the satisfaction of his mother-in-law, Charlotte's husband received one of them; it was unthinkable that he should remain a mere baronet, and he was quickly created Earl of Lichfield, partly no doubt to spite Frances whose husband's death had left the title vacant.

At the age of eight, George, anticipating a possible marriage with Lady Betty Percy, became Earl of Northumberland, with the added titles of Viscount Falmouth and Baron Pontefract. The Falmouth title had been vacant since Charles Berkeley's head had been blown off at the battle off Folkestone, and it was perhaps in his memory, or perhaps to pay off old scores against Lady Falmouth for daring to cast her eye on Henry Jermyn, that the Duchess decided to annexe it for her family.

Altogether the Duchess was more than holding her own. Louise de

Kéroualle, from whom so much had been expected, had borne the King a child, but in other ways had proved something of a disappointment. From the start the French Ambassador Colbert de Croissy had sounded a warning note; he had seen too much of the Duchess of Cleveland to be sure that she would easily relinquish her hold. 'I think it safer', he wrote, 'while undermining that lady, to keep her on our side by appearing to be with her'. This advice, so typical of the tortuous diplomacy of the day, was after Arlington's own heart. He was more than ready to cultivate Louise while marrying his little 'Tata' off to the Duchess of Cleveland's son. He saw in the French girl the perfect mistress; for one thing, she was a lady, which made her far more valuable than 'the comediennes and the like, on whom', as he put it, 'no honest man can rely, by whose means the Duke of Buckingham was always trying to entice the King, in order to draw him away from all his Court and monopolize him'. At the same time she was less likely to be meddling and interfering after the style of the Duchess of Cleveland. 'The young lady', he told Colbert, 'must be counselled to manage well the good graces of the King, not to speak to him of affairs, and not to show any aversion to those who are near him, and, in short to let him find only pleasure and joy in her company.'

The Earl of Arlington did what he could to guide Louise along the lines he himself had laid down. He invited her to Euston and made sure that the King came over frequently from Audley End to see her. Nobody, as John Evelyn put it, was 'more hospitably easy to be withall than my Lord Arlington'. Lady Arlington made her contribution by advising Louise 'either to yield unreservedly to the King, or to retire to a French convent'. Louise did not prove easy to woo or swift to succumb, but in the luxurious atmosphere of Euston Hall she at last relaxed. Evelyn was shocked to see that during the King's visits, she was 'for the most part in her undress all day, and that there was fondness, and toying'. It was believed that Louise was first made a 'misse' at Euston, but she showed little gratitude to the master of the house for providing the opportunity. As Colbert de Croissy was later to report, 'Arlington neither likes nor esteems Mlle de Kéroualle, and reproaches her with having as soon forgotten the obligations he conferred on her, as any of the good dinners she has eaten'. Colbert himself had hoped that so long as Louise behaved discreetly she might well exclude all the King's other attachments and provide the French with a valuable ally, but he had to admit he too was disappointed. Louise proved too selfish to live up to the high standards expected by the French diplomatic service. Nor did she succeed in ousting the other mistresses. Nell Gwynn still shared the King's affection, as well as his time and his largesse, amusing him with imitations of the French mistress— 'if me taut me was one bad woman, me would cut mine own trote'. The Duchess of Cleveland at first gave way to furious tantrums when she heard about Louise's success, but she soon calmed down when the King still came to visit her, even if it was less frequently than before.

In the summer of 1673 the French mistress was created Duchess of Portsmouth and the King found himself involved in heavy expenses with two Duchesses to maintain as well as Nell Gwynn who eschewed the need for titles but was not averse to taking her share of the material spoils. It was said that £100,000 was given away in the short space of five weeks, the major share going to the two Duchesses. But in July 1673 the King reputedly gave Nell an outright gift of £20,000, thus 'angrying much my Lady Cleveland and Mademoiselle Carwell [anglicized version of Louise de Kéroualle]'. The story went that the two Duchesses invited Nell to dinner and were not too heartbroken when she nearly choked herself to death on a napkin. For a day or two there were rumours that Nell had died as a result of this unusual accident, but they were quelled as soon as Nell appeared as usual in the Park, as large as life and as lively as ever.

When Settle's *Empress of Morocco* was performed at Court, the Earl of Rochester added a prologue which was spoken by Lady Elizabeth Howard. It was addressed to the King in the guise of a message from Youth and Beauty; and the three mistresses were there to hear it —all sitting together in the same row:

> And hither come with such a force of charms
> As may give check even to your prosperous arms
> Nor can you scape our soft captivity,
> From which old age alone must set you free.
> 'Tis well, for your own part, great Prince,
> 'Gainst us you still have made a weak defence.

The King certainly could not resist a 'force of charms', and he found that it was as hard to dismiss an old mistress as it was easy to acquire a new one. He dealt with the quarrels in his seraglio with his usual ability to stand aside and let events take their course, happily conferring titles on his mistresses and sons, and remaining immune to innumerable jibes such as the lines which ran:

> This making of bastards great
> And duchessing every whore.

The rivalry between the ladies was often intense; when the others acquired fine coaches, the Duchess of Cleveland paraded through the Park with a magnificent equipage drawn by eight horses, saying that she was ready to progress to twelve if her rivals tried to outdo her.

When the Duchess of Portsmouth's son was granted the much sought-after title of Duke of Richmond, the King had to placate Cleveland by decreeing that both her elder sons should also become dukes. In the undignified race between the ladies to see who could gain precedence for their offspring by acquiring the first patent, the King stood aside in his usual manner and left it to the Lord Treasurer to sign the papers. The Duchess fell into a spectacular rage when she found that she had been beaten at the post by Portsmouth, and rather than face her the Lord Treasurer quickly escaped to Bath.

It was true that the King visited Louise every morning at nine o'clock, never staying for less than an hour; it was also true that since she was a lady by birth and not a termagant by nature, like some others who could be mentioned, 'persons of breeding could, without loss of dignity, go to her rooms' to pay their court both to her and to the King. But as her position with the King became more established, she became more and more disliked. Her extravagance was notorious, and at a time when the French were becoming increasingly unpopular, her nationality was in itself a drawback. The Duchess of Cleveland, whether she was a termagant or not, always had her admirers and her following at Court, but the Duchess of Portsmouth relied entirely on the King's favour. She had no relations in England to help her, and she seldom put herself out to help anyone else. The nearest she came to nepotism was to import her nondescript sister to England, quickly marrying her off to the spendthrift Earl of Pembroke, a rake who had twice been accused of murder, and who might well have conveyed to his wife the disease which Louise herself contracted as a result of the King's 'misconduct with trulls'.

Colbert de Croissy, who had been so convinced in 1671 that the Duchess of Cleveland's influence was on the wane and that all the trouble and money lavished on her 'to get her round to the Spanish side' had been thrown away, soon realized that he had been wrong. For after ten years as the King's *maîtresse en titre*, after several lovers, after three sons and three daughters, the exotic Duchess was still more entwined with Court politics than the well-bred Louise or the witty Nell would ever be.

CHAPTER EIGHTEEN

LANDLADY CLEVELAND

T HE DUCHESS of Cleveland's cupidity seemed to be endless, and with the blood of the Baynings flowing in her veins it was not surprising that she brought to her activities a business acumen that was outstanding in a woman of those times. Apart from the gifts and grants she obtained from the King, she augmented her fortune by accepting bribes from those who knew that by means of her influence they could gain wealth, position and power. When Lord Robartes, who had gained the post of Lord-Lieutenant of Ireland through the Duke of Buckingham's influence, was removed after a very short term of office, his successor, Lord Berkeley of Stratton, may have owed his success to the tact that he had offered a bribe of £20,000 to the Duchess. And in 1672 he was forced to come over to England to pay 'ten thousand pounds in rent to his landlady Cleveland'.

Sir Robert Howard, by now one of the most influential men in Parliament and at Court, had turned his attention to other matters besides the examination of the naval accounts and those who administered them when the King finally made it clear that he was satisfied no monies voted for the war had been devoted to other uses. Well known for his tendency to hold forth in the House on every kind of subject, Howard had begun to devote his energies increasingly to financial matters for which he had a particular flair. He was foremost among those who were searching about for new methods of raising money for the King so that he would be able to equip an efficient fleet. His policy was to levy duties on an increased number of commodities such as wine, vinegar, linen, brandy and currants.

Howard himself undertook to raise £400,000 by the methods he himself advocated. Known in the past as an Undertaker for the King in Parliament, and then as a 'roller out' who was concerned to destroy the careers of many of the King's servants, he was now described by Marvell as one of:

> . . . the five recanters of the House,
> That aim at mountains and bring forth a mouse.

He was now prepared to dedicate himself to the King's service with his associates, but of course only at a price. Although described by one commentator on his appointment as Secretary to the Treasury as a 'mushroom upstart', his climb to a position of such importance had been slow and steady, and if his astuteness in managing his own financial affairs was anything to go by he was exceptionally well fitted for the task. He had found himself in the position of being able to help the King with sizeable loans, and this stood him in good stead when he decided to form a syndicate for the collection of customs duties and the new tax on wines. Howard had been mercilessly caricatured as Sir Positive At-All in Shadwell's play, *The Sullen Lovers*—'so foolishly Positive, that he will never be convinced of an error, though never so gross'—and he certainly showed immense confidence and even audacity in his bold attempt at acquiring the valuable right to farm the taxes. His scheme was to engage his own tax collectors and to extract a commission for the syndicate, as well as a monopoly of the profitable right to obtain a rake-off on every wine licence issued.

Although the King was in a very real sense indebted to Howard, there was wisdom in making sure that every possible influence was exerted on behalf of the syndicate in order to obtain the right to farm the taxes on the most favourable terms possible. The most obvious person to approach was the Duchess of Cleveland whose continuing influence at Court could not be ignored and who was, in addition, related to Howard himself through Lady Suffolk. His friend, Lord St John, who had also been pilloried under the name of Woodcock in *The Sullen Lovers*, was the Marquess of Winchester's son and owed his courtesy title to the fact that like the Duchess's grandmother Barbara St John, he could trace his lineage back to the first Lord St John of Basing. The other members of the syndicate were Sir John Bennet, the Earl of Arlington's brother, and an uncle of Isabella, with Sir William Bucknell, a London brewer:

> Whilst Positive walks Woodcock in the dark,
> Contriving projects with a Brewer's clerk,

as Marvell put it. To make sure that they secured the tax farm monopoly, the syndicate did not hesitate to sign and seal £10,000 to the Duchess in return for her services. But for once Howard's instincts were wrong and he spoiled his case by pressing for better and better terms, until in the end the syndicate lost its contract and Ashley and Clifford arranged for the money to be collected by the King's own commissioners, thus dispensing with the entrepreneur.

Having pocketed her bribe, the Duchess of Cleveland was unconcerned at Howard's failure, and when in 1673 the wine licences were taken into the King's hands, a pension of £5,500 was granted to be paid to the Duchess for life in Lord Grandison's name. There were rumours that she had been granted the reversion of all the King's leases, as well as a valuable right to control appointments in the Customs House, to take a commission on the duties levied on the Green Wax, all this and 'indeed, what not?' as Marvell was prompted to enquire. In October 1672 she added a further £6,000 from the excise revenues with remainder to her son Charles and his heirs, the sum made over as usual in the names of her trustees Lord Grandison and Sir Edward Villiers. In addition all her sons received grants of £3,000.

Six months after she became a Duchess, the King granted his mistress the house at Nonsuch with its surrounding parkland, with the remainder to Charles and George. Gramont had it that the King only granted these honours on condition that she gave up Jermyn for ever, that she agreed not to rail any more at her rivals and that she accepted everything 'without any constraint on the King's behaviour to her'. In 1673 her fortunes continued to augment with astonishing rapidity. Camouflaged as usual in the form of gifts to her uncles, the Duchess's new acquisitions included lands in the Duchy of Cornwall, a warrant for £5,000 as a free gift, as well as the wine licences. She was granted the Manor of Somersham and five other manors in Huntingdon, given in reversion to Lord Grandison for her life and after her death to the Earl of Southampton and his male heirs, 'the residue of the revenue to be divided into moieties, one whereof to the Lord Euston and his heirs, and the other to the Lord George and his heirs'.

There had been rumours that Roger would return to England when his wife was created a Duchess, but he wisely stayed away, and the property in King Street, now known by the imposing name of Villiers House, was let to the combined Councils for Trade and Plantations which met for the first time in October 1672. It was not long before her Grace ruthlessly demolished the fairy-tale Palace of Nonsuch with its gilded domes and magnificent decorations, selling the materials for a good price and letting the land with considerable profit. She also sold off Berkshire House and most of the garden, and with the proceeds built herself a smaller property, Cleveland House, on a choice site abutting on the Park which she had reserved for herself. When planning her new garden she asked the advice of her old friend the Earl of Chesterfield. He now spent his time almost exclusively at Bretby with his third wife Elizabeth Dormer who had brought him the kind of domestic happiness which had previously eluded him. His greatest pleasure in life was to return to Derbyshire after one of his rare visits to London, smelling the perfumes of the flowers and cleansing the city air from his lungs. All his energies were now devoted to the improvement of his estate, and particularly of his garden which Marshal Tallard was to

6

pronounce the finest in Europe with the exception of Versailles. He was
planning a fine avenue of Spanish chestnuts, sunken gardens, an aviary,
labyrinths, a tea house, a hydraulic clock chiming the hours to the tune
of 'Lillibullero' and waterworks with several fountains, one with a
jet of fifty feet.

Chesterfield responded with alacrity to the Duchess's appeal for help.
'The greatest pleasure of my thoughts is in thinking how to serve your
ladyship', he wrote in his old style. He ordered for her fountain a statue
of Cupid kneeling on a rock and shooting water from his bow in the
direction of heaven. 'My meaning in it is', Chesterfield explained, 'that
your ladyship, not being content with the conquest of one world, doth
now by your devotions attack the other. I hope this style hath too much
gravity to appear gallant, since many years ago your ladyship gave me
occasion to repeat:

> Vous m'ôtez tout espoir, pour vous, belle inhumaine,
> Et pour tout autre que vous, vous m'ôtez tout désir.'

While she improved her own property, the Duchess did not relax
her efforts to acquire other people's. To the consternation of the Earl
of Essex, the Lord-Lieutenant in Ireland, she renewed her claim to
Phoenix Park, causing him to explain, as Ormonde had done before
him, that Dublin Castle had no land attached to it apart from the Park,
'nor any house to retire to for a little air upon occasion of sickness';
without it the Governor would not have 'the command of a buck for his
own table or a little grass to turn out his horse'. Essex did his best to
suggest alternative land, amounting to 30,000 acres, although he had to
admit that some of it was unprofitable and scattered about several
counties. The Duchess cared little about the Lord-Lieutenant's horses.
She was preoccupied with the task of providing for her own and her
children's future. There was bound to come a time when her beauty
would fade, but during the early seventies she made the most of her
continuing good looks to amass money and property on a grand scale
against the time when she no longer had any influence. The strength of
her character is shown in the extent of her gains, and in the awe with
which she was regarded by her contemporaries, men and women alike.
She aroused curiosity and admiration wherever she went, even though
she was a hated papist and an adulterous one at that. When she went
to Oxford to arrange for her sons' education, her visit caused such a stir
that on the morning before she went away she sat for at least an hour
in her coach so that 'everybody might see her'. She revelled in her
notoriety, capitalized on her beauty, and made the most of the fact that
for the first time she was likely to benefit from a sympathetic Lord
Treasurer. Lord Clifford, after filling the post of Treasurer of the

Household for four years was appointed Lord Treasurer in 1672. This development augured well for the Duchess, since Clifford was pro-Catholic and a good friend of the Duke of York.

Working with the members of the cabal, who were all signatories of the *traité simulé*, the King muzzled his Parliament by the simple ruse of omitting to call its Members to Westminster. But he could not control the thinking of the country at large, or prevent apprehension spreading about his Catholic friendships, his secretive dealings with France and his determination to establish his own financial independence. Although he cheerfully told Colbert de Croissy that the announcement of his conversion, when it came, was not likely to cause too great a stir, the Duchess of Portsmouth was nearer the mark when she said that once the secret was out everybody would desert him. The Duchess of York's conversion did nothing to allay the ever latent fear of popery, and when after her death in 1671 it became known that the Duke planned to marry a Catholic—Maria Beatrice, a sister of the Duke of Modena—this seemed to confirm that James had already turned to Rome himself.

Since no Parliament was called between April 1671 and January 1673 the King had to rely on the money he managed to extract from the French, together with the wine licence rents and taxes already voted by Parliament. Lord Clifford, sharing the King's Catholic sympathies as well as his determination to renew the struggle with the Dutch, averted a financial crisis by introducing the Stop of the Exchequer. This brought to a halt the payment of heavy interest on large sums of money borrowed from the banks. It was a drastic measure, in a sense a confession of bankruptcy, but at least it ensured that for the time being the money raised through taxation could be used for current expenditure and in particular for fitting out the fleet.

The members of the cabal were all in favour of some measure of religious toleration, and it was easy to imagine, in the isolated world of Whitehall, that a Catholic revival was not an impossibility. Up to now, whenever the King had attempted to improve the papists' lot, Parliament had cancelled out his efforts with a call for even harsher laws against recusants, and his need for money had always forced him to succumb. Now he felt that his independence of Parliament, however temporary it might turn out to be, gave him a chance to exercise what he believed to be his lawful prerogative. In March 1672 he issued a second Declaration of Indulgence which was far less tentative in tone than its predecessor. The Declaration called for the suspension of the penal laws against nonconformists of all kinds, allowing Protestant dissenters to meet openly in premises licensed for the purpose, while Catholics were granted the privilege of holding services in private houses. Two days later, war was declared on the Dutch.

As usual the King's aims were larger than his resources. In conjunction with the French, the English fleet was to deliver a blow against the Dutch naval forces which would clear the way for a landing in Holland. But again the sea battle, which took place in May, proved inconclusive, and the English fleet suffered much damage and many casualties. For the rest of the summer persistent bad weather prevented both the English and the Dutch fleets from venturing out to do battle, but the French meanwhile swept forward into the Dutch provinces by land, making it increasingly evident that it was they who would possess all the bargaining power when the time came to draw up treaties and divide the spoils. And so the money made available by the Stop of the Exchequer had brought no tangible returns and by the end of 1672 it was evident that to avoid complete bankruptcy the King would be forced to call a Parliament.

At Christmas time it was noticed that the Duke of York was missing when the King attended Holy Communion, and the Parliament which met in February 1673 had good grounds for suspecting that there had been much Catholic infiltration at Court. The fact that during the long recess the King had on his own authority issued the two vital declarations of war and indulgence seemed to suggest that he was all too prepared to exceed his prerogative and, if given a chance, to bring in an era of arbitrary government. The Parliament was prepared to teach him a lesson. While granting him a generous sum of over £1,000,000, Members made it clear that they would exact their own terms more harshly than ever. First they demanded the withdrawal of the Declaration of Indulgence and he himself had the humiliation of breaking the Seal on March 7. They then brought in a Test Act which stipulated that nobody would be allowed to hold office unless they were prepared to take the sacrament according to the Anglican rites, and to swear the oaths of Supremacy and Allegiance. So, once again, in imitating his French cousin by asserting his prerogative in religious matters, he had produced exactly the opposite of his original intention.

The measure struck personally at the King. He was forced to remove from his Household all Catholics except his barber. His brother James, who once again refused to take the sacrament at Easter time, resigned his post as Lord High Admiral. The Duchess of Cleveland was deprived of her post as Lady of the Bedchamber to the Queen. Lord Clifford, who had staked his future on the chances of a Catholic revival, had made it clear by his open and violent opposition to the Test Act, where his own sympathies lay.

For the Duchess the loss of her post in the Queen's Household was not too serious, since Catherine had by now retired to a separate establishment at Somerset House, a prey to headaches and general ill-health.

But the probable fall of Lord Clifford was far more serious, for he had been responsible for signing many of the remittances which had helped to build up her fortune. None too sure whether her interests would be looked after by Clifford's successor, she wrote pressing him to despatch outstanding business on her behalf, explaining that the situation would have been less serious had she not been heavily committed in setting up and furnishing her new house. Believing herself 'sartan' of the money, she had been buying up furniture and plate. A few days later she told Clifford that she had spoken to Sir Robert Howard at Whitehall and had asked him whether all her business had been despatched. 'He told me that the Forest of Dean was not', she reported, 'so I spoke with the King and he says that tomorrow if your Lordship will offer him the warrant he will sign it. I do beg of your lordship that you will be pleased to put an end to all my concerns that are before you tomorrow or else I shall despair of having them done when your lordship has quitted.'

Lord Clifford's Catholic sympathies were well known and he was too honest a man to cling to office. He handed over amicably to Osborne and retired from the scene, dying soon afterwards, some said by his own hand. His departure heralded the disintegration of the cabal. This assortment of men had been described in a satirical catalogue of a sale at the Royal Coffee House as 'Lot 17: A very fine cabal cage with 5 or 6 canary birds all of differing notes to make a better consort'. Now even the King, with his genius for bringing different elements together, could not prevent the ensuing discord. The old enmity between Buckingham and Arlington broke out again. Bitterly disappointed by the progress of the war and by his own failure to gain the command of land forces promised to the French, Buckingham refused to be wooed even with the promise of pensions and appointments. He devoted his energies to the negative task of rallying support in the campaign to bring Arlington down, working on everybody he could think of—'the debauchees by drinking with them, the sober by grave and serious discourses, the pious by receiving the sacrament'. Arlington, for his part, resigned at last to the fact that he would never achieve his ambition of becoming Lord High Treasurer, gradually showed signs of losing his appetite for the political game he had played for so long.

In Parliament, Members made up for their enforced silence by giving vent to their many grievances. The Ministry was blamed for fostering popery, and inevitably its financial policies came under fire. Not surprisingly the large sums squandered on the King's mistresses during the previous two years did not go unnoticed, and the two Duchesses attracted extra venom on account of their faith, while Louise suffered even more as a result of a general dislike of the French alliance. In the mock catalogue of the Royal Coffee House sale the lots included one whole piece of the Duchess of Cleveland's honesty, two ells of Nell Gwynn's virginity in three pieces, and two dozen of French wenches the one half paid by His Majesty to keep him right to the Protestant religion, the other to incline him to the Catholics.

The Duchess of Portsmouth showed signs of alarm as criticism became more vocal; she went so far as to win favour by attending an Anglican church—'as one whore comes over to the Church of England, so another, the Duchess of Cleveland, went to the popish church 14 years ago' was how Anthony Wood put it. The English Duchess, if she had her qualms, still managed to live much as she had done before, only with greater circumspection. When mention was made in the House of £400,000 which it was believed the two Duchesses had in the main received, trouble seemed certain, but Lord Clifford's thoughtfulness in removing himself to another world made an examination of such benefits difficult to carry out. The Duchess of Cleveland had gathered in as much as possible while the going was good and now she was prepared to live quietly on the proceeds, managing her affairs as usual with considerable astuteness and making sure that she had good advisers. When the question of wine licences remained unsettled at the time of Clifford's fall, she asked that her own solicitor might be used in the negotiations, 'for', she wrote, 'he that is in is neglectful'. She decided in the end to choose a share of the customs duties rather than relying on the wine licences. 'You have doubtless heard', Andrew Marvell wrote to Sir Henry Thompson, 'that the Duchess of Portsmouth has £1,000 a year settled out of the wine licences, she of Cleveland having chosen hers out of the excise as the more secure and legal fond.'

When there was talk of impeaching the mistresses on the grounds that they kept the King in a state of continual poverty, Lord Mordaunt remarked, 'but no, we ought rather to be grateful to them for making the King subservient to his Parliament'. On the whole there was little that anybody could do to touch them so long as they enjoyed the King's favour. While the members of the cabal faced the wrath of Parliament —Lord Ashley was dismissed in the autumn of 1673 for his opposition to the Test Act, and Lauderdale too was under fire—the Duchess of Cleveland lay low and emerged more or less unscathed. Sir Thomas Osborne, who had quickly been created Earl of Danby, filled the gap left by the disintegrating cabal, keeping a firm grip on expenditure and encouraging to the full an Anglican policy with no concessions for nonconformists of any hue. The 'grinding and terrible laws' embodied in the Act of Uniformity were rigorously enforced; godly and moderate preachers were silenced along with fanatical ranters, and many meetings were dispersed. But the greatest fury was directed against the recusants as the real nature of the Grand Design became clear, and as fears for the Protestant succession were aroused by the Duke of York's marriage with the Catholic Mary of Modena.

Unlike his predecessors in the cabal, Danby possessed the ability to formulate a coherent policy as well as the determination to carry it out. But he still had to work with the delicate balances and shifting alliances which had existed under the rule of the cabal, and which the King knew so well how to handle. Although his main concern was to keep the King on good terms with his predominantly Anglican Parliament, he was at the same time forced to work amicably with the two men who wielded the greatest personal influence with the King—the Duke of York and the Earl of Lauderdale—who both strongly supported the non-conformist cause. There were others who had to be placated, such 'small things' as Bab May, who still enjoyed his long-standing privilege of selecting those who were allowed to share the King's leisure hours. The Duke of Buckingham also had to be taken into account, for his magnetism was perennial and he could always charm the King with his wit and mimicry. Ominously enough he had already perfected an impersonation of the formidable Lady Danby.

With the help of judicious bribes the Lord Treasurer worked hard to establish his own position and to reinforce the King's support in Parliament. Danby's painstaking studies of the different power groups, with notes as to how each member should be approached, show his determination to steer the ship of state rather than let it be buffeted by every wind that blew. Wherever possible he put his own relations into strategic places in the administration, and he wooed other office-holders with the promise of preferment. But however hard he worked there were still many imponderables; there could be no guaranteeing the votes of men who did not scruple to accept bribes from two sources at once, perhaps balancing Danby's contributions against the well-organized generosity of the French or Spanish Ambassadors.

As the new pattern of power gradually emerged, the Duchess of Cleveland, like everybody else, had to take stock of the situation and decide where future loyalties lay. The fact that the Duke of York was still influential with the King augured well, and Sir Robert Howard's continuing presence at the Treasury also helped to keep her position stable. Howard was thought to have 'a great place at Court', and at the same time he jarred strongly with Danby; as the Earl of Essex put it, the enmity of the two men made 'all matters of the Treasury go ruggedly'. Although Sir Robert acquired the post of Auditor of the Exchequer, he was reluctant to relinquish the Secretaryship of the Treasury, and his presence caused continual friction. He succeeded in obtaining for his son the reversion of a place as teller in the Exchequer, and this manoeuvre was matched by Danby who gained a similar reversion of the Auditor's place for his younger son Lord Dumblane, placing his brother-in-law and henchman Charles Bertie in the Secretary's place when Howard was finally persuaded to give it up.

In April 1675, articles of impeachment were drawn up against the Earl of Danby. Some thought that Sir Robert Howard could have had a hand in promoting them, although in fact the Earl of Arlington was the main instigator of the attack. Since the first article concerned the alleged perversion of the normal methods of accounting in the Exchequer, Sir Robert, thanks to his long-standing involvement with government finance, was likely to be aimed at as much as Danby himself, and he parried a suggestion that all the Exchequer books should be examined, with the remark, 'You may then be said truly to stop the Exchequer'. Both he and Danby survived the attack and continued their wrangling, but as Danby began, in contemporary parlance, to stand 'a little more on his own bottom', and to break free from the Duke of York and the Earl of Lauderdale, it is probable that Howard moved back to his old allegiance with the opposition party.

Strong though the Anglican party was in Parliament, the opposition was by no means quiescent, and those with nonconformist sympathies gravitated towards the masterful Lord Ashley, now created Earl of Shaftesbury. Sir William Temple, writing in October 1673, named Shaftesbury as the prime mover in the Lords, and Howard in the Commons, of a Bill to make provision for the King's divorce as a method of safeguarding the Protestant succession. The possibility of dispensing with the infertile Catherine had always been close to the Duke of Buckingham's heart, and it is probable that the Duke was still able to rally old supporters such as Howard and Sir John Trevor. The opposition groups did their best to secure a dissolution of the present Parliament in the hope of obtaining another that might prove less belligerently Royalist and Anglican and at the same time more sympathetic towards the nonconformist cause. In the face of persecution Catholics and some Protestant dissenters were ready to work for their common good, and it seems that the Duchess of Cleveland was prepared to throw in her lot with Sir Robert Howard and the Duke of Buckingham's other supporters; it is significant that one of Danby's working lists recorded the fact that Sir John Trevor could best be approached through her influence.

In spite of all his careful research the Earl of Danby could never be totally sure of the way the different power groups were constituted. Loyalties wavered, outlines remained uncertain, divisions appeared and disappeared. And at the centre of it all was a King who could be relied on for nothing so much as his ability to say one thing and do another. As fast as Danby initiated a strong enforcement of the penal laws, the

King would put in his own personal pleas for leniency. His lack of resolution caused Danby much annoyance and left others in a state of bewil-
derment. As Sir William Temple put it when discussing the question
of a royal divorce, 'The King seems sometimes very earnest in it, and
sometimes cold, and in all . . . matters is either so uncertain or disgusted
that those who are nearest him know not yet what will be the issue.'

It was in the field of foreign relations that the King's subtleties were
the most difficult to fathom. In his anxiety to bring the King in line
with the feelings of the majority of parliamentary Members, Danby
continually advocated a speedy end to the war and a cessation of the
French alliance. Arlington, one of those who had been at the heart of
the negotiations with France in 1670, now turned about with his usual
facile flexibility and urged the King to listen to Danby's counsels and
the voice of his Parliament. The King's description of Arlington's
insistence was that he 'wearied' him into the idea of an early peace;
probably the prospect of pleasing the Commons and so extracting a
generous grant of money was what weighed with him most. And having
broken with the country he had wooed so assiduously through Minette,
Charles now played the game of European diplomacy with some success,
until his duplicity had become such a byword that nobody trusted him
any longer.

For the time being the King was happy to hold the balance in Europe
as he had for so long contrived to do in England, standing between the
coalition of Protestant powers and the might of France, flirting with
Spain, with the Dutch, with the French, and turning London into a
paradise for those who were prepared to live on the foreign gold doled
out by competing Ambassadors. And when in the autumn session of
1675 the Commons stingily voted the King an inadequate grant for the
navy, and refused to help pay off outstanding debts, the King had no
scruples about going back to the French in secret to beg for more. He
prorogued Parliament in November 1675, letting Members know that
he did not expect to recall them for over a year.

Relieved from the harassment of Parliament, the King settled down
to some peaceful months enjoying life with the help of money which
was to be paid over to him by his cousin in quarterly instalments. He
was soon hatching plots to enter into a new secret alliance with France,
while Danby, unsuspecting, continued to impress on him the advantages of aligning himself with the Dutch. The Duke of York was prepared to support his brother in his relations with France, although in
the sphere of domestic politics he had been veering towards the opposition party; on 19 June 1675 the Earl of Essex heard from one of his
correspondents that the Duke was trying to bring in Shaftesbury,
reverting to the old belief that Protestant nonconformists, if returned

6*

to power with the help of Catholic support, might well prove more tolerant. Sir Edward Seymour noted 'a strict conjunction between the fanatic and papist to dissolve this Parliament', both groups hoping that if there were an election, a new Parliament might be returned with a predominance of Members ready to support the cause of toleration. Danby, for his part, did his best to insure against such an eventuality by bringing in a Bill which was likely to be more far-reaching in its effect than the Test Act; the oath of non-resistance which had to be taken by clergymen was to be extended to Members of Parliament, Justices of the Peace and office holders. Had Danby succeeded in putting this Bill through, many conscientious dissenters would have found it difficult to take the oath by which they had to promise that they would not endeavour to alter the Protestant religion, and so he would have rid himself of many opposition Members both in Parliament and in the administration. But the autumn session finished without Danby achieving his aim, and with the opposition disappointed in its hopes of a disso- lution.

A lengthy prorogation was just what the King needed to expedite the negotiations he had already initiated with France. Since he could not persuade Danby to join him, he drew up on 3 February 1676 a secret treaty in his own hand which he sealed himself, Ruvigny, Colbert de Croissy's successor as resident Ambassador, signing on behalf of Louis XIV. It is probable that he did not take his brother into his confidence, for he had become increasingly irritated by James's fidelity to the non- conformist cause and by his vexing sincerity in openly declaring his conversion to the Catholic faith. And if the King was working inde- pendently and secretly, in the manner that suited him best, James was capable of carrying on his own campaign to further the cause of the opposition, cultivating the French on his own behalf and perhaps planning for the day when he could rid himself of his Protestant allies and help his brother to rule without a Parliament—financed, of course, by France.

The King, the Duke of York, Danby, Shaftesbury, the French Am- bassadors and everybody else, were all working to consolidate their various positions, and as always the women had to be taken into account. The French Ambassador saw to it that the ladies received their share of bribes, and Danby placated the Duchess of Portsmouth with liberal grants. The situation was complicated at the beginning of 1676 by the arrival on the scene of a new candidate for the King's favour and the French Ambassador's money. Just as beautiful as the three reigning mistresses and even more outrageous than the Duchess of Cleveland, the scintillating Duchesse de Mazarin landed at Torbay in January 1676, accompanied by the Comte de Gramont, a multitude of servants and a much-favoured blackamoor boy. Hortense Mancini, dark haired, with blue-black eyes, was the fourth of the five famous nieces of Cardinal Mazarin, and the King had known and courted her when he was still in exile. Her husband had been created Duc de Mazarin, but finding him an insufferable eccentric, she abandoned him, spending several years travelling on the Continent and gaining considerable notoriety thanks to her amours with both men and women. She had a partiality for dressing as a man, and it was in this guise that she first appeared in England.

Nobody seemed to have doubted that the Duchesse was of the calibre to make a new mistress for the King. The only uncertainty lay in her choice of a sponsor. If she were to be introduced into the royal bed, nobody yet knew whether her presence there would benefit the French or their enemies; it was said that she had quarrelled with Louis XIV on account of his failure to extract on her behalf a larger pension from her husband. Significantly enough, she was related to the Duchess of York, and it seemed certain that the Duke intended to make her very welcome at St James's Palace. The Montagu clan also had designs on her, for Ralph Montagu, who had come over from Paris, made a point of waylaying her on her way to London and carrying her off to his sister's house in Covent Garden. Lady Harvey, who had not been cured of her Sempronian tendencies by the histrionic skill of Mrs Corey, soon arranged for the King to meet Hortense at her house. At the same time Ralph Montagu fancied himself to be half in love with her—in spite of his portly figure he liked to think of himself as something of a squire of dames.

While speculation grew about the new arrival's place in the complicated pattern of diplomacy, the gossips of the town were provided with further ammunition when the Duchess of Cleveland left for France only a few weeks after the Duchesse de Mazarin set foot in England. The Comte de Gramont exchanged one Duchess for another and undertook to accompany Cleveland to Paris. Ruvigny reported on February 3 that her departure was imminent, and it seemed that she intended to travel in style with two coaches and a string of horses, taking with her four of her children—Henry, Duke of Grafton, George, Earl of Northumberland, as well as Charlotte and Barbara. Charles she left behind to pursue his unacademic way at Oxford, while Anne stayed with her husband. The document in which Ruvigny wrote his instructions that she and her party should be exempt from customs duties, did not meet with her approval; in her opinion Louis XIV should have referred to her children as 'cousins'. She urged the King to lodge an objection to such a slight on young noblemen liberally endued with royal blood. When he resisted her demand, she tore the document up in a rage. But she did not part with him on bad terms, for before she left he bestowed on her the offices of Chief Steward of Hampton Court and Keeper of the Chace.

The French customs officials were warned that to cross the Duchess of Cleveland would be to invite a scene and they had orders to exempt her from all dues. She was seen off by 'several persons of quality', who accompanied her to the waterside. When she arrived in Paris she installed herself in the Convent of the Immaculate Conception of our Blessed Lady in the Faubourg Saint-Antoine on the left bank of the Seine. There were many theories concerning the reasons for her journey, although few people can seriously have believed that she was retiring from the world she had conquered with her beauty, in order, as Chesterfield had put it, to attack a higher realm with her devotions. Some said that she had been forced to go abroad because she had been 'pillaged' by Churchill—rumour had it that £100,000 had already passed into his pocket, which was to come in useful later when he married the forceful Sarah Jennings. But whether or not she had really crossed the Channel in order to escape her creditors, or to devote her time to prayer and meditation, or even simply to arrange for the education of her children, it soon became clear that she did not intend to spend her time in Paris exclusively immured within the walls of the Convent of the Immaculate Conception.

CHAPTER NINETEEN

A CONVENT IN PARIS

THE IDEA of a convent education for her daughters understandably appealed to the Duchess of Cleveland, and her husband Roger Castlemaine was equally convinced of its value. Lady Anne had spent a year at Chaillot, the convent founded by the Queen Mother, as well as some months at Pontoise in Normandy, under the care of the English Abbess, Lady Neville. Roger also advised his brother Philip Palmer to send his daughter Phoebe to Pontoise, assuring him that it would not cost him more than £30 a year, 'and there she may stay', he added, 'until she is fit for marriage, receiving in the meantime a virtuous and good education and thus you know people of the best fashion beyond sea bred their children'.

Philip Palmer took his brother's advice in principle, but chose the Convent of the Immaculate Conception rather than Pontoise, and Phoebe was admitted there in December 1671 'for education by the Earl of Castlemaine'. In April 1672 the Abbé Montagu received her into the Catholic Church, but she had left Paris for Liège where she took her first habit, before the arrival of her uncle's wife. However two of Roger's other nieces, Jane and Barbara Darrell, aged seven and six, the daughters of Roger's sister Catherine, who had been associated with her brother in his espionage work just before the Restoration, were being educated there. The Duchess made arrangements for Charlotte and Barbara too to be brought up under the care of the Abbess, an Englishwoman named Elizabeth Timperley, and of the nuns, who were always known as the Blue Nuns because this was the colour of their ceremonial cloaks. The Convent, which was set in its own large garden, benefited as a result of the Duchess's munificence; she donated sums ranging from £50 to £1,000 and paid for improvements costing 280 pistoles which included the construction of a new staircase, alterations in the kitchen and wainscoting in the refectory.

There was some talk of John Churchill following his mistress and daughter to Paris; certainly in November 1676 he applied to join a French regiment, but at this stage the man who was later to become the victor of Blenheim and Ramillies was thought to be too fond of his

pleasure to make a good officer, and Louvois put it bluntly when he
wrote that Churchill would give 'more satisfaction to a rich and faded
mistress, than to a monarch who did not want to have dishonourable,
and dishonoured, carpet knights in his armies'. So he stayed in England,
and his parents did their best to marry him off to an ugly heiress.

Cut off from her lover and from the society which she had dominated
for so long, the Duchess at first found it somewhat difficult to adjust
to life in Paris, and in April 1676 it was reported that 'Lady Cleveland
is not, they say, much satisfied in France, because the greatest ladies
do not visit her'. But if the ladies were not over anxious to make her
acquaintance, there was no similar reluctance among the men, and
before long she had captured the affection of an Archbishop, an Ambassador, and a Gentleman of the Chamber to Louis XIV. When she had
been in Paris for less than a year it was reported that 'she followeth
her old employment very hard there, especially with the Archbishop of
Paris who is her principal gallant'. Her association with the King's
servant, the Marquis de Châtillon, was more circumspect; the Marquis,
a refined but impecunious young man, was indiscreet enough to write
her a number of love-letters, but the affair was carried out cautiously
enough to avoid causing a stir. It seems likely that the Duchess selected
her French lover not for his aristocratic looks but for his proximity to
King Louis, and King Charles may well have instructed her to make
up for his loss of Madame by picking up what information she could;
it is even possible that the Duke of York was using her to further his
interests in Paris. She was far more likely to fathom the workings of the
French King's mind by establishing an intimate relationship with one
of his servants than by exercising the right he had granted her of sitting
on a *tabouret* in the Queen's presence on formal occasions at Versailles.

Alongside her liaison with Châtillon, the Duchess succeeded in
conducting an affair with Ralph Montagu, the approach being made
by way of the marital aspirations of her son George. Montagu was
gifted with the ability to lure rich widows into his net, and in 1673
he married as his second wife Elizabeth Wriothesley, the widowed
Countess of Northumberland, who was endowed with beauty, £6,000
per annum and a much sought-after daughter, Lady Betty Percy. The
Duchess of Cleveland had always planned to capture Lady Betty for
George and in her endeavours to achieve the match she paid frequent
visits to the Montagus' house in Paris. At first Lady Betty's mother
treated the Duchess somewhat coldly, resenting her appropriation of
the Northumberland title for her son, but gradually the clever Duchess
triumphed, and within a year Montagu was able to report that the two
ladies were visiting each other frequently.

The task of marrying off his nine-year-old stepdaughter was one which appealed to Ralph Montagu, and he was perfectly ready to play one candidate off against the other while gaining the maximum benefit for himself. His first choice had been Charles FitzCharles, the King's son by Catherine Pegge, who was generally known as Don Carlos. This idea was favoured by Danby, who wanted to find another Protestant bastard who could be balanced against the Duke of Monmouth. It seemed that the King preferred to put forward the Duchess of Cleveland's son, and further complications were caused by the fact that under the terms of her husband's will, Lady Betty's mother had surrendered custody of her daughter as soon as she remarried; it now lay in the power of the child's grandmother, the dowager Countess of Northumberland, to make any decisions concerning Lady Betty's future, and she favoured Lord Ogle, the Duke of Newcastle's son. As Montagu put it to the Earl of Danby, 'I believe there will be that disagreement between the grandmother and mother that it must naturally come before the King and Council . . . I make no doubt but the daughter will declare for marrying where the mother pleases and not where the grandmother desires'.

Although even Montagu had to admit that Lady Betty was too young to enter into any binding association which might make her miserable all her life, the competition mounted and at one time all three suitors were in Paris. The Duchess of Cleveland called on the patient Sir Edward Villiers to intercede for her, and he expressed himself much 'rejoiced' to see that his niece was on such good terms with Lady Betty's mother. Sir Edward, who with his wife had been given the task of bringing up the Duke of York's two daughters Mary and Anne in the Protestant faith and watching over their education at Richmond Palace, was always ready to make himself useful. He furthered the cause by writing to Ralph Montagu, assuring him that the entire Villiers family could vouch for the fact that the King had 'engaged himself to my Lady Duchess of Cleveland to do all he can to procure this match for my Lord Northumberland, who himself is already cunning enough to be enquiring of me after my Lady Betty Percy, and has taken such an aversion to my Lord Ogle about the report that when they meet at my house he is always ready to laugh or make mouths at him, so that the governor now will scarce let them meet'.

Sir Edward's description suggests that his great-nephew had not reaped any appreciable benefit from the attentions of his Oxford tutor, Edward Barnard, who had found himself able to stand his task for only a very limited time. 'My friend Mr Barnard', Humphrey Prideaux explained in a letter, 'who went into France to attend upon two bastards of Cleveland, hath been so affronted and abused there by that insolent woman that he hath been forced to quit that employment and return.'

The Duchess reserved her amiability for men of importance, including Ralph Montagu, who succumbed to her attraction 'out of inclination, her own charms being inevitable'. The need to discuss possible plans for a marriage between George and Lady Betty gave them plenty of chance to meet, and the Duchess was soon to tell the Ambassador that ten days out of his company were more grievous to her than to him; as Sir William Temple put it on one occasion, the ladies were always Ralph Montagu's best friends as a result of 'some secret perfections that were hid from the rest of the world'. With the skill of an agent who had in her time been in the pay of both the Spanish and the French, the Duchess encouraged him to open his heart so that he gave away all his aspirations, telling her how he hoped to become one of the Secretaries of State and eventually Lord Treasurer in Danby's place.

Danby had no inkling that his trusted agent in Paris was capable of plotting his downfall. He relied on Montagu to keep the French in a reasonable frame of mind while he himself pursued his pro-Dutch policies. At home he continued to dole out honours, appointments and pensions to strengthen the King's party, and he even became involved in the sphere of female diplomacy, favouring the Duchess of Portsmouth with generous gifts of money and in the process alienating Nell Gwynn, who felt disgruntled because he refused to grant the title she now felt she had earned as a result of her amorous activities. The Duchess of Portsmouth was said to have received £50,000 in two years, but even so the Lord Treasurer could not be confident that he had backed the right horse.

The French Ambassador, Ruvigny, had been recalled soon after the King's signing of his own secret treaty, and his successor, Honoré de Courtin, was especially chosen for his ability to mix with the highest society. He spent much thought on the subject of the mistresses, trying to establish, after patient research, which of them was uppermost in the King's affections. Although the Duchess of Portsmouth was the lady most likely to be of help to him, he discovered that she was often in bad health, paying frequent visits to Bath to seek out a cure. 'I have ascertained beyond doubt,' he wrote, 'that [the King] passes his nights much less often with her than with Nell Gwynn.' Courtin found the newcomer much more attractive than any of the others. The Duchesse de Mazarin, in fact, would have been the most useful agent of them all, had it not been for the disconcerting fact that she seemed to be out of sympathy with her own country. 'She's beautiful, has the air of high breeding, is full of talent, and yet modest and unassuming', Courtin wrote. 'Were I no older than you, I should be madly in love with her. But I am forty-nine, and the thick air of London depresses me.'

Courtin was puzzled by his compatriot's behaviour. She deliberately hid everything from him, so much so that he began to wonder whether she was not actually plotting against the French. To complicate matters, she had an unusual power to attract women younger than herself, and soon the fifteen-year-old Duchess of York, as well as the Duchess of Cleveland's daughter Anne, had fallen under her spell. The Duke of York bought her a newly-built house in St James's Park and she spent a great deal of time at St James's Palace, playing romping games with the young Duchess. Lady Harvey also gave her innumerable invitations and was soon described as her 'intimatest' friend, but it was the Countess of Sussex who struck up the closest relationship with Hortense. 'Every evening', Courtin wrote, 'I witness scenes at her rooms so astounding that a description of them could not fail to set even a great minister like you laughing'. The two women amused themselves with dogs and sparrows; they spent their afternoons playing battledore and shuttle-cock, and in the evenings retired to the Duchess of Cleveland's old lodgings over the Holbein Gate. The King had not forgotten the way upstairs, and he often joined them, giving orders that nobody else should be allowed in. Anne was expecting a child, and was not in good health, which gave the Duchesse ample cause to stay with her, and the King plenty of excuse to visit her. Like Roger Castlemaine, the King treated Anne as if she were his own daughter, and it was reported that he had collected together all the best pearls he could lay his hands on to make a necklace for her worth £8,000.

Hortense and Anne decided to take a course of fencing lessons, and one evening they demonstrated their skills in St James's Park, having carried their drawn swords down to the Park under their nightgowns. They made a number of fine passes, much to the admiration of several men who happened to be standing by. Their action, however, scan-dalized those who heard about it; Anne's mother wrote from Paris remonstrating with the King for allowing such behaviour, while her husband naturally felt that it was hardly the most suitable activity for a woman with child. She was sent off to her husband's family castle at Hurstmonceux where, having lost her baby, she consoled herself with some hunting expeditions. But she still pined for her friend, and spent so much time kissing the Duchesse de Mazarin's portrait that there were fears for her health, not to mention her sanity. She was sent off to her mother in Paris, where she was immured in the nunnery at Conflans, and the Duchess found her useful as a go-between, enclosing letters for the Marquis de Châtillon in packages addressed to the convent.

Soon after the departure of the Countess of Sussex, the King demanded the return of his daughter Charlotte who had become a charming and agreeable girl, far more amenable than her sister. She soon went through a second wedding ceremony with the Earl of Lichfield and settled down to a long and happy marriage. As far as the King was concerned, she was no substitute for Anne whose departure had removed the Duchesse de Mazarin's constant availability. However attractive the French Duchesse might be, and however successful in gaining the King's affection, she had not succeeded, any more than the others, in monopolizing his favour. As the Duchess of Portsmouth's health began to improve so she regained her importance both for the King and for the French Ambassador. And Nell Gwynn's impudence had lost none of its fascination; during the summer and autumn of 1677 the Cockney mistress gave Danby good cause to regret the fact that he had ignored her requests for titles and favours.

When Parliament met after the long prorogation, opposition Members tried to prove that there should be an automatic dissolution. The wisest did not press the point, but Buckingham, who was not noted for his sagacity, soon found himself in the Tower as a penalty for persistence. In the summer he petitioned for his release on the grounds of ill health, saying that he had 'contracted several indispositions and desired a month's air'. Once this concession had been achieved, Nelly and her 'merry gang' easily persuaded the King to grant Buckingham complete liberty.

Friendship with Nell stood Danby's enemy Sir Robert Howard in good stead when, in the autumn, there was an investigation into alleged irregularities at the Exchequer. Howard was suspected of at best failing to report a deficiency and at worst of conniving at the introduction of lead coins into money bags to help hide the shortage. At the start of the enquiry the King had refused to speak to Howard when he had seen him at Newmarket, but less than six weeks later he was allowed to kiss the royal hand. He escaped conviction, remained in possession of his post as Auditor of the Exchequer and continued to harry and annoy the Lord Treasurer. His lucky escape was officially due to the fact that the main witness proved unreliable, but his friendship with Nell, for whom he acted as trustee and financial adviser, most certainly militated in his favour.

The last months of 1677 were the most fruitful in the whole of Danby's career, in spite of his failure to rid himself of Buckingham and Howard. The marriage of the Duke of York's daughter Mary to William of Orange and the Anglo-Dutch treaty which was signed at the end of the year seemed to be a vindication of all his policies. And yet the Parliament which was called in January 1678 proved disappointingly unready to vote supplies for a war against France unless the King made public all secret alliances. Refusing to surrender what he considered his rightful prerogative to make decisions concerning peace or war, the King had to resort to his usual and by now monotonous tactics of adjourning Parliament. Danby, for his part, fearful of losing his hold with the King, at last succumbed to the lure of French money. Misguidedly Danby revealed his intention in letters to Ralph Montagu, who encouraged him to set the price high. On 18 January 1678 Montagu wrote, 'be pleased to let me know what they offer, and I dare answer to get our master as much again, for Barillon's orders are to make the market as low as he can'.

Montagu himself was confident that he was on the verge of achieving his ambition to become Secretary of State. Henry Coventry was shortly to retire, and with the help of his sister, Montagu had been carefully preparing the ground for his own appointment. Danby himself had earmarked the position for the pro-Dutch Sir William Temple, whose support and experience he greatly needed, but as Montagu put it to Charles Bertie, Lady Danby's brother, 'One must never despair, no more than I do of being Secretary of State, if Lady Danby continues her favour to me and can work off Sir William Temple'. Provided he was prepared to name Montagu as his successor, Henry Coventry was to be offered £10,000 as an inducement to speed his departure, and although Danby did not favour such ruses, Montagu felt confident of success. It was only when he heard rumours that the Duchess of Cleveland was planning a visit to England that he began to experience some qualms. Although her pretext for making the journey was a plan to break off the match between Henry and Isabella, Montagu suspected that there was a more sinister reason for her decision, and he now began to regret his indiscretion in revealing the extent of his ambitions.

Realizing that the Earl of Arlington was not as powerful as he had been, the Duchess found Isabella a rather less attractive proposition than Lady Betty Percy, and she was now planning to marry Henry off to the more eligible heiress while reserving George for the infant daughter of Ralph Montagu and the Countess of Northumberland. Since Arlington was in fact so out of favour, there were some grounds for thinking that the match could have been broken off without the Duchess stirring from Paris; all the same she seemed certain to go, and was reported to be 'not a little vexed at the trouble my Lord Arlington puts her to by the journey and taking her children from their exercises'. Montagu believed that she had received a letter from Henry Savile who was hoping to enlist her support for a plan to bring in Laurence Hyde, the Duke of York's brother-in-law, as Secretary of State. Montagu warned Charles Bertie that there was a great cabal, organized by Nelly and the Duke of Buckingham, to ensure that no friend of Danby's would be successful. Laurence Hyde and the Duke of Buckingham were known to be good friends, and they were both influential figures in the opposition. Buckingham had stayed at Hyde's house on the first night

after his release from the Tower, and Hyde himself was on good terms
with his brother-in-law and had been closely involved in the negotiations
leading to the treaty with the Dutch—a treaty much favoured by the
Duke and by his new son-in-law William of Orange. Savile's reward
for 'engaging' influential people on Hyde's behalf was to be in a position
'at the Robes' which Hyde would vacate on becoming appointed
Secretary of State.

In Montagu's opinion everything added up to a very menacing plot,
and he was sure that the Duchess had been assigned her role even if it
was only to intercede with the King on Savile's behalf so that he would
be allocated some extra money and given leave to sell his place in the
Bedchamber. Fearing that she might reveal some of his confidences, he
was determined to blacken her name before she had an opportunity to
ruin his chances of promotion. He therefore told Bertie that he could
pass on all the information to Lord and Lady Danby, only keeping the
source secret for the time being, 'for else', he explained, 'it would hinder
me knowing many things that may be for their service'. Montagu self-
righteously added that he thought it 'not very well in Mr Savile, who
has those obligations to my Lord Treasurer, to manage such an affair
underhand. For my part, I care not for the place except I come in with
his favour and kindness.'

Although he was an ill-favoured man, 'not at all beholding to nature',
Ralph Montagu was adept at gaining the affections of young ladies; he
had, for example, fathered a child by Jane Middleton, the beautiful but
wanton girl who had always been 'most tiresome when she wished to
be most brilliant'. Now he turned his attentions to the youthful Countess
of Sussex who was more than receptive, and his efforts were rewarded
when he managed to take possession of some of the Marquis de Châtillon's letters which it was Anne's duty to deliver to her mother. These
incriminating missives were duly despatched to the King by Montagu
—timed to arrive in England during the Duchess's stay.

The Duchess set off for England in March 1678, still giving as her
reason the necessity for breaking the marriage settlement with Isabella,
and also expressing her intention of collecting the rents due to her as
Steward of Hampton Court and Ranger of Bushey Park. She had no
cause to believe that the King would not greet her as an old friend,
even though the Duchess of Portsmouth was his favourite—so much
so that he 'spoke to her of everything that was on his mind and received
all her insinuations'. Danby still supported Louise, and the Earl of
Sunderland, a passionate advocate of the Anglo-French entente, also
cultivated her friendship, much to the disapproval of his wife who
labelled her a harlot, a cheat and an abominable jade. Disappointed in
the Duchesse de Mazarin, the French were using her in their renewed

campaign to keep the English well out of the way in their struggle to subdue the Dutch. Ruvigny's son had been sent over to join the new Ambassador, Paul Barillon, a wise choice since he had an entrée into opposition circles through his cousin, Lady Russell. With great subtlety he worked on leading members of the anti-Court party, reminding them that they had found it unwise in the past to trust the King with money and arms. Distributing bribes to the Duke of Buckingham, Henry Sidney and others, and arranging to converse persuasively with other men of importance, Ruvigny succeeded in making the opposition withdraw its support for the war which it had once advocated. The King, realizing that he was again facing difficulties over the question of supply, as usual turned to the King of France for help, but with less response than formerly. The success of Ruvigny's mission was already so marked that Louis had achieved his aim of neutralizing the English simply by distributing money and words of wisdom in the most unlikely places.

If Henry Sidney and other opposition members had called the Duchess of Cleveland back to England to plead their cause with the King, her work had already been done for her by the time she arrived. In addition, she found the King strangely cold, and not at all inclined to take up with her just where he had left off. He was uncooperative when she requested him to extricate Henry from his marriage vows, and made no attempt to plead her cause with Arlington. All the same Sidney reported to Montagu that she appeared to be in good heart and in good health; Montagu, who had by this time forwarded to the King her correspondence with Châtillon, replied hypocritically that he was glad to hear it. 'I will always lay on her side against everybody', he wrote, adding for good measure, 'I am a little scandalized you have been but once to see her—pray make your Court oftener for my sake, for no man can be more obliged to another than I am to her on all occasions, and tell her I say so, and, as my Lord Berkeley says, give her a pat from me. If you keep your word to come in June, I fancy you will come together, and I shall not be ill pleased to see the two people in the world of both sexes I love and esteem the most.'

The Duchess of Cleveland in fact left London in May without having given away any of Montagu's secrets. She returned to find Paris buzzing with talk about the behaviour of her daughter Anne. During her absence the Countess of Sussex, who was not inclined by nature to live demurely in a convent, had bribed the Abbess to let her come and go as she wished, and she had finally left Conflans, settling herself at the Convent of the Holy Sepulchre in the Belle Chasse, where she was free to do as she liked. It seemed that she had spent a great deal of time at her mother's house, remaining shut up alone with the British Ambassador until five o'clock in the morning, and only allowing his

servants to wait on them. Montagu, it was said, had provided three
women to attend her, with a Switzer to stand at her door; he had also
arranged for a consort of music to play for her, and his wife had been
taking her everywhere—to Court, to a fair, and to supper at the Hôtel
de Ville on St John's day. She had built up a fine collection of clothes
and had ordered furniture to be specially made for her apartments.

To find her own lover consorting with her daughter was enough of a
shock for the Duchess, but worse was to come when she realized that
Montagu had betrayed her affair with Châtillon to the King. Montagu
himself was spreading it about that Charles had written to him giving
orders that all her children were to be taken from her, and all her pensions stopped. She knew now the reasons for the King's curious coldness, and she probably suspected that Montagu had revealed her political
as well as her amorous intrigues. And if she had refrained from warning
the King against Montagu during her visit to England, she now had no
scruples about reporting his confidences. 'I am so much afflicted', she
told the King, 'that I can hardly write this for crying, to see a child that
I doted on as I did on her should make so ill a return and join with the
worst of men to ruin me. For sure never any malice was like the Ambassador's, that, only because I would not answer to his love and the impor-
tunities he made to me, was resolved to ruin me.'

The Duchess explained to the King that she had always respected
the Ambassador's trust, and would never have thought of betraying
the details of his nefarious plots if he had not dealt treacherously with
her. 'For he had neither conscience or honour and has several times told
me that in his heart he despised you and your brother; and that for his
part he wished with all his heart that the Parliament would send you
both to travel; for you were a dull governable fool and the Duke a wilful
fool.' She explained that Montagu aimed at grabbing the Secretary's
place before Sir William Temple could be appointed. Lady Harvey
was involved in the plot and had been trying to persuade Coventry not
to resign until the time was ripe for Montagu to leave Paris; Lady
Danby too was prepared to work on her husband and to persuade him
to bestow on Montagu the Secretary's post; 'and when I have it',
Montagu had told the Duchess of Cleveland, 'I will be damned if I do
not quickly get to be Lord Treasurer; and then you and your children
shall find such a friend as never was. And for the King, I will find a
way to furnish him so easily with money for his pocket and his wenches
that we will quickly out Bab May and lead the King by the nose.'

As for her affair with Châtillon she was sure that the King would
understand, and she knew that Louis did not believe Montagu's story
since he had said that in any case it was a private matter in which he
did not propose to meddle, especially as 'all the world knew that now

all things of gallantry were at an end with you and I'. What upset her most was the fact that the whole matter had created such a stir, when all the time she had been trying to follow his instructions to make the least noise possible. 'Oh, this noise that is had never been had it not been for the Ambassador's malice', she told the King.

It was the Duchess's belief that the King did not have it in his nature to be cruel to any living thing. His reply to her letter was so kind that it bore out her theory. 'I received your Majesty's letter last night with more joy than I can express', she told him, and went on:

this proceeding of yours is so generous and obliging that I must be the worst woman alive were I not sensible. No, Sir, my heart and soul is touched with this generosity of yours, and you shall always find that my conduct to the world and behaviour to your children shall always render me worthy of your protection and favour; this pray be confident of.

The King enclosed a letter for Anne which the Duchess despatched immediately by one of her gentlemen. He was informed through the grille at the convent door that the Countess was ill and had been so delirious for two days that she knew nobody and referred to everyone who came near her as 'My Lord Ambassador and my Lady'. Subsequent messengers all met with a different excuse and were told that the Countess was asleep or had just been let blood. The Duchess had the King's letter translated into French, and sent it to her old friend the Archbishop of Paris in the hope that he would intervene; however all he did was to send a priest in his own coach and the Duchess began to fear that he too was in the plot.

The Duchess's waiting-woman Pigeon finally gained admittance. She found Montagu sitting in the parlour with Lady Sussex who said, 'Mistress Pigeon, if the King knew the reasons I have for what I have done he would be more angry with my lady than with me.' Pigeon replied discreetly that 'these were things she did not enter into'—all she knew was that she had orders to take back the King's letter when the Countess had read it. There was an undignified wrangle; the Countess refused to part with the letter, the Ambassador took her side, Pigeon stood firm, and Montagu self-righteously remarked that since Lady Sussex was the King's daughter 'it was not suitable for her to live with my Lady Duchess who led so infamous a life'.

Whatever Montagu might feel about her reputation, the Duchess for her part had a low opinion of the Convent of the Holy Sepulchre, and she was determined that Anne should be removed from it at once. 'She must be ruined if you do not tackle some speedy course with her', the Duchess told the King. She suggested that it would be a chastening experience for Anne to be moved to the Convent at Port-Royal, where there would be nobody to wait on her except a couple of nuns, and where she would not be allowed to receive any visitors without the Duchess's written permission. 'I cannot so far conquer myself to see her daily', the Duchess told the King, 'though your Majesty may be confident that as she is yours I shall always have remains of that kindness I had formerly, for I can hate nothing that is yours.'

This show of solidarity between the King and the Duchess filled Montagu with alarm. He realized now that he had in his turn been betrayed by the woman who had bewitched him into revealing his inner-most thoughts. To win back the King's favour he wrote to his sister asking her to enlist the Earl of Danby's help in promoting the match between George and Lady Betty—a union which the King was known to favour. The best way of succeeding, he thought, was to persuade the King himself to write to Lady Betty's mother. 'The way of doing it', he explained, 'is for the King to order my Lord Treasurer to write to her a very civil letter upon the same occasion, and send it enclosed in his . . .'

Montagu made hasty arrangements to go over to London where he had an audience with the King but was unable to reverse the harm wrought by the Duchess of Cleveland. The fact that he had left his post in Paris without permission gave the King an excuse for depriving him of all his places. The pro-French Earl of Sunderland was appointed Ambassador in Paris, and left accompanied by the Duchess of Cleve-land's friend Henry Savile. His best chance of achieving his ambitions was to throw in his lot now with the French and to make himself useful to the opposition in its campaign to bring about the fall of Danby.

Barillon had asked Louis to furnish him with 20,000 crowns to help cover the cost of a programme of bribery intended to throw England into such political confusion that she would be incapable of making any significant contribution to the war either on the side of the French or of the Dutch. Montagu was quickly added to the list of 'persons to whom gratuities may be offered'. The idea was to pay him £1,000 on condition that he would produce Danby's more incriminating letters at the most propitious moment. So it was that even when she had left England to attend to the education of her daughters, the Duchess of Cleveland continued to influence the course of events.

CHAPTER TWENTY

THE END OF THE REIGN

THE DUCHESS of Cleveland had done more than warn the King of Montagu's designs—she had revealed the scope of the opposition plot to dislodge Danby and establish a ministry drawn from the anti-Court party. She had hinted that men like Montagu had it in mind to send both the King and the Duke on their travels and to set up a republican government. What the Duchess may not have known was that the moment was now ripe for the opposition party to dispense with the Catholic connection which had in any case been a matter of convenience only. Backed up by French money, Shaftesbury felt strong enough to make his final bid for power without Catholic support. Caring less about the complexion of English affairs than they did for the need to make the whole country impotent in the war against the Dutch, the French were ironically enough prepared to help exclude the Duke of York from the succession. Equally ironically, the Catholic Duke had spent the past months championing the cause of his Protestant son-in-law against the French.

So it was that one day in August, as the King took his usual walk in the Park, he was warned that before long he would become the victim of a Jesuit assassination attempt. Calm and perceptive as always, the King refused to take the information seriously until he had been given a chance to check its veracity. Detailed accusations were later brought forward by Israel Tonge, an eccentric Anglican clergyman, and by Titus Oates, a recent Catholic convert who had been reared in an Anabaptist family. The homosexual Oates, bizarre in looks, with a short neck and an enormous mouth, proved to be utterly brazen and irrepressible. Although the King himself was able to point out serious flaws in his evidence, he refused to keep silent or admit defeat, and there were plenty of people at that particular time who were more than ready to believe anything detrimental to the Catholics. Tonge had spent some time in an English Jesuit seminary in Spain, and the experience had taught him to understand the secret aspirations of his fellow Catholics —their hopes of promoting their faith in England with the help of the French, and their impatient desire to see James established on the throne. Building on the basis of this knowledge, the grotesque perjurers drew up a fictitious list of conspirators who in the eyes of a public rendered hysterical by the revelations, had only to be named to be proved guilty.

Playing on the traditional English fears of popery, of foreign interference, of standing armies and arbitrary government, Shaftesbury seized his chance to get rid of Danby, to establish the Protestant succession by discrediting the Queen and to satisfy the almost pathological desire of his party to obtain a dissolution. He achieved his first aim, for Danby had been rapidly losing popularity as a result of his failure to take the Popish plot seriously; Montagu's lodgings were searched after carefully timed accusations that he had dealt with the papal nuncio in Paris, and Danby's letters naming the high price he was prepared to demand from the French for the King's support helped to precipitate his downfall. When articles of impeachment were drawn up against Danby, the King dissolved the eighteen-year-old Parliament, thus satisfying another of Shaftesbury's ambitions.

On the question of the succession, however, the King remained adamant. He stood by his Queen as loyally now as he had done before when Buckingham had first mooted the idea of a divorce. He insisted that he could not see an innocent woman wronged, and it was his support which saved Catherine when she was accused of propagating the Catholic faith, and even of plotting to poison her husband. Proclaiming that he had never been married to any other woman, he steadfastly parried all suggestions of divorce, insisting that his brother was the only legitimate heir and declaring that he would rather see Monmouth hanged than masquerading as a pretender to the throne.

The King himself, with his easy nature and his warm humanity proved to be the best defence against those whose ultimate aim was the abolition of the monarchy. His ability to bend helped him to avoid breaking under the impact of the forces that now assailed him. The anti-Catholic ferment was far greater than the unrest which had prompted the publication of The Poor-Whores' Petition; at that time people had been reminded of the dark days preceding the death of Strafford, and now more than ever it seemed that the King was in the same predicament as his father, with his favoured minister on trial and his Queen under attack. As always he avoided a confrontation, and his calmness, bolstered by well-disciplined guards who ensured the safety of the Palace, helped to avert the crisis. There were enough opposition men like Sir Robert Howard, who nursed a deep dislike of Danby, but who were also faithful supporters of the King, wishing only to see him work harmoniously with a loyal Parliament; as Howard put it, 'I am confident the Parliament would give him that ease that is due to his excellent nature, and I cannot but wish that all interpositions, like so many eclipses, between him and them were removed'.

For the grandees of the nascent Whig party who had played so coolly on the religious hysteria of others, the next years were to bring the satisfaction of a large parliamentary majority, with Danby in the Tower and the Catholic heir to the throne well out of the way. The King had to accept the introduction into his councils of men he deeply disliked; all the same, like Clarendon, like the cabal, like the rival mistresses, they were forced to learn the lesson that although he could be cordial and apparently receptive to advice or insinuation, he would always follow his own sound political instincts. He was strong enough to protect his Queen and his current mistresses, although he could do little to save some of Catherine's servants from the scaffold and many Catholic priests who suffered the same fate.

It was evident that England was no place for a royal mistress of the Catholic persuasion who had surrendered her place to others. The Duchess of Cleveland's political usefulness had come to an end at the same time as the alliance between Protestant and Catholic nonconformists was pulled apart by the spurious revelations of Tonge and Oates. Her friendship with Montagu had come to its dramatic conclusion, she was cut off from her cousin Buckingham by the great religious divide, and her greatest ally, the Duke of York, had become the focus of a vicious and prolonged attempt to exclude him from the succession.

The Duchess's estrangement from Montagu had put an end to her hopes of marrying Henry and George to the Countess of Northumberland's daughters. It was said that she did her best to acquire one of Louis XIV's natural daughters for Henry, but when this failed she reverted to the old plan to make him Arlington's heir. Fortunately she had failed in her attempt to extricate him from his earlier marriage vows. The Earl spent much of his time at Euston Hall, although he had been appointed Lord Chamberlain to compensate for his loss of the Secretaryship, and the King still liked him well enough to gratify 'the dearest wish of his heart by commanding the remarriage of the Duke of Grafton to the Lady Isabella Bennet'. In July 1679 there were reports that the Duchess of Cleveland was heading for England, and the King was said to have given the Commissioners of the Treasury fair warning to look to themselves, 'for that she would have a bout with them for money, having lost £20,000 in money and jewels in one night at play'. The remarriage in fact did not take place until November 6; it was celebrated by the Bishop of Rochester in the Lord Chamberlain's lodgings at Whitehall in the presence of the King. Lady Isabella was now twelve years old, and already showed signs of becoming such a paragon that she would have made a fit bride for any prince in Europe.

This was John Evelyn's opinion, and he feared that she was being thrown away on an unworthy object. He expressed his misgivings to Lady Arlington, who replied that 'the King would have it so, and there was no going back', and so, as he put it, 'this sweetest, hopefullest, most beautiful child, and most virtuous too, was sacrificed to a boy, that had been rudely bred, without anything to encourage them but his Majesty's pleasure; I pray God the sweet child find it to her advantage'. Afterwards, at an informal supper, the King sat between 'the Duchess of Cleveland (the incontinent mother of the Duke of Grafton) and the sweet Duchess the bride'. Evelyn had to admit that the young Duke was very handsome—'by far surpassing any of the King's other natural issue'— and the diarist had hopes that if Henry fulfilled his ambition of pursuing a naval career, he might well emerge 'a plain, useful, robust officer, and were he polished, a tolerable person'.

The Duchess left for Paris soon after the remarriage, making arrangements to let Cleveland House to the Portuguese Ambassador. John Evelyn dined there only a few weeks after her departure and he much admired the house and garden, although, with its sumptuous staircase and gallery, he found it 'too good for that infamous ——'. The vicissitudes of political life also prevented the Yorks from enjoying their home at St James's Palace, for although the Duke had been called back from Brussels when the King fell dangerously ill the previous August, his presence in London caused too much tension for safety. He had taken his Duchess to Edinburgh, leaving Shaftesbury's party still in the ascendant.

Throughout the following year the persecution of the Catholics continued. There were fears that the Duke of Monmouth would be established as the King's lawful heir, and many believed that the country was once again on the verge of civil war. All the same the King kept calm and more often than not he was in buoyant spirits, for, as Sir John Reresby put it, it was not in his nature to perplex himself. Rejecting the more violent expedients advocated by the Exclusionists or by his brother, he followed as moderate a course as possible, all the time encouraging those who although they might have been anxious to supplant Danby, still remained loyal to the monarchy and were unlikely to entertain any thought of rebellion. Among such moderates were the Hyde brothers, Henry 2nd Earl of Clarendon, and Laurence, created Earl of Rochester in 1681, who had looked to the Duchess of Cleveland for help when he had set his sights on the Secretaryship in 1678. Although in December 1680 the aged William Howard, Viscount Stafford, was sent to the scaffold, and the second Exclusion Bill passed its third reading in the Commons before being thrown out in the Lords, strong voices were raised in the Duke of York's favour, and some even had the courage to point out that Exclusion could prove even more dangerous than popery.

In February 1681 Shaftesbury and Buckingham organized an efficient election campaign, their propaganda machine spreading the doctrine that royalism and popery were almost synonymous. Many people were victimized for past or present loyalty to the Crown, and Samuel Pepys was among those who were forced to spend some time in the Tower on a tenuous charge of popery, his support for the Duke of York now telling against him. The French continued dispensing their largesse wherever they saw a possibility of creating discord. But all the time the King held to his belief that the extremism of his enemies carried within it the seeds of its own destruction. He waited coolly for the inevitable reaction which was not long in coming. By the end of 1682 Shaftesbury had been arrested, Monmouth was in hiding, and the revelation of the Rye House plot had brought two prominent Whigs, Lord Russell and Algernon Sidney to the scaffold. The King renewed his financial dependence on France, which enabled him to live independently of his Parliament, and succeeded for the rest of his reign in characteristically holding the balance between moderates and Tory extremists.

The improved situation for Catholics made it possible for the Duchess to visit England some time in 1681, and Luttrell reported that Cleveland House was being made ready for her arrival. She was probably present when the King presented the Duke of Grafton with his commission as Colonel of the Foot Guards at a review of the Household troops in Hyde Park. At the beginning of 1682 she was back in Paris where she was joined for a while by the Duchess of Portsmouth, the other half of what was described as 'the beastly brace'. Whether the two ladies actually met or not is unknown, although an apocryphal encounter was described in some scandalous verses entitled *A Dialogue between the D of C and the D of P at their meeting in Paris with the Ghost of Jane Shore*. The Duchess of Portsmouth had arrived furnished with a letter from Charles requesting Louis to grant her the right already enjoyed by her rival, to sit on a *tabouret* when she went to pay her respects to the Queen. As it turned out the French were so appreciative of all the work she had accomplished on their behalf, that they greeted her as if she were a Queen herself, and when she visited the Capuchins, they came out to meet her in procession, with cross, holy-water and incense. In general, the welcome she received 'threw her all in a heap, she not expecting so much honour' and she returned to England with her reputation much enhanced—'the homage paid her by Louis XIV being like sunshine, gilding and glorifying an insignificant object' as Barillon put it.

The Duchess of Portsmouth's loyalties were far less constant than the Duchess of Cleveland's, and she was always ready to sell her support

to the highest bidder. When Danby fell from favour, she quickly transferred her patronage to Shaftesbury and his party; she worked for the
French only when it suited her, and now she abandoned the Exclusionists, realizing that after all James was likely to be the next monarch,
and not wishing to jeopardize her chances should the King die. The
Duke of York himself admitted that he owed his return in part to her
intervention; John Churchill did his best to negotiate a pension for
Louise, as generous as the one enjoyed by his former mistress Barbara,
to be paid for out of the Post Office Revenues which had been granted
to the Duke of York for life—all this on condition that she persuaded
the King to have his brother back in London. In fact, as always, the
King in the end probably made up his own mind to let James return
'for good and all' regardless of the advice of the mistress, the French,
or of anybody else.

Whether or not the King's own good nature and wisdom lay behind
the decision, the Duke of York was allowed to join the royal party at
Newmarket in March 1682 and the brothers returned to London together
in early April. The following month the Duke fetched his wife from
Edinburgh and brought her back to St James's Palace. By that time the
Duchess of Cleveland had already taken up residence at her house just
across the road, and it was said that the King was so pleased to see her
back that he celebrated by visiting her five times a day. In June Louise,
his beloved 'Fubbs', returned to England, and re-established herself as
his principal mistress and companion. But the Duchess of Cleveland
was also to be seen frequently at Court, and the King continued to find
pleasure in Nell's company. The Queen too remained in the picture;
she had grown fonder than ever as a result of her husband's loyalty
during the nightmare days of the Titus Oates revelations; even now
tears came into her eyes when the Duchess of Portsmouth waited on her
at table and laughed at her discomfiture.

The women in the King's life had all, in their time, possessed varying
degrees of political importance, but now their era of influence was over.
At last people had begun to appreciate the special nature of the King's
authority; in the past they had complained about the reign of the mistresses, of the dictatorship of ministers, or the power of factions. But
recent events had proved that however malleable he might appear to
be, he possessed a hard core of certitude which enabled him to resist
the pressure of extremists, foreigners, mistresses or any other unconstitutional forces. His refusal to let the Rye House plot develop into a
Tory version of the Titus Oates affair, proved his own strength, and
the fact that he had not succumbed to his brother's insistent and vindictive advice reassured those who had feared the ferocity of a Royalist
reaction.

Retaliation came; the Whiggish party was chased from positions of trust, purged from Whitehall, from the counties and boroughs. The High Tories, successors of the Cavaliers who had greeted the King on his return from exile, expressed their loyalty almost as enthusiastically as their predecessors. When the King visited Oxford, the scholars went mad with joy, and thousands of people flocked to him to be touched for the King's evil. The Duke of York was frequently at the King's side, gradually reassuming his position with a place on the Privy Council as well as his old post of Lord High Admiral. The details of the administration were left to a group of able men whose political convictions were not too rigid—the competent but unexciting Sidney Godolphin, who shared the King's love of horses and racing, the Earl of Rochester, the ambitious and somewhat enigmatic Earl of Sunderland, and Lord Halifax, a self-styled trimmer. With the help of 'the Chits' as they were called, the King carried on for three years without a Parliament, relying on French subsidies, an improved revenue from sources at home and the prosperity which automatically resulted from his ability to stay out of the European conflict. Although the Turks had swept into Europe and now stood at the gates of Vienna, although France was ravaging the Netherlands and his nephew continually appealed to him for help, Charles remained aloof, advising William to make peace as soon as possible. He abandoned Tangier, to avoid the expense of maintaining the garrison, and encouraged his seamen to put their energies into developing their country's trade all over the world.

The King himself now lived more soberly and simply, dividing his day into 'an exact distribution of his hours, both for his business, pleasures and the exercise of his health'. He walked by his watch, and when he glanced at the time 'skilful men would make haste with what they had to say to him'. His principle pastime was fishing:

> Fine representative, indeed, of God,
> Whose sceptre's dwindled to a fishing rod.

More than ever now, he showed his pleasure in the enjoyment of his own family and he remained incorrigibly fond of his natural children. Although, for his brother's sake, he could never openly forgive Monmouth, he always felt an affection for his treacherous eldest son, and sent him money when he was in exile in the Netherlands after the discovery of the Rye House plot. There were no restrictions on his love for the sons of his two Duchesses and he could favour them without constraint, bestowing on them some of the honours he felt bound to wrest from his first-born. Portsmouth's son, the Duke of Richmond, became Master of the Horse, and in 1682 the Duke of Grafton was created a vice-admiral after the death of Prince Rupert. In March 1684 Evelyn saw the King at the altar rail on Easter Sunday, accompanied by the sons he had fathered by three different 'prostitute creatures'—the Dukes of Northumberland, Richmond and St Albans—'the three boys entering before the King within the rails, at the right hand, and three bishops on the left'.

Both the King and the Duke nursed a particular affection for the Duchess of Cleveland's virtuous daughter Charlotte Lichfield. James frequently wrote to her during his exile in Scotland, and the King too carried on an affectionate correspondence, signing himself 'your kind father Charles Rex', and referring to her as his 'dear Charlotte'. On one occasion he wrote to tell her that he had made arrangements for her to receive 500 guineas, and he commissioned Christopher Wren to design town houses both for her and her sister Anne, his only stipulation being that Charlotte's house should not be built too high in case it spoiled Anne's view. It was said that the King liked Charlotte to sit beside him and tickle his bald pate when he had his after-dinner nap.

The King's son Henry had become a personable young man who was taking his naval career seriously. During the course of his service he had acquired an unfashionable sun-tan, and his father was relieved to hear that he was going on a visit to Holland; 'by the time he returns', the King wrote to Charlotte, 'he will have worn out in some measure the redness of his face, so as not to fright the most part of our ladies here'. In 1683 a son was born to the Duchess of Grafton, which the Earl of Arlington was 'so joy'd with that some says he will smother it with kisses'.

Although the King was apparently in good health and seemed likely to enjoy a prolonged and peaceful latter end to his reign, he himself did not neglect to ensure the future of his dependants in the case of his death. All the time he was setting aside small sums of money which mounted up to a large fund for the benefit of his children. He arranged to pay off the debts for his daughters' wedding clothes and in 1684 made secret service payments to the Duchess of Cleveland of £1,599. There was a certain urgency about all this, for his agreement with the French for the payment of subsidies had almost run out, and it was likely that he would soon be facing the old familiar financial troubles. The Earl of Rochester's management as First Lord of the Treasury had become suspect, and in the autumn of 1684 he was 'kicked upstairs' into the less influential post of Lord President of the Council.

In November 1684 the Queen's birthday was celebrated more lavishly than usual with a firework display on the Thames outside the Palace at Whitehall and a ball afterwards, where the clothes of the dancers struck Evelyn as being richer than any seen since the King's restoration. Altogether the Court seemed in a mood of carefree enjoyment, and

Evelyn was shocked by the standard of behaviour when he visited White-hall one Sunday evening in January 1685. There was a great deal of gaming in progress, as well as 'luxurious dallying and prophaneness', and the King was 'sitting and toying with his concubines, Portsmouth, Cleveland and Mazarin &c, a French boy singing love songs, in that glorious gallery, whilst about twenty of the great courtiers and other dissolute persons were at basset round a large table, a bank of at least 2,000 in gold before them'.

The King's health had from time to time given cause for concern, and he had suffered attacks which his physicians labelled fits of the ague. But the thought of him falling seriously ill was something which most people preferred not to contemplate. On February 2, just under a week after the scene described by Evelyn, his servants noticed as he was dressing that he continually stopped talking in the middle of a sentence, as if he had forgotten what he intended to say. He then fell back in his chair unconscious, where he remained for the rest of the day insensible, in spite of all the efforts of the physicians to bring him to his senses with spirits, strong purges and blistering plasters. After they had clapped a hot warming-pan to his head he regained conscious-ness and stared wildly round, asking, 'What is the matter with me?' to which his brother unequivocally replied, 'You have had a fit, sir.' The Queen and the Duchess of Portsmouth waited on him faithfully, but never at the same time. He hung on to life for several days, apologizing, with typical wryness, in his famous phrase, for being 'so unconscionable time a-dying'.

It was the King's brother, prompted, perhaps, by the Duchess of Portsmouth, who asked him whether he would like a priest to be called. He replied immediately, 'For God's sake, brother, do, and please to lose no time.' Father Huddleston, who had helped him escape after the battle of Worcester, was quickly called, the room was cleared, except for the Lord of the Bedchamber and the Captain of the King's Guards, and the King then expressed a desire to die in the faith and communion of the Catholic Church. He expressed sorrow for the sins he had commit-ted, and particularly for deferring his conversion for so long, making a confession of his whole life and pronouncing the act of contrition 'with great piety and compunction'. Afterwards he received the sacrament and Father Huddleston left him 'in so much peace of mind that he looked approaching death in the face with all imaginable tranquillity and Christian resolution'. He asked his brother to care for all his children —Nelly's Duke of St Albans, Louise's Duke of Richmond, and all the Duchess of Cleveland's brood. Then, when the end was near, he asked his attendants to draw up the curtain and open the window so that, as he put it, 'I may behold the light of the sun for the last time.' So he

7

died as he had lived, relishing the evidence of the senses, and extracting from his last moments the maximum physical satisfaction, as he had always done, with his great capacity for life and love.

When the King breathed his last, his chamber was crowded with doctors, Privy Councillors and Ambassadors, who all expressed deep sorrow. But it was on the faces of the common people outside the Palace that grief was most apparent; many of them felt that they had lost a friend, for the King had always been the most approachable of monarchs, never afraid to walk informally in the Park, never succumbing to the fears of assassination which frequently assailed his brother. His familiar figure, so often to be seen as he stood at the edge of the canal, feeding the ducks, or walking briskly with a crowd of unruly dogs at his heel, was greatly missed, and although at first there was universal loyalty for his successor, the serious-minded, pompous James II was no substitute for his humorous, roguish, warm-hearted brother.

CHAPTER TWENTY-ONE

COUNSELLOR CASTLEMAINE

IN MANY hearts grief at the King's death was quickly followed by
anxiety for the future, and his mistresses, so long dependent on his
protection, had good cause to feel apprehensive. As the chosen
tool of men who had always been the new King's enemies, Nell Gwynn
could hardly feel optimistic, especially as the Duke of Buckingham's
retirement from the political scene to distant Yorkshire had left her
without a patron. It was fortunate that Charles had put in a special plea
for her on his death-bed, imploring his brother to 'Let not poor Nelly
starve', and that James responded by paying off most of her debts and
granting her a pension.

The Duchess of Portsmouth's problems were even more acute, for
she was still looked upon as a foreigner and she was also deeply in debt.
When she took refuge with the French Ambassador after the King's
death she made herself more unpopular than ever. James refused to
let her withdraw to France until she had paid off her debts and returned
some Crown jewels which were said to be in her possession. He had
always disliked her for her influence over his brother and for her dealings
with the French; he also found it hard to forgive her for collaborating
with his political enemies, even though she had tried hard to regain his
favour during the last two years of Charles's reign. He made some use
of her as a go-between in his relations with France, but the fact that he
was determined to manage without French money deprived her of her
usefulness. He did not scruple to deprive her son, the Duke of Richmond, of the post of Grand Equerry which had been promised to him
by his father—a position which James considered unsuitable for a boy
of thirteen. Nor was he ready to confirm the income his brother had
granted her. 'The disgust so caused . . . provoked her into using plain
speech', Barillon told Louis.

For the two other Duchesses the outlook was more favourable. Mazarin
was lucky enough to be related to the new Queen, while Cleveland now
reaped the benefit of her consistent support of the cause which was
nearest the new King's heart. She had championed the policy of toleration from the days when Clarendon's friends had wryly observed that

she was 'the fiercest solicitor' the persecuted Presbyterian ministers
could hope to find. Ever since she had become the Yorks' neighbour at
St James's, she had remained on consistently good terms with the Duke,
and during the Exclusionist crisis she had preferred to remain in Paris
rather than risk the necessity of making up to his enemies. It was evident
that the new King liked her and was genuinely fond of her children,
whom he trusted in a way that he could never trust the Duke of Monmouth. At the coronation in April 1685 the Duchess of Cleveland was
among eight others of similar rank who had a place in the procession,
and her son Henry also took part as Lord High Constable of England.
When only two months later the Duke of Monmouth mounted his ill-
advised expedition, Grafton was in command of a regiment and fought
with some distinction at Sedgemoor on his uncle's behalf against his
rebellious half-brother.

King James from the start of his reign dedicated himself to the cause
of toleration, following a course which his brother had been forced to
abandon. He proceeded at first with caution, assuring his loyally monar-
chist Parliament that he intended to respect the Church established by
law. In return he received a generous grant of money which enabled
him to remain independent of French bribery and helped him to build
up a useful standing army. With trade expanding, the customs and
excise yielded plentiful dues, and his natural frugality helped to make the
money raised go farther; the Court became less extravagant and osten-
tatious, and the King himself set the example by banishing his mistress
Catherine Sedley from the Court. In retaining the moderate Ministers
appointed by his brother—Clarendon, Rochester and Halifax—he created
a good impression, and made it possible to release priests from prison
and introduce some of his Catholic friends into Court places without
attracting too much attention. He also experienced the infinite pleasure
of consigning Titus Oates to a session in the pillory.

Although the perennial fear of popery had been in abeyance once the
hysteria whipped up by Shaftesbury had been allowed to subside, it
was still latent and easily aroused. At the same time a similar dread of
the republican tendencies of some Protestant nonconformists haunted
all those who could remember the days of the Civil War and the interregnum, while the furore aroused by the Exclusionists was naturally
very much to the fore in James's own mind. It is possible that had he
been able to go forward with his aim of introducing liberty of conscience
for all dissenters, quietly, and in his own time, he might in the end have
carried Parliament with him, overcoming other people's fears of popery
and his own of republicanism. But the actions of others were to arouse
all the old misgivings, causing him to accelerate his campaign and
jeopardize his position with precipitate measures in favour of the Catho-

lics. On the one hand Monmouth's rebellion made him determined to wipe out all disaffected elements and to maintain order with the help of a standing army. On the other the French King's revocation of the Edict of Nantes made English Protestants fear that James intended a similar campaign of persecution with all the paraphernalia of enforced conversions, whippings, heavy fines and general harassment. Mutual fear and distrust tended to tear the Catholic and Protestant dissenters apart whenever they were bettering their circumstances with a joint campaign, and when James came to issue his own Declarations of Indulgence he found himself facing the same opposition that had confronted his brother in earlier times.

Many Anglicans might have been prepared to give their guarded support to a greater measure of tolerance for all dissenters, but as the King increasingly drew Catholics into his councils, and gave dispensations to many others, enabling them to hold office in defiance of the requirements of the Test Act, the old fears of a Catholic autocracy began to grow and spread. Always critical of his brother's lack of persistence and firmness, James was determined to succeed in his aim of repealing the Test Act and of suspending the penal laws. Many of his Catholic friends watched apprehensively realizing that he was proceeding too fast and gradually losing the balanced approach which might have proved the key to success. Never remarkable for his tact, he embarked on a series of actions calculated to arouse the resistance of Anglicans and Protestant dissenters alike. Catholics were admitted to the Privy Council and appointed to university posts where they were allowed to celebrate Mass and were exempted from attending Anglican services. Christ Church, the college which had benefited as a result of the generosity of the Duchess of Cleveland's grandfather Viscount Bayning, was provided with a Catholic Dean, John Massey—a successor to the Dr Fell who had not altogether relished his task of educating the Duchess's sons. Permission was given for the printing of Catholic books, and Catholics were granted commissions in the army. The Duchess of Cleveland's husband, the Earl of Castlemaine, was despatched as an Ambassador Extraordinary to Rome, and Count Ferdinando d'Adda was received in July 1687 at Windsor as if he were the Pope's official nuncio. It was probably no coincidence that Sir Robert Howard's play *The Committee*, so Royalist in outlook and so full of unkind caricatures of Protestant dissenters, was revived several times in 1686; the King and Queen took a box for a performance in April, and in November it was put on at the Palace at Whitehall, as well as at Oxford in July.

The King's open encouragement of Catholics made people doubt his sincerity when he insisted that his aim was to benefit dissenters of all kinds. Count d'Adda himself viewed developments with some misgiving; he had originally come to England in an unofficial capacity and he had already seen enough to know that the King was likely to undo any of the good he had so far been able to achieve by receiving him with great ceremony at Windsor and providing him with a procession of sixteen coaches. In Rome, Pope Innocent XI, well alerted by the militancy of Louis XIV to the dangers of imposing the Catholic faith on unwilling people, was so alarmed by the course of events that he gave a cool welcome to the envoy from England. Had the King's chosen ambassador been of a different cast of mind, had he proceeded discreetly and attempted to reassure the Pope, he might have made a better impression. But his zeal was not, and never had been, tempered by wisdom.

Roger Castlemaine had at one time seemed likely to spend his life either in exile or in prison. In 1677 he had been accused of condoning the popish plot and had found himself in the Tower under suspicion as a secret priest, although he had finally been acquitted in 1680, by which time many of the witnesses had been discredited. The new reign brought him the opportunities which had for so long eluded him thanks to his religious affiliations and his unfortunate marriage. He had made his name during the difficult years as a religious apologist and a historian, and besides writing *The Catholique Apology*, he had also published accounts of the wars between the Venetians and the Turks, and between the English and the Dutch. During his sojourn in the Tower he wrote *The Compendium: or a Short View of the late Trials in relation to the Present Plot against His Majesty and the Government* as well as a treatise concerning a horizontal globe he had invented himself—*The English Globe: being a stable and immobil one, performing what ordinary Globes do and much more, invented and described by the Rt. Hon. the Earl of Castlemaine*. Although depicted by one modern historian as a 'swaggering incompetent' and by another simply as 'fatuous', the Earl's mental powers were not negligible. Boyer described him as a learned person, well versed in mathematics, and Pepys pronounced his *Apology* 'very well writ indeed'. With the help of his early legal training he had conducted his own defence with considerable competence. Although Castlemaine's qualifications were not impressive, he was among the more intelligent Catholics available for office and as Sir Daniel Harvey's deputy in Turkey he had gained some diplomatic experience. It was unfortunate, however, that he lacked the tact and restraint necessary for the delicate mission with which he had been entrusted.

During the early weeks of 1686 the Earl of Castlemaine was busy preparing an impressive equipage which afforded 'discourse to the busy and over curious'. He ordered a 'great sea chest' costing £20 and hinges at £2 to house the silver plate which had been assigned to him. His instructions, grandiosely and more than unwisely, directed him to 'reconcile the kingdoms of England, Scotland and Ireland to the Holy See', and a Privy Seal was passed for a generous allowance of £100 a week. He set out from Greenwich on 15 February 1686, and stayed in Paris for a few days, taking the opportunity of visiting his nieces who were still in the care of the Blue Nuns, and donating 480 livres to the Convent. The English in Paris made sure that he was not asked to perform any official functions during his stay, for they were sure that inexperienced as he was, he was more than likely to commit a diplomatic *gaffe*. He entered Rome in great style on Easter Sunday, installing himself in a fine palace with the King's arms over the door as well as the Pope's, not to mention 'several devices of the Catholic religion triumphing over heresy'. Back in England engravings were made at the King's expense depicting the Ambassador's triumphal entry and his audience with the Pope, but Innocent XI was rather less impressed; he found Castlemaine pompous and self-important; the hot-tempered envoy and the equally irascible ecclesiastic were inclined to jar 'in almost every point they went on'. Castlemaine did nothing to remove the Pope's disapproval of James's impetuous policy, and he was equally unsuccessful when he attempted to obtain a Cardinal's hat for Mary of Modena's uncle. He became so importunate that whenever he appeared the Pope 'was seasonably attacked with a fit of coughing', much to the amusement of the papal entourage. Thick-skinned though he was, he began to realize that he was not being treated with the respect he felt that his mission merited, and when in the heat of the moment he threatened to leave Rome, the Pope gratefully accepted his offer, suggesting that he should rise early and rest in the afternoon since it was dangerous in Italy to travel in the heat of the day. Although on the return journey most of his belongings fell a prey to Algerian pirates, he managed to arrive back with the ambassadorial silver plate still in his possession.

Back in London, Castlemaine joined his cousin, the Earl of Powis and other men of '*esprit médiocre*', who made up the inner circle of counsellors and who met every Friday evening at the Earl of Sunderland's or Will Chiffinch's lodgings. More balanced men were doing all they could to temper the King's rashness, even persuading him to reassure the Protestants by showing open favour to his non-Catholic mistress, Catherine Sedley, to the extent of creating her Countess of Dorchester. This move did not, of course, please the Queen, as the French Ambassador was quick to report. 'The King,' he wrote, 'promises that he will not see Sedley again. He loves his wife. *Elle est Italienne et fort glorieuse.*' The parading of a Protestant mistress was in any case an inadequate gesture when it came to allaying the fears of subjects by now thoroughly alarmed at the appearance of Catholic officers in the army, particularly in Ireland, and by the encampment at Hounslow each summer of the efficient military force which the King had built up, some said for the purpose of subduing London. Surrounded by second-rate men who lacked experience in posts of high responsibility, the King pressed ruthlessly on in his determination to be rid of the penal laws and the Test Act. For all their failings, Castlemaine and his cousin Powis were among the more able Catholics who surrounded the King, and there was even some talk of sending Castlemaine to Ireland as Lord-Lieutenant in place of the fanatical Tyrconnel; whether he would have proved more or less inept is a matter for speculation. As it turned out he was used to carry out the King's policies nearer home, for he was appointed to the Commission of Regulation which master-minded the campaign to remove from all public bodies any member who was not prepared to support the King's policies. Other members of the committee were the Earl of Sunderland, the hated Judge Jeffreys, the Earl of Powis and the increasingly influential Jesuit Father Petre.

The King, like his brother before him, had come to realize that the best method of silencing his critics was to remove their main platform, in other words to prorogue or dissolve Parliament. But he now believed that since he had no son and the Crown was likely to devolve on his eldest daughter Mary, it was essential that he should obtain a repeal of the Test Act and penal laws with the legal sanction of Parliament. To this end he had determined to acquire a House of Commons that would be sympathetic towards his policies. It was the task of the regulating committee to bring this about. And while Castlemaine was busy with his new and exacting task, the King continued to extend favours to the Duchess of Cleveland's children, making sure that none of them would have any excuse to show the disloyalty that had driven their half-brother Monmouth to rebellion. In February 1686, just at the time when their mother's husband was leaving for Rome, all the Duchess of Cleveland's children were invited to dance at the Queen's Candlemas entertainment dressed in different national costumes. The arrangements had to be hastily cancelled when the Duke of Grafton became involved in a duel and killed Jack Talbot, a brother of the Duke of Shrewsbury. It seemed that Henry had inherited the duelling tendencies of his grandfather, Lord Grandison, for later in February Evelyn reported that he had killed the Earl of Derby's brother 'upon an almost insufferable provo-cation'—there most probably had been reflections on Harry's parentage. Although King James strongly disapproved of the 'unchristian custom of duelling', Henry was not punished for his crimes, but he left the Court for a while.

The King was sufficiently concerned for his brother's children to take an interest in their matrimonial prospects, and he had been making plans to marry George to a daughter of the Duke of Newcastle, who was ironically enough a sister of the Lord Ogle who had eventually won the hand of Lady Betty Percy; he was not amused when he heard that his nephew had been 'bubbled into marriage' with Catherine, the widow of Thomas Lucy of Charlecote. As the bride was the daughter of a poulterer and was reported to be rich 'only in beauty', she was not considered to be of the right calibre for a Duchess. George, whose dark looks betrayed his origins, had inherited his father's susceptibility where ladies were concerned, and he persisted in his fondness for her in spite of the family's disapproval. Henry, playing the part of the elder brother, spirited Catherine away to a convent in Flanders, doing all he could to extricate George from such an unsatisfactory liaison, even taking legal advice concerning the possibility of a divorce. The King was not prepared to sanction such a solution, especially as Catherine was a Catholic, and George continued to write to her by every post, while the ladies at Court expressed their horror at the thought of one of their sex being abducted against her will. And when the gossips were not mulling over the question of George's marriage they were probably discussing his mother's latest aberration, for there were rumours that at the age of forty-five she was expecting a child by the actor Cardonnel Goodman. 'In the meantime', as Peregrine Bertie put it, 'their gracious mother is brought to bed of a son which the town has christened Goodman Cleveland.'

The Duchess's latest lover had turned to acting when his unreliable character had barred him from other careers. He had been expelled from Cambridge for defacing the Duke of Monmouth's portrait and he was later deprived of his place as a Page of the Backstairs, on a charge of negligence. Having parted with his meagre fortune to buy his way into Court employment, he was left with nothing except a gentlemanly manner and a fine appearance. Deciding to make capital out of these qualities, he joined the King's Company at Drury Lane, where he was soon playing the lead parts in *Julius Caesar*, *Othello* and *Alexander the Great*. In October 1684 he had pleaded not guilty to the curious charge of 'conspiring and endeavouring to hire one Amidée to poison the Dukes of Grafton and Northumberland'. He was fined £1,000, but paid off the money with his share of the haul in a highway robbery. The Duchess, always indulgent to those she loved, repaid him for his attempt to poison her sons by obtaining a pardon for all his crimes. In return he showed his affection by refusing to let any performance in the theatre begin until he was sure that she was in her seat. One night when they told him that the Queen had arrived in the auditorium he immediately asked, 'Is my Duchess come?' and on hearing that she had not, he declared with

7*

an impressive string of oaths that the curtain was not to be raised until she appeared. Fortunately she entered the theatre almost at once, which 'saved the affront to the Queen'.

Nothing more was heard of the son that the Duchess was reputed to have borne to the man who was known to his friends as 'Scum'. But the relationship continued, and as friends and supporters of the King both the Duchess and her lover must have viewed with concern the dramatic events that led up to what Mary of Modena was to describe to the Pope as the *'Eretica Usurpatione'*. The Duchess's sons were more closely involved with the King's cause—particularly the Duke of Grafton in whom James had confided a great deal of trust. When the Duke of Somerset had refused to conduct the reception of Count d'Adda at Windsor on the grounds that the ceremony was treasonable, the King had delegated the task to his nephew, and Grafton had obediently carried it out. His compliance encouraged the King to let him keep his command in the Guards, while his brother George was given a position of trust in the Household Cavalry. James's attempt to procure a sympathetic Parliament through the efforts of the Commission of Regulation was matched by a similar campaign to fill the key army posts with men he thought he could trust—Catholics, relations, old friends. But many of the men he believed in were beginning secretly to rebel against policies which seemed to threaten the monarchy and the established Church. Even John Churchill, who owed him so much, whom he had favoured, promoted, trusted and raised to the peerage, had seen that he must choose a different master. Like many others, Churchill had watched with apprehension as the moderates, particularly the two Hydes, Clarendon and Rochester, had been removed from the King's councils. It was made clear to men in authority that they must change their faith or lose their position; Sunderland, whose preoccupation with his own career was stronger than his loyalty to any particular religious dogma, announced his conversion and stayed in the inner circle of power. Churchill and Grafton were also retained, although they did not turn Catholic, the King relying on the loyalty of both, certain that gratitude would guarantee their constancy.

The King hoped that the regulators would have completed their work in time for him to call a co-operative Parliament in November 1688. In April of that year he issued his second Declaration of Indulgence, with instructions that it should be read in all churches. The Bishops, recognizing their inability to enforce this order, petitioned the King to withdraw it, and in reply he prosecuted them on a charge of seditious libel. Seven of them were sent to the Tower; they travelled by barge down the river, and when they disembarked at Tower wharf they were met by a large crowd of people all on their knees, begging their blessing and praying for them as they passed by. On June 30 they were acquitted amid scenes of rejoicing; the King, on a visit to his much-prized army at Hounslow, was displeased to learn that an outbreak of cheering among his soldiers was provoked by the news that the verdict in the Bishops' trial had been favourable to the established Church. That same evening seven men including the Earls of Shrewsbury, Devonshire and Danby, Bishop Henry Compton and Henry Sidney, signed a letter inviting William of Orange to intervene in a situation that had become increasingly dangerous for the established Church and for all Protestants.

The invitation had been precipitated by the birth of a son to the Queen ten days before. So long as James had no heir there had been good cause for patience, in the knowledge that both his daughters and their husbands were true to the Protestant faith. But now the prospect of a Catholic succession lent urgency to plans which before had been moving forward only tentatively. In Holland, William began to assemble his forces for an armed expedition to England, and at home the disaffected made secret plans for his reception. Among those who pledged their support was the man who was trusted implicitly by the King; on August 4 Lord Churchill wrote a letter to William assuring him that he put his honour into the Prince's hands, 'in which I think it safe'. He added that he was 'resolved to die in that religion that it has pleased God to give you both the will and power to protect'. This was the man to whom James had given his 'entire confidence', so much so that when William had already landed the King appointed him Lieutenant-General and second in command under the Earl of Feversham.

One of the first of the deserters was Lord Cornbury, the Earl of Clarendon's son. It was said that Churchill and others received the news 'going hand in hand along the gallery in the greatest transports of joy imaginable'. By this time Churchill knew that he had the Duke of Grafton on his side, and together they did all they could to persuade Grafton's brother George to join them. At a council of war held on November 23 at the King's army headquarters near Salisbury, Churchill and Grafton advocated an advance on the enemy, but the King was more inclined to take Feversham's advice and to retreat to a defensive line along the Thames. That same evening Churchill and Grafton left the King's camp and rode fifty miles to join forces with William.

Their defection came as a bitter blow to the King, and when he heard that his daughter Anne and her husband had also abandoned him he felt utterly undermined. He had always cherished the family spirit, and to find such divisions among those endowed with Stuart blood was unforeseen and unimaginable. But when he was asked whether he would accept an offer to have Churchill and Grafton murdered he could not bring himself to eradicate an old friend and a brother's son. The fight went out of him as he saw his friends and relations desert him. He had striven to achieve what he believed to be right and he was deeply pained to find that his righteouness had done nothing except make him the victim of ingratitude and treachery.

The King's main concern now was for the safety of his wife and of Prince James Edward whose birth had helped to bring so much trouble on his parents. Lady Powis had been appointed the Prince's governess, and she and her husband succeeded in conveying him to France. The King's supporters had to fend for themselves, and the Earl of Castlemaine, unlike his cousin Powis, left it too late to escape to the Continent. As a member of the Privy Council and of the Commission of Regulation, as well as a former envoy to the Pope and a signatory at the Prince's christening, he had little to hope for once the King and Queen had fled. He left London for Wales, where he had inherited considerable property, and lay low, hoping to live there unnoticed.

There had been no spectacular reconciliation between the Earl of Castlemaine and his wife during his brief period of prominence, and she had shown no signs of attaching herself to the ultra-Catholic party. Now her long-established adherence to the Catholic faith seemed likely to be offset by the fact that her sons had gone over to William. It was her uncle, the ever-useful Sir Edward Villiers, who was entrusted with the task of escorting Queen Mary II to England when arrangements had been made for her to assume the crown jointly with her husband. Sir Edward's wife had been responsible for bringing up both Mary and Anne in the Protestant faith during their childhood at Richmond. The new Queen, who had no wish to leave the quiet domesticity of her life in Holland, made little attempt to cultivate any of the ladies at Court, let alone the formidable array of her uncle's and her father's former mistresses. William's asthma and Mary's dislike of social life made them spend as much time as possible at the Kensington house they had bought from the Earl of Nottingham. The Duchess of Cleveland did what she could to ingratiate herself by placing Cleveland House at the disposal of the Dutch Ambassadors sent over by the States-General to congratulate William and Mary at the time of their coronation. She fared rather better than Catherine Sedley, Countess of Dorchester, who had greeted the new Queen with the witty but none too endearing comment, 'I have sinned *with* your father, but you have sinned *against* him.' Catherine remarked self-righteously that the Queen was forced to 'admit of ladies I should be very sorry to be compared to, for instance the Duchesses of Mazarin and Cleveland . . . I am sure it goes much against my stomach to name myself with them'.

The Catholic mistresses might be allowed to haunt the Court, but the Duchess of Cleveland was soon to find out that her financial prospects were not favourable. Promises made in what had been, for her, happier times, were conveniently forgotten and the new Postmaster-General, Major Wildman, even refused to pay her pension. She received a quarter's payment in 1690, but further appeals were in vain. Any advantage that she might have hoped to gain from Grafton's defection were quickly disappointed, for William viewed his illegitimate cousin with dislike, fearing his influence in the naval and military sphere. Grafton was inclined to indulge in 'unwary speeches', and it caused no surprise that he and King William fell out, both their 'natures being stiff'. Early in the new reign there were authentic rumours that the Duke, while retaining his pensions, was to be put out of all his places. He was in fact divested of his army command, but was allowed to keep his title of vice-admiral and was put in charge of a man-of-war, the *Grafton*. At the battle off Beachy Head in June 1690 he found a chance to prove his loyalty when he conducted himself with such outstanding gallantry that the Queen mentioned him specially in a letter to William III who was away campaigning in Ireland.

King James II had established a strong foothold in Ireland, and Marlborough put forward a plan to seize the ports which were being used by the Jacobites to bring in supplies and reinforcements from France. On 17 September 1690 the Duke of Grafton set sail from Portsmouth, carrying troops under the command of his mother's former lover, to be used against his uncle. Their first target was the town of Cork, and towards the end of September, Marlborough disembarked with 6,000 men some miles down the coast. Grafton also landed with a detachment of seamen and made himself responsible for placing the besieging batteries. Once again he acquitted himself bravely, showing the same spirit his grandfather, Lord Grandison, had displayed in the attack on Bristol many years before. He was wounded in the ribs and died ten days later, saying that although he died content, he wished that he was leaving his country in a happier and more tranquil state. They brought him back to Euston for burial, and the beautiful sweet-natured Isabella, who was never heard to say an unkind word about anyone, who was painted by the great Court artists and eulogized by poets and wits, was left to bring up the son she had borne to the man of whose death Fleetwood Shepherd wrote:

> G—— rot him
> That shot him.
> The son of a whore:
> I say no more.

Had Grafton lived it is possible that he might have remained on good terms with the King, assuaging any fears that his mother could nurse secret Jacobite sympathies. As it was there was little to recommend the Duchess to the Calvinistic William and the pious Mary. Roger Castlemaine was arrested at Oswestry in October 1689 and he soon found himself back in the familiar surroundings of the Tower. Although he was released on bail, he was among those who were exempted from the general pardon granted under the Act of Indemnity. In the Tower at the same time was the Earl of Arran, heir to the Duke and Duchess of Hamilton. His parents had welcomed William III to England, but Arran himself had sent a message to the new King making it plain that his loyalties still lay with James II. He had married Lady Anne Spencer, the Earl of Sunderland's daughter, who had become a Lady of the Bedchamber to Mary of Modena, and in spite of his previously dissolute and extravagant life he had settled down to matrimony surprisingly well. The formidable walls of the Tower at least provided him with a safe refuge from his many creditors, and when he was released in November 1689 he turned his back on the temptations of London life, making straight for the family seat in Scotland. He was joined by his wife, who died of puerperal fever in June 1690; reputedly stricken with grief, he made his way back to London.

The capital was in a state of alarm, with the King away in Ireland and fears of an imminent French invasion growing after the defeat of the English fleet off Beachy Head. The Jacobites for the first time allowed themselves to feel a modicum of hope; there were secret meetings and some arms and ammunition were accumulated. It is probable that James's supporters used the Duchess of Cleveland's house as a rendez-vous, and that the Earl of Arran was among those who went there to formulate plans for an uprising in the event of a French landing. In any case he met the Duchess's daughter Barbara Churchill, who had come over to London after becoming a novice with the Blue Nuns in 1689. In the heady atmosphere of those tense weeks Arran fell in love with the beautiful novice; they experienced a few weeks of happiness before he was arrested on a charge of corresponding with the exiled Court and was sent once again to the Tower. He was joined there by many other known Jacobites, including the Earl of Castlemaine. While Arran was there he learnt that Barbara Churchill was expecting his child.

The death of their son's wife had come as a bitter blow to the Duke and Duchess of Hamilton. For years they had tried to steer him into a suitable marriage, when he himself had thought of matrimony, if he thought of it at all, as nothing more than a chance to pay off his debts with a large dowry. Now, after all their hopes, he had become a widower with no legitimate heir, and had lost his heart to an unsuitable girl. They were more than anxious to extricate him from his liaison with Barbara so that on leaving the Tower he would be able to give his mind to the task of finding a new, and desirable, wife. After some bargaining they procured his release on condition that Barbara returned immediately to France. She was looked after by her mother at Cleveland House until March 1691, when she gave birth to a son, Charles Hamilton, and only a fortnight later she went back to the convent in Paris, making her profession there as Barbara Fitzroy, daughter of King Charles II, to be known in her religion as Bernadette.

In 1691 the Earl of Castlemaine was tried on a charge of failing to return plate worth £4,000 which had been granted him for his mission to Rome. He pleaded that a warrant had been issued by James II authorizing him to keep the plate for his own use, but it was believed that the warrant was invalid as it had not been passed prior to the abdication. It was an unwritten law that ambassadors were allowed to regard their plate as a personal perquisite, but the extravagance of Castlemaine's equipage as well as the doubtful legality of his mission, attracted a fine of £2,500, a more than just punishment for his ostentation. Again failing to procure a pardon, he was allowed to join the exiled King at Saint-Germain in 1692 and records show that he stayed there for the next two years, standing as godfather to three children born in that unhappy Court. He was reunited with Anne Sussex, whom he still regarded as his daughter, even though Mary of Modena treated her as if she were of royal blood, creating her a Lady of the Bedchamber and allowing her to be seated in the presence of French princesses and duchesses.

Charles Hamilton was brought up at Cleveland House by his grandmother who meanwhile continued her association with Cardonnel Goodman. The actor had rounded off his melodramatic career by throwing in his lot with the Jacobites. The fact that he had defaced a portrait of the Duke of Monmouth at Cambridge suggests that he had for long been a devotee of James II. Now he and his associates met regularly at the Dog Tavern in Drury Lane, carousing to the sound of kettle-drums and trumpets, and behaving as indiscreetly as the old Royalists of the interregnum. As plots for an armed rising were formulated and plans reached completion for an assassination of the King, the conspirators grew more confident, and one evening, having imbibed rather too freely, they lit a bonfire in the street and forced onlookers to drink to the Prince of Wales. Cardonnel was arrested and on hearing the news the Duchess of Cleveland took the precaution of having two cases of carbines she had been harbouring removed from her house to his. She then went off to Tunbridge Wells as if nothing had happened and was frequently observed at the gaming table, surrounded by gallants.

Throughout the nineties the Duchess struggled to balance her gambling debts against payment of arrears long overdue, but all the old sources of income had gone and there was nobody now who could plead for her. While in prison Cardonnel turned informer and implicated many people in Jacobite plots, including Sir John Fenwick who eventually went to the gallows, after himself accusing a number of other prominent men. The Duchess was lucky to escape unscathed, in view of the fact that her husband, her lover, her daughter Anne and her daughter Barbara's lover were all involved with the exiled Court. In 1696, when the Earl of Castlemaine was unwise enough to come over to England, he was promptly arrested under the writ issued in 1690 which was still in force although Queen Mary had died of smallpox in 1694. To the original accusation of treason was now added a charge of failing to obey a summons to attend the Irish Parliament. After another spell in the Tower he was released on condition that he left the country immediately. Cardonnel was also released as a reward for turning informer and he too went abroad only to find himself imprisoned in Paris on a charge of informing against Catholics.

Many of the old familiar faces were now missing from the London scene. Shaftesbury and Arlington were dead and neither the Duke of Buckingham nor Nell Gwynn had lived to rejoice at the departure of the Catholic King. Gone were the halcyon days when the Duchess of Cleveland could look to the King and his heir for protection, when Bab May and Chiffinch had seen to it that all the avenues to wealth and favour were open to her and when her friends held most of the important posts in the Exchequer. The Court was no longer a fruitful hunting-ground for the ambitious and the acquisitive. As a widower William withdrew more than ever into his male circle of advisers and favourites; when he remembered how easily many had changed their allegiance at his own arrival he doubted whether there was anyone he could really trust. He could not even be sure of Marlborough; the Queen had been convinced that he was treasonable and he was among those Fenwick had accused of corresponding with Saint-Germain. Clarendon and Rochester were still in eclipse, and although Danby came back into prominence for a while he once again found himself facing impeachment in 1694. The facile Sunderland quickly shed his Catholicism to please the new monarch and William was prepared to overlook past actions and make use of his political expertise. Forgiveness and mercy were William's best weapons for countering the constant menace of a rival just across the Channel who had a better claim to the throne than his own. So he tolerated the Jacobites, keeping a close watch on their activities but letting them live unmolested so long as they were harmless and there was no immediate danger of an assault from overseas. The Duchess of Cleveland could even have been useful to him as a decoy for the disaffected, but that did not mean he showed her any favours or went out of his way to help her out of her financial difficulties.

The Duchess of Cleveland was £10,000 in debt and still the King made no attempt to come to her aid. It was not until 1699 that he relented and orders were issued for payments to be made of £100 for twenty-three weeks; for the remainder of her life she received regular payments of her pension. Altogether she fared rather better than the Duchess of Portsmouth who was not granted the smallest sum throughout William's reign and was never allowed to set foot in England. The Duchesse de Mazarin, however, did receive an annual pension of £2,000 from 1698 onwards, which did something to relieve her chronic insolvency—at one time so acute that she relied on her admirer, the philosopher Saint-Evremond, to provide the butter for her table. She did not enjoy her grant for long, for she died soon afterwards, her death hastened by the 'intemperate drinking of strong waters'—white wine, anis, absinthe and Irish whiskey.

Queen Catherine, too, had gone, forced to leave Somerset House on a suspicion of caballing against the government, and she had finally returned to Portugal. There were few people left now who had graced the Court during the Duchess's heyday. Her fortunes had declined; she had found it necessary to leave Cleveland House and move to a property in newly-developed Arlington Street and then again to Park Street off St James's. She was separated from her husband, her lover and two of her daughters, and she had lost her most personable son. Her charms had at last begun to fade and her signature was shaky, but there was to be one last episode in her life that for sheer melodrama lived up to her undying reputation for the exotic and the outlandish.

CHAPTER TWENTY-TWO

HANDSOME FEILDING

THE DEATH of two kings, James II in 1701 and William III in 1702, brought some easing of the tension for those of Jacobite persuasion. The Earl of Castlemaine was allowed to return to England and he spent his last years quietly in Wales, but the Countess of Sussex stayed in France where she was treated with great respect. She remained separated from her husband, but this did not prevent her complaining about his extravagance.

By now the Duchess of Cleveland had no desire to regain her former position and in any case life at the Court of Queen Anne was not much more diverting than it had been in the time of William and Mary. The Queen was often ill and for most of her reign was dominated by the cantankerous Sarah Marlborough or the insinuating Abigail Masham. Mary de la Rivière Manley, author of the scurrilous *Adventures of Rivella* and *The New Atlantis*, painted the Duchess's declining years in lurid colours, claiming that she was querulous, fierce, loquacious, excessively fond or infamously rude, and hated by her family. Mary herself lived in the Duchess's house for some years, and was her constant companion at the gaming table, the Duchess believing that she brought her luck. She no doubt witnessed at close quarters the sombre moods of old age and obscurity which had replaced the calculated and fascinating rages the Duchess had displayed at the height of her power. All the same, in spite of Mrs Manley's strictures, the Duchess still possessed enough charm to attract one last admirer, and her family stood by her in the troubles which this final amour brought in its wake.

In 1705, after over forty years of a marriage that had been a mere mockery, the Duchess was widowed when Roger Castlemaine died. He was buried at Welshpool, and Anne, whom he had appointed one of his trustees, inherited his house near the Strand, his leaseholds in the county of Monmouth as well as his plate and jewels. Within four months the Duchess was married again—or so she believed.

Throughout her life she had been drawn to men of unusual good looks, even though in character they were often feckless and usually in the end unfaithful. Her new inamorato, Robert Feilding, was in the same mould; in his youth he had always 'passed like an inundation over the fair sex', and he would no sooner sit down in his pew on a Sunday than all the eyes of the ladies would be fixed on him and a murmur would run through the church that Handsome Feilding had arrived. It was impossible to list his mistresses, for 'the whole sex was his seraglio', and he had proved irresistible to the 'ready chambermaid or the distant baroness' alike. Having married two heiresses in succession, the second of whom had died in 1698, he was now, like the Duchess, free to choose another mate. There was a certain distinction in following in the footsteps of a King and of two of the most distinguished actors of the day, although Beau Feilding would have been happier if the Duchess's pension had been somewhat more generous.

Feilding, whose father lived near Solihull in Warwickshire, came of the same family as the Earl of Denbigh who had married the Duchess's great-aunt Susan Villiers. The Feildings claimed descent from the Counts of Habsburg, and this fact accounted for the spread eagle which Feilding liked to have emblazoned on his coach. Dressed magnificently in clothes that were distinctly out of date, he would be seen driving through the town with a crowd of urchins running behind. He would call out to them, 'Good bastards, go to school, and don't loose your time in following my wheels; I am loath to hurt you, because I know not but you are all my own offspring . . . Why, you young dogs, did you never see a man before?'—and the reply would come, 'Never such a one as you, noble General.' He had commanded a regiment with the Imperial army and later had served under James II, being one of the Catholic officers whose presence had caused so much fear and suspicion. He kept the memory of his military adventures green by calling for his tea to the sound of a drum, while his long-suffering valet had to shave him to the sound of a trumpet.

At this time Feilding was living in Pall Mall, not far from the Duchess's house in St James's. As fellow Catholics and supporters of James II they had probably been well acquainted for years, and when Roger died, Feilding lost no time in suggesting that he would make a worthy successor to all the Duchess's former lovers:

Madam,
   It is not only that Nature had made us two of the most accomplished of each sex, and pointed to us to obey her dictates in becoming One; but that there is also an ambition in following the mighty persons you have favoured. Where Kings and heroes, as great as Alexander, or such as could personate Alexander, have bowed, permit your General to lay his laurels.

The Duchess responded favourably to this appeal and on November 25 she married the man who was at least ten years her junior, the ceremony being performed at her own house by Father Duarte, a chaplain to the Portuguese Ambassador. Among the witnesses was General Sackville who had been a leading member of King James's Court at Saint-Germain. As soon as the ceremony was over Feilding moved in with his bride and began systematically to fleece her; according to Abel Boyer he would in the end have divested her of everything, including the furnishings, if her grandson, the young Duke of Grafton, had not stood by her. It was he who discovered that Feilding had 'solemnized or pro-phaned' a marriage with one Mrs Wadsworth only a fortnight before his so-called wedding with the Duchess.

When the truth was revealed the Duchess flew into a rage in her old style—perhaps rather more justifiably than on previous occasions. Feilding, however, was her equal. He threatened to kill her, broke open her safe and stole £100 and proceeded to beat her until she managed to reach the window and cried murder to the crowd that had gathered out-side. Feilding rounded off the incident by seizing his blunderbuss and letting it off indiscriminately. The Duchess was reduced to a state of collapse, and Luttrell reported on 11 May 1706 that the physicians despaired of her life. Feilding meanwhile was arrested and committed to Newgate, but he was later released on bail, with the Duke of Devon-shire and the Earl of Denbigh standing surety. Fearful of her own safety, the Duchess fled from her house and sought the protection of her son and grandson; this Feilding styled an elopement, and he published an advertisement warning tradesmen 'upon no account whatever to trust, or give credit, to the said Duchess, whose debts he will in no wise satisfy'.

The bigamy trial opened on December 4 at the Old Bailey and sentence was not passed until May of the following year. As the trial proceeded it became evident that Feilding himself had become the victim of a monstrous and humiliating deception. He had bribed a hairdresser, Charlotte Villars, to introduce him to a rich widow named Anne Deleau —he had checked the will himself in the Doctors Commons and disco-vered that she had been left the worthwhile sum of £60,000. Mrs Villars, realizing that Feilding was up to no good, but still anxious to pocket the £500 he had offered her as a reward for bringing about the introduction, decided to play 'trick for trick'. She brought Mary Wadsworth, who had recently been released from Bridewell, to Feilding's lodgings dressed in widow's clothes and in a mourning coach. Feilding, lamentably taken in, showed her all his fine clothes and furniture and paid Margaretta Galli to sing love songs as he did so. When he proposed to her, Mary with 'seeming modesty checked his forward behaviour', but he made her promise not to put off their marriage longer than the following

Wednesday. Preparing for this great day he wrote 'Nanette' a succession of love letters referring to Mrs Villars as 'Puggy'—'You and Puggy have nothing to do but come at bed-time so we may go to bed and lie till morning when Puggy may come again and call you'. He ordered his landlady to make up white ribbon with gold fringe into garters for the bride, buying scarlet gloves for the ladies and white gloves for himself; somewhat hypocritically he bespoke a ring engraved with the words *Tibi Soli*. A fire had been lit and there were clean sheets on the bed, and when the ladies arrived, he promptly locked them in and set off at a gallop to procure a priest, driven by the thought of £60,000 in his pocket. The Emperor's Envoy, Count Gallas, provided him with the priest who was known as the Father in Red on account of his red habit. A fortnight later he went through a second ceremony with the Duchess, subsequently returning to his lodgings where he supped with Mary off boiled chicken.

When sentence was finally passed, the Duchess's son, grandson and sons-in-law were in Court to hear the verdict. They learnt that the Duchess's marriage had been proved void, and although Feilding finally received a pardon from Queen Anne and lived happily with Mary whom he referred to in his will as his 'dear and loving wife', he was ordered to surrender to the Duchess his gold ring and the seven love letters he had written to 'Nanette'. It was said that Feilding 'ended his dolors in a garret' and he certainly fell into debt, spending some of his last years in the Fleet prison.

The humiliation of her so-called marriage and all the publicity of the trial took their toll of the Duchess's health. She withdrew from London to a house in the Mall at Chiswick, spending the last year of her life away from the world in the company of her much-loved grandson, Barbara's son, Charles Hamilton. On 11 August 1709 she made her will and at about the same time she was struck down with dropsy which 'swelled her gradually to a monstrous bulk'. The famous good looks were at last destroyed, and on October 9, within a few weeks of her sixty-ninth birthday, she died. The Duke of Grafton arranged her funeral which took place at Chiswick parish church. He had always been her friend and she made him her residuary legatee, although in fact she had little to leave. What remained of Nonsuch went to Charles, Earl of Southampton, with the Cleveland title, which lapsed on the death of his son in 1774.

In the same year Ralph Montagu too breathed his last, passing on to his son John the dukedom bestowed on him by Queen Anne, leaving him the much improved Boughton House with its fine new wing built in the French style, a memento of that distant time in Paris set in the Northamptonshire countryside and filled with treasures that were a reminder of the days when he had been the intermediary of Kings—pictures, clocks, mirrors and a writing-desk, the gift of Louis XIV, inlaid with pewter and brass, mother-of-pearl and ebony. John had been wise enough to marry Mary, daughter of the great Duke of Marlborough who owed the foundation of his fortune to the Duchess but chose to forget his debt of gratitude when she later asked him to lend her money at the gaming table.

The girl who had first come to London in 'a plain country dress' had put behind her the impoverishment of her youth and left a well-established family. The dynasty of the Graftons, founded with the help of her charm, ambition and match-making ability, has survived right down to the present day. She left her sons and daughters well furnished with fine titles and good prospects. The Countess of Lichfield was able to live a prosperous life of conventional domesticity with her many progeny. Anne, Countess of Sussex, was widowed in 1715 and married two more husbands—Lord Teyhnam who shot himself in a fit of madness, and Robert Moore, whom she was to outlive by twenty-seven years. Barbara Fitzroy, after the peccadillo which resulted in the birth of the charming Charles Hamilton—who was to have a brief moment of fame as a second in the duel when his father the Duke of Hamilton died of a severed artery and Lord Mohun also lost his life—lived a saintly life as a nun, becoming a prioress at the Convent of Saint-Nicholas, where she died in 1731.

More lasting than the beautiful house the Duchess built or the fortune she amassed or the family she left behind, was the legend that has come down over the centuries. She has lived on through the testimony made by her contemporaries—a woman of incredible beauty, insatiable appetites and limitless ambition. As one versifier put it:

> Cleveland, I say, was much to be admired,
> For she was never satisfied or tired.

She was described by Reresby as 'the finest woman of her age', by Boyer as the handsomest and by Oldmixon as 'the lewdest as well as the fairest of all King Charles's concubines'. Bishop Burnet commented on her extraordinary beauty which, he wrote, 'was of long continuance', but he added that she was 'vastly expensive' and stuck at nothing that served her appetites and passions. As Wycherley put it in his dedication to the play Love in a Wood, 'You have that perfection of beauty (without thinking it so) which others of your sex but think they have'. From Lely's portraits and Pepys's diary she emerges as a woman of dazzling good looks and vibrant character; both painter and diarist appear to have been almost hypnotized by her beauty. Pepys found her entrancing whether she was covered in jewels at a ball, or asleep in a coach with her mouth open, or clapping a man's hat on to protect her hair from the wind, or in a crowded box at the theatre sticking on a beauty spot to hide a rising pimple.

When the Duchesse de Mazarin's sister was about to arrive in England in 1682, Chesterfield noted that there was much speculation at Court as to whether she would prove to be 'a beauty, a misse, a wit or politician'. The Duchess of Cleveland's distinction—John Evelyn would probably have found a less complimentary word—was that she combined all these qualities in a single person. Burnet wrote that he never heard anybody commend her except for her beauty, and commentators in general have failed to notice her consistent loyalty to the cause of religious toleration, which accounted for her lasting friendship for James and her fluctuating relationship with the Duke of Buckingham—her amity giving way to alienation whenever he supported Protestant dissenters at the expense of the Catholics. Although she had consorted with some of the Jacobites during the reign of William and Mary, she had made no attempt when James was on the throne to assume those ultra-Catholic doctrines favoured by her husband which had brought disaster to the Catholic cause. She had done her best to help extend the privileges of her fellow Catholics, and Protestant dissenters as well, but had drawn back when James began to embark on his more unrealistic policies.

During Charles's reign the presence of his mistresses at Whitehall and in the purlieus of St James's had been a factor that every aspiring politician and courtier tended to take into account. Although the Spanish and French Ambassadors had in the end been forced to concede that in spite of all their bribes 'King Charles was not disposed to communicate his affairs to women', yet, as Lord Arlington put it, the mistresses still had the ability to 'injure those whom they hate, and in that way ruin many affairs'. The noble Lord Grandison, who had spilled his blood in the service of a monarch, might well have been scandalized had he lived to witness his daughter's own particular method of keeping the Villiers family tradition alive. Studying the workings of the Court, making herself expert in the valuable trade of perquisites and titles, manipulating and 'rigging' those in power, but above all gaining the affection and friendship of a King and his brother, the Duchess had followed in the footsteps of her uncle, the great Duke of Buckingham. When the mantle of favour had finally fallen from her shoulders, it had been taken up, strangely, by another member of the family, Elizabeth Villiers, the daughter of 'honest Ned', who for a while played the part, albeit far more discreetly than her cousin, of royal mistress, in her case to William III.

The irrepressible Nell Gwynn, observing the Duchess of Cleveland looking at her with an expression that could hardly be interpreted as one of unadulterated approval, had clapped her on the shoulder and said 'she perceived that persons of one trade loved not another'. But the

Duchess's strength had lain in her ability to deal with every threat, accepting the King's need for novelty, while never losing her power to enchant him. For over a decade she had been a person nobody could afford to ignore, dominating the Court with her beauty, her wit and her opportunism, embodying the sensual brilliance of the reign of Charles II, the zest for life that often plunged over into excess, and the humanity and enjoyment of that pleasure-seeking Court.

SELECT BIBLIOGRAPHY

An alphabetical list of works referred to in the notes on pages 213–228 with a key to the abbreviations used. Details of works which are only mentioned once or twice are given in full in the notes.

ANDREWS, ALLEN: *The Royal Whore* (1971).

ASHLEY, MAURICE: *Charles II, the Man and the Statesman* (1971).

—*James II* (1977).

BARBOUR, VIOLET: *Henry Bennet, Earl of Arlington* (1914).

BOD.: Bodleian Library, Ashmole Mss. Carte Mss., Clarendon Mss.

BOSWELL, ELEANORE: *The Restoration Court Stage, 1660–1702* (1966).

BOYER, ABEL: *Annals of the Reign of Queen Anne* (1722).

BRAMSTON, SIR JOHN: *Autobiography* (1845).

BROWNING, ANDREW: *Thomas Osborne, Earl of Danby and Duke of Leeds 1632–1712*, 3 vols. (1944–51).

BRYANT, ARTHUR: *The Letters, Speeches and Declarations of King Charles II* (1935).

—*Charles II* (1932).

BUCKINGHAM, GEORGE 2ND DUKE OF: *Works*, 2 vols. (1721).

BURNET, GILBERT: *History of his Own Time*, 6 vols. (1833).

CSPD: *Calendar of State Papers Domestic.*

CSPV: *Calendar of State Papers Venetian.*

CARTE, THOMAS: *The Life of James, Duke of Ormonde*, 6 vols. (1851).

CHAPMAN, HESTER: *Great Villiers: a Study of the 2nd Duke of Buckingham* (1949).

CHESTERFIELD, PHILIP 2ND EARL OF: *Letters* (1829).

CHRISTIE, W. D.: *A Life of Anthony Ashley Cooper, 1st Earl of Shaftesbury* (1871).

CHURCHILL, WINSTON S.: *Marlborough, his Life and Times* 2 vols. (1947).

CLARENDON, EDWARD HYDE 1ST EARL OF: *A History of the Rebellion*, ed. W. D. Macray, 8 vols. (1888).

—*Life, written by himself and a Continuation of his Story of the Grand Rebellion*, 3 vols. (1827).

—CCSP *Calendar of Clarendon State Papers*, ed. W. D. Macray, H. O. Coxe, F. H. Routledge and Sir Charles Firth, 4 vols. (1876–1932).

—CSP *Calendar of Clarendon Papers*, ed. W. H. Bliss, W. D. Macray, and O. Ogle, 3 vols. (1867–86).

CLARK, G. N.: *The Later Stuarts, 1660–1714* (1961).

CLARKE, J. S.: *The Life of James II*, 2 vols. (1816).

COOK, AURELIAN: *Titus Britannicus* (1685).

CREWE, NATHANIEL: *Memoirs* (1895).

DALRYMPLE, SIR JOHN: *Memoirs of Great Britain and Ireland*, 3 vols. (1790).
DAVIES, GODFREY: *The Early Stuarts 1603–1660* (1959).
—*The Restoration of Charles II, 1658–1660* (1955).
DNB: *Dictionary of National Biography*.
Dorney Court Muniments.
DOWNES, JOHN: *Roscius Anglicanus, or an Historical Review of the Stage*, ed. Montague Summers (1928).
ELLIS, G. A.: *The Ellis Correspondence*, 2 vols. (1829).
Essex Papers, ed. O. Airy and C. E. Pike, 2 vols. (1890, 1913).
EVELYN, JOHN: *Diary and Correspondence*, ed. E. S. de Beer, 6 vols. (1955).
FEILING, KEITH: *British Foreign Policy 1660–72* (1968).
—*A History of the Tory Party 1640–1714* (1950).
FITZROY, A. W.: *Henry, Duke of Grafton* (1921).
FORNERON, H.; *Louise de Kéroualle* (1887).
FOXCROFT, H. C.: *The Life and Letters of George Savile 1st Marquis of Halifax*, 2 vols. (1898).
GRAMONT, COMTE DE (ANTHONY HAMILTON): *Memoirs*, trans. Peter Quennell (1930).
GREENE, GRAHAM: *Lord Rochester's Monkey* (1974).
GREY, ANCHITEL: *Debates of the House of Commons 1667–1694*, 10 vols. (1763, 1769).
HMC: Historical Manuscripts Commission Reports.
HALEY, K. D. H.: *The First Earl of Shaftesbury* (1968).
HARDACRE, PAUL: *The Royalists during the Puritan Revolution* (1956).
HARTMANN, C. H.: *Charles II and Madame* (1934).
—*Clifford of the Cabal* (1937).
—*The King's Friend* (1951).
—*The King my Brother* (1954).
—*La Belle Stuart* (1924).
—*The Vagabond Duchess* (1926).
Hatton Correspondence, ed. E. M. Thompson, 2 vols. (1878).
JESSE, J. H.: *Memoirs of the Court of England during the Reign of the Stuarts*, 6 vols. (1901).
JUSSERAND, J—J.: *A French Ambassador at the Court of Charles II* (1892).
KENNET, WHITE: *A Complete History of England*, 3 vols. (1719).
KENYON, J. P. *Robert Spencer, Earl of Sunderland* (1958).
—*The Popish Plot* (1972).
—*The Stuarts* (1966).
LEE, MAURICE D.: *The Cabal* (1965).
LISTER, T. H.: *The Life and Administration of Edward, 1st Earl of Clarendon*, 3 vols. (1838).
LUTTRELL, NARCISSUS: *A Brief Historical Relation of State Affairs*, 6 vols. (1857).
MANLEY, MARY DE LA RIVIÈRE: *The New Atlantis*, 2 vols. (1720).
MARVELL, ANDREW: *Poems and Letters*, ed. H. M. Margoliouth, 2 vols. (1971).
MILLER, JOHN: *Popery and Politics in England, 1660–1688* (1973).
MILWARD, JOHN: *Diary*, ed. Caroline Robbins (1938).
MORDAUNT, JOHN: *Letter Book 1658–60* (1945).
NICHOLAS, EDWARD: *Correspondence*, ed. G. F. Warner, 3 vols. (1886–97).
OGG, DAVID: *England in the Reign of Charles II*, 2 vols. (1956).
OLDMIXON, JOHN: The Critical History of England, 2 vols. (1728–30).

OLIVER, H. J.: *Sir Robert Howard* (1963).

PEPYS, SAMUEL: *Diary*, ed. Robert Latham and William Matthews, 9 vols. (1970–76).

POAS: *Poems on Affairs of State 1660–1688*, 4 vols. (1963–8).

PRIDEAUX, HUMPHREY: *Letters*, ed. (1875).

PRO: Public Record Office.

RERESBY, SIR JOHN: *Memoirs*, ed. Andrew Browning (1936).

ROCHE, T. W. E.: *A Pineapple for the King* (1971).

SAVILE, HENRY: *Correspondence* (1858).

SCOTT, EVA: *The King in Exile* (1904).

—*The Travels of the King* (1907).

SECRET SERVICES: *Moneys received and paid for the Secret Services of Charles II and James II 1678–88* (1851).

SERGEANT, PHILIP: *My Lady Castlemaine* (1912).

SIDNEY, HENRY: *Diary*, ed. R. W. Blencowe, 2 vols. (1843).

SINGER, W. S.: *Correspondence of Henry Hyde, 2nd Earl of Clarendon, 2 vols.* (1828).

STEINMANN, G. S.: *A Memoir of Barbara, Duchess of Cleveland* (1871).

STRICKLAND, AGNES: *Lives of the Queens of England*, vol. V (1854).

SYLVESTER, MATTHEW: *Reliquiae Baxterianae* (1696).

THURLOE, JOHN: *A Collection of the State Papers*, ed. Thomas Birch, 7 vols. (1742).

UNDERDOWN, DAVID: *Royalist Conspiracy in England 1649–1660* (1960).

VAN LANNEP, WILLIAM: *The London Stage, 1660–1800*, vol. I (1963).

WILLIAMSON, JOSEPH: *Letters,* ed. W. D. Christie, 2 vols. (1874).

WILSON, J. H.: *All the King's Ladies* (1958).

—*A Rake and his Times* (1954).

WOOD, ANTHONY: *Life and Times*, ed. Andrew Clark, 2 vols. (1892).

NOTES

Chapter 1: THE SILKEN HEIRS

Page

1
The duel: HMC de Lisle, VI, 200.
Lord Grandison: Clarendon, *Life*, I, 120.
The Villiers ladies: D. H. Willson, *King James VI and I* (1956), 426.

2–3
The Baynings: CSPD 1639, 539; Lawrence Stone, *The Crisis of the Aristocracy 1558–1641* (1965), 85, 120, 355, 497–8, 535; *Death Repealed by a Thankful Memorial sent from Christ Church in Oxford celebrating the noble deserts of the Right Honourable the late Lord Viscount Bayning of Sudbury* (1638), 15, 21.

3
The christening: Sergeant, 5, from the Register of St Margaret's Church.

4
The King goes north: Clarendon, *Life*, I, 129.
The coach mares: Harry Verney, *The Verneys of Claydon* (1968), 31.

4–5
Grandison's character: Clarendon, *Rebellion*, IV, 151–2.
His military exploits: ibid, III, 259, 343, 610, 628, 631; G. Goodwin, *The Civil War in Hampshire* (1882), 24, 60; HMC 5th Report, 191; John, Vicars, *Parliamentary Chronicle* (1644), 227, et seq; C. V. Wedgwood, *The King's War 1641–1647* (1958), 125, 153; Peter Young, *Edgehill 1642* (1967), 88, 114, 182–3, 185, 210–11.

5
The King at Oxford: HMC Ormonde, II, 406–10.

6
The siege of Bristol: Eliot Warburton, *Memoirs of Prince Rupert and the Cavaliers* (1849), II, 233–4, 236–7; Wedgwood, op. cit., 232–6.

Chapter 2: THE TRIBE OF FORTUNE

7
Francis Villiers: Chapman, 41; HMC de Lisle, VI, 573; Marvell, I, 329–332.

8
Music during the interregnum: Ian Spink, *English Song* (1974), 96–7.
Barbara arrives in town: Boyer, 48.

9
The tribe of fortune: John Forster, *Sir John Eliot* (1865), I, 377.
Grandison in Dunkirk: CSP, III, 357, September 13, 1657.
The world of espionage: CCSP, III, 87, 263.

10
Lady Anne Hamilton: John Anderson, *Memoirs of the House of Hamilton* (1825), 146; Rosalind K. Marshall, *The Days of Duchess Anne* (1973), 25–6, 105.
The 2nd Duke of Buckingham: Madame d'Aulnoy, *Memoirs of the Court of England* (1707), 13–14; Kenyon, *The Stuarts*, 50; Reresby, 24.

Chapter 3: LOVE ON LUDGATE HILL

Page

11   *Chesterfield's experiences :* BL Add. Mss. 19, 253, ff. 206–9.

12   *Cromwell rejects kingship :* CCSP, III, 269; Thurloe, VI, 200.
      Frances Cromwell : BL Add. Mss. 19, 253, ff. 203–4; Hardacre, 121; HMC 5th Report, 177, 183; Thurloe, V, 146.

12–13   *Buckingham's marriage :* CSP, III, 171, 373; Marvell, I, 84, 'Upon Appleton House', lines 705–6; Thurloe, VI, 580, 616.

14–15   *Chesterfield and Barbara :* Chesterfield, 80–105.

15–16   *Roger Palmer :* Boyer, 48.

Chapter 4: MRS PALMER

17   *Royalists in 1658 :* Underdown, 230–1.
      They rarely confer together : CCSP, III, 359, September 12, 1657.
      Richard Cromwell succeeds his father : CSP, III, 407–8.
      The Great Trust : Davies, *Restoration*, 125–6.

18   *Barbara's marriage :* Andrews, 13.

19   *Narcissus :* BL Add. Mss. 19, 253, f. 203.

19–20   *Chesterfield in gaol :* ibid, f. 46; CSPD 1659–60, 164, 186, 240; Mordaunt, 19, 23, 70, 78, 88.
      Royalists in prison : ibid, 36, 60.
      Brodrick works up support : Bod. Rawlinson, A 259, f. 43, C 179, ff. 206–34.
      The King's instructions : Mordaunt, 157–60.
      The situation improves : ibid, 77, 174.

21   *Brodrick and Palmer :* CCSP, IV, 552, 557, 561, 585, 608, 621–2, 655; Bod. CSP, III, 665; Bod. Clarendon Mss, 69, f. 101, 71, f. 237; Underdown, 304, from Brodrick Mss. I, 28, 33–8.

Chapter 5: OUR COUSIN VILLIERS

23   *Smallpox :* Bod. Clarendon, Mss, 69, ff. 129–30, 21 February 1660.

24   *Chesterfield's duel :* Mordaunt, 166.
      Paris : Chesterfield, 111-12; Alan Fea, *Some Beauties of the 17th Century* (1906), 171.
      Lady Byron : Pepys, VIII, 182.
      Lucy Walter : CCSP, III, 341; Clarendon, *Life*, II, 252; Thurloe, V, 160–1, 178.

25   *The exiled Cavaliers :* Nicholas, III, 92.
      Proposed marriages for the King : ibid, 54, 68, IV, 112; Scott, *Travels of the King*, 95, 429, 436.

26   *The resolution of the Commons :* Commons Journals, VIII, 8; CSP, III, 737.
      Rise in the price of commodities : CSPV 1657–9, 197, 284.
      Lambert's escape : Pepys, I, 109, 15 April 1660.
      May Day : ibid, 121,
      The calamities of 18 years : CCSP, IV, 687.

27   *The Lord Mayor and the milkmaid :* ibid, 671.
      No cipher needed : ibid, 685.
      Whitehall prepared : CSP, III, 739–40; Davies, *Restoration*, 346
      John Mordaunt's misfortune : Mordaunt, 164.

Page
27–8   *The return:* Clarendon, *Life*, I, 327; CSP, III, 742; Evelyn, III, 246;
        HMC Le Fleming, 25; Lister, II, 10.
28   *The first night:* Boyer, 48; Jesse, IV, 244; Kennett, III, 164–5; Mrs
        Jameson, *Memoirs of the Beauties of the Court of Charles II* (1838), I,
        71–2; Rugge's Diurnal, BL Add. Mss. 10, ff. 98–102; Steinmann, 21–3.

Chapter 6: THE RETURN OF THE KING

29   *Mrs Monck:* CCSP, IV, 644; CSP, III, 739.
30   *Petitioners and place-seekers:* CSPD 1659–60, 404–31; Clarendon, *Life*,
        I, 323–4, 326, 332; Hardacre, 149, 152–3; Mordaunt, 164.
31   *'We did both sinfully entangle':* Scott, *The King in Exile*, 162.
        'Those who murmured': Lister, II, 36.
        Buckingham: Reresby, 24.
32   *Roger Palmer's appeal for preferment:* CSPD 1660–1, 104; 1661–2, 165,
        303.
        The Howards: ibid, 1660–1, 55; 1661–2, 236, 256, 270, 277; Davies,
        Restoration, 133n; DNB; Oliver, 7, 11, 38–9.
33   *The King's easy nature:* Burnet, I, 169.
        Parties on the river: Gramont, 143.
        'An abundance of gallantry': Evelyn, III, 249.
        Music party at the Palmers: Pepys, I, 199.
        The rope dancers: Boswell, 350; DNB Jacob Hall.
        Italian opera company: Boswell, 114–15.
34   *'We see what he can do':* Scott, *Travels of the King*, 423.
        The army is disbanded: Lister, II, 30–1.
        The King's appeal to the Commons: Bryant, *Letters*, 103.
        The death of the Duke of Gloucester: Clarendon, *Life*, I, 392.
        Anne Hyde: Burnet, I, 303; CSP, III, 274–5; Clarendon, *Life*, I,
        371–385; Lister, II, 68; HMC Report 5, 158.
34–5   *The Duke of York and Barbara Palmer:* Pepys, I, 265–6.
35   *The King's proposed marriage:* CSP, III, Supplement, vii; Clarendon,
        Life, I, 489, 492, 507; HMC Report 5, 158; Lister, III, 128–9, 133,
        138–9; Nicholas, III, 113, 118.
36   *Misfortune in the royal family:* Marvell, II, 13, 17.
        The January rising: Burnet, I, 287–8; Cook, 242; Lister, II, 62–4;
        Marvell, II, 16; Reresby, 24.
36–7   *The new Parliament:* Parliamentary History, IV, 178–81, 194–200.
        The King's speech: Bryant, *Letters*, 11–12, 8 May 1661.
        The Portuguese Ambassador leaves: CSPV 1661–4, 6; Pepys, II, 128.

Chapter 7: THE JOVIAL CREW

38   *The birth of Anne Palmer:* BL Add. Mss. 7006, ff. 171–6.
        Pepys at the theatre: Pepys, II, 80, 139, 164, 174.
39   *Women actors:* HMC Rep 5, 158; Wilson, *All the King's Ladies*, 6, from
        Thomas Jordan, *Loyal Poesie* (1664); Wood, I, 405–6.
        The vices of the Court: Burnet, I, 313; Evelyn, III, 308; Pepys, II, 50,
        156, 167.
40   *Clarendon's speech:* Lister, II, 60.

Page

40   *The King's intention of sticking to his wife :* Fane, Commonplace Book, II, 170–77.
     'Our most religious King' : Burnet, I, 332.
41   *The Earl of Worcester:* Bryant, *Letters*, 98.
     Sir Robert Howard: Oliver, 38–9.
42   *The warrant for the title :* Burnet, I, 65–6; Clarendon, *Life*, II, 170–77.

Chapter 8: THE QUEEN AND THE ENCHANTRESS

43   *The King writes to Catherine :* Bryant, *Letters*, 115, 2 July 1661.
     Factions at Court : Pepys, III, 15, 68, 82.
44   *Lady Castlemaine and the King :* ibid, 87–8.
     The Queen on board ship : ibid, 90.
     Sarah : ibid, 251.
     The Queen arrives : Bryant, *Letters*, 125–8; CSPV 1661–4, 137, 143–4.
45   *Her looks :* HMC Le Fleming, 28; Evelyn, III, 320–1.
     Lady Suffolk : CSPD 1661–2, 329.
     Uncertainty of the King's affections : Chesterfield, 117–20; Reresby, 40–1.
46   *If my nose be handsome :* Pepys, III, 277.
     Lady Castlemaine's smocks : ibid, 87.
     Roger Castlemaine's misfortunes : Boyer, 39.
     Charles Palmer : Pepys, III, 146–7.
     The flight to Richmond : ibid, 147.
46–7 *Her husband's bond :* Dorney Court Muniments, 362.
47–50 *The quarrel over Lady Castlemaine's appointment :* CSPV 1661–4, 171–2; Clarendon, *Life*, II, 168, 173–4, 180–1; Strickland, V, 528.
50   *The Portugal music :* CSPV 1661–4, 62, 164, 185.
     The Queen's arrival in London : Evelyn, III, 333; Pepys, III, 175, 23 August 1662.
     'The insolency of the dame' : Bod. Carte Mss. f. 9.
51   *'The happiest man in the world' :* Bryant, *Letters*, 127.
     'Unsanctified enjoyments' : BL Add. Mss. 19, 253, f. 6.
     Father Talbot : Carte, IV, 368–9; Bod. Carte Mss. ff. 22, 25.

Chapter 9: THE HOUSE IN KING STREET

53   *Hyde's attitude :* CSP, III, 65; Burnet, I, 172.
     He is accused of working for Thurloe : Thurloe, VI, 835; CCSP, IV, 627.
     The book of inscriptions : ibid, III, 123–4.
53–4 *Hyde's difficulties in exile :* ibid, 195; CCSP, IV, 637.
54   *The King and the Council :* Ogg, I, 189–90.
     The King 'new-chafed' : Clarendon, *Life*, II, 193.
     The King's letter : Bryant, *Letters*, 129–30.
55   *Clarendon's head on the stake :* Carte, IV, 152; Bod. Carte Mss. 32, f. 25.
     Elizabeth Weaver : Pepys, IX, 19.
     The King's friends : Lister, III, 222; Pepys, III, 245, 302.
55–6 *O'Neill's wife :* Bod. Carte Mss. 32, f. 9.
56   *The Countess of Penalva :* ibid, ff. 14–15, 23.
     The high game : Pepys, III, 237.
     The Earl of Bristol : Clarendon, *Life*, II, 256.

Page

Bennet's nomination as Ambassador : Barbour, 53–4; le Comte d'Estrades, *Lettres, Mémoires et Négociations* (1743), I, 232.

Two parties : CSPV 1661–4, 172.

57   *Montagu's position :* Bod. Carte Mss. 32, f. 120.

The ball in King Street : Pepys, III, 215, 6 October 1662.

58   *Buckingham's character :* Gramont, 140; Burnet, I, 174–6.

His religious standpoint : Lee, 162–3; Fane, Commonplace Book, 164.

Church music : Evelyn, III, 347; Pepys, I, 195.

The King's religious attitude : Burnet, I, 169.

59   *Meetings at Lord Manchester's lodgings :* Feiling, *Tory Party*, 128.

Lady Castlemaine supports Presbyterian clergy : Bod. Carte Mss. 32, f. 3; Haley, 163.

Bennet's character : Bod. Carte Mss. 32, ff. 15–26; CSPV 1661–4, 203; Clarendon, *Life*, II, 230; Pepys, II, 282.

59–60   *The office of the King's Privy Purse :* G. E. Aylmer, *The King's Servants* (1961), 35.

60   *Sir Charles Berkeley :* Clarendon, *Life*, II, 229; Hartmann, *The King's Friend*, 7; Pepys, III, 282.

Sir William Morrice : Lister, II, 8.

60   *Sir Edward Nicholas :* Clarendon, *Life*, I, 319–20; CSPV 1661–4, 203; Lister, III, 223.

61   *Discontent at Court :* Bod. Carte Mss. 32, f. 68.

Rumours of pregnancy : ibid, f. 43; CSPV 1661–4, 184; Pepys, III, 191, 217.

The Castlemaines are estranged : ibid, III, 248.

Clarendon's economies : CSPV 1661–4, 197–8, 206, 217; Lister, III, 238–9, 244; Pepys, III, 260, 302.

The young men get uppermost : ibid, 227.

The Declaration of Indulgence : Feiling, *Tory Party*, 128–9; Miller, 51–66, 101.

The Chancellor's fall prophesied : Pepys, III, 290; IV, 123, 137.

62   *His gout :* Burnet, I, 172; Clarendon, *Life*, I, 231; CCSP, III, 287.

Henry Jermyn : HMC Le Fleming, 29.

The King bewitched by Castlemaine : Pepys, III, 282, 15 December 1662.

Chapter 10: THE COMMITTEE

63   *New Year 1663 :* Bryant, *Letters*, 137; CSPV 1661–4, 221, 223, 250; Evelyn, III, 346; Gramont, 171; *Jusserand*, 91; Lister, III, 239; Pepys, III, 300–1; PRO 31/3/110, f. 499.

64   *Declining moral standards at Court :* Pepys, IV, 113, 134, 271.

Lady Chesterfield : Gramont, 156–7, 172, 198–9; Hatton, I, 64; Pepys, III, 248; IV, 19.

65   *Lady Castlemaine's influence with the King :* Pepys, III, 289; IV, 1, 57.

Her lodgings : ibid, 112, 164; Lorenzo Magalotti, Travels of Cosmo III (1829), 369.

The Wild Gallant : Pepys, IV, 56; Dryden, *Works*, vol. I, 45–6; vol. VIII, 3–91.

66   *Lady Gerard :* ibid, 68.

The Garter ceremony : ibid, 112; Bod. Carte Mss. 32, f. 268.

The Committee : Sir Robert Howard, *Four New Plays* (1662) or *Five New Plays* (1692).

Page
67   *The King and Parliament in 1663 :* Bryant, *Letters,* 139, 142, 144; Miller, 101; Pepys, IV, 205–6.

67–8   *Bristol and the impeachment :* Clarendon, *Life,* II, 258–263; CSPV 1661–4, 255–6; Haley, 168; PRO 31/3/112, ff. 35, 78–9, 106, 110–11; Pepys, IV, 222–4.

68   *The warrant :* CSPD 1663–4, 160.
          The Lady loses her hold : Pepys, IV, 182, 222; Bod. Carte Mss. 32 ff. 597–8, 708, 716.
          The Committee and Frances Stuart : Gramont, 110–12, 137–40; Hartmann, *La Belle Stuart,* 29 et seq; Pepys, IV, 37–8, 48, 366.

69   *All the tricks of Aretin :* Jusserand, 89–90; Pepys, IV, 136–7, 213.

70   *The Lady decamps to Richmond :* Hartmann, *La Belle Stuart,* 38–40; Pepys, IV, 238; PRO 31/3/112.
          The Duke of Buckingham's party : Pepys, IV, 238.
          Berkeley fetches the King from the Council : ibid, 255–6.
          Improvement in the Queen's looks : ibid, 177, 216, 272; Bod. Carte Mss. f. 405, 15 May, 1663.
          The Duchess of Richmond's party : Hartmann, *La Belle Stuart,* 50–1.
          The party on July 13 1663 ; Pepys, IV, 230.

71   *The visit to Oxford :* Bryant, *Charles II,* 231; Jusserand, 92–3; Hartmann, *The King's Friend,* 106; Wood, I, 494.
          The Queen at Tunbridge Wells : Bod. Carte Mss. f. 598; Jusserand, 190.

72   *The chine of beef :* Pepys, IV, 334.
          The Queen's illness : ibid, 343, 348, 352, 357; Bryant, *Letters,* 147–9; PRO 31/3/112, ff. 187, 189, 206, 234.

73   *'Is the King above or below?' :* Pepys, V, 20.
          Lady Castlemaine's amours : ibid, V, 21.

74   *'How loose the Court is' :* ibid, IV, 371.

Chapter 11: THE NEW MANAGERS

75   *Lady Castlemaine's conversion*: Clarendon, Life II, 219; Oldmixon, II, 577; Pepys, IV, 431.

75–6   *The King's religious views :* Bryant, *Letters,* 109, 152; Jusserand, 95; Pepys, V, 12.

76   *The new managers :* Barbour, 78–80; Feiling, *Tory Party,* 116; Haley, 170, states that there is no surviving evidence of a political combination against the Chancellor.

77   *The King and Frances Stuart :* Pepys, V, 20.
          Lady Castlemaine at the Playhouse : ibid, 33.
          The calash : Gramont, 144–6.
          The Queen's bedchamber : Pepys, V, 188.

78   *The King plays the good husband :* Bryant, *Letters,* 158.
          His illness : ibid, 161; Jusserand, 87; Pepys, V, 126.
          Portraits : R. B. Beckett, *Lely* (1951), Pls, 78, 90, 100, 101; Thomas Hearne, *Reliquiae Hernianae,* ed. P. Bliss (1869), II, 57–8; Oliver Millar, *Sir Peter Lely* (1978), pls 38, 45; David Piper, *Catalogue of Seventeenth-Century Portraits in the National Portrait Gallery* (1963); Pepys, III, 113, 230; V, 200, 209, 254.

78–9   *Edward Montagu's flirtation with the Queen :* Boyer, 46; Pepys, V, 153.

Page

The birth of Charlotte, and the incident in the Park: Jusserand, 85, 90, 229; Pepys, V, 245, 294; Sergeant, 114.

80   *The King's speech*: Bryant, *Letters*, 170–1.
      The Duke returns from Portsmouth: Pepys V, 339, 7 December 1664.

81   *The Commission of Prizes*: Clarendon, *Life*, II, 341; Haley, 175; PRO Shaftesbury Papers, XL, 39, 41.
      Talk of triumphs and victories: Barbour, 83.
      The masque: Evelyn, III, 397; Pepys, VI, 29; Bryant, *Letters*, 177.
      The luxury of the times: Pepys, VI, 41.

82   *The Duke and the fleet*: Clarendon, *Life*, II, 353.
      The King's dislike of disputes: Bryant, *Letters*, 151.
      His French: Jusserand, 143.
      The Ambassadors: CSPV 1664–6, 94, 95, 110, 115, 125; Haley, 178–9; Hartmann, *La Belle Stuart*, 78–81; Jusserand, 233–4.

83   *Molina's feast*: Jusserand, 152.
      'Incense': Hartmann, *La Belle Stuart*, 81.
      Fitzharding's house: Clarendon, *Life*, II, 358; Pepys VI, 39, n.
      His wife: Hartmann, *The King's Friend*, 132.
      Castlemaine in England: Pepys, VI, 41, 55–6; Sergeant, 118–19.
      Buckingham takes offence: Clarendon, *Life*, II, 356–7.

84   *Lady Castlemaine asleep in the Park*: Pepys, VI, 60, 19 March 1665.
      The rings: Extracts from the Ledgers of Alderman Edward Backwell Barker, Williams and Glyn's Bank Ltd.
      The Duchess of York in a darkened room: CSPV 1664–6, 59.

Chapter 12: A CATALOGUE OF DISASTERS

85   *The naval battle, June 1665*: Ashley, *James II*, 81; CSPV 1664–6, 137; Evelyn, III, 410, 412; Pepys, VI, 116, 120, 128–9.
      The death of Falmouth: ibid., 123.

86   *Duke of York to stay ashore*; Clarendon, *Life*, II, 399.

86–7 *The plague*: Walter G. Bell, *The Great Plague in London* (1924); CSPV 1664–6, 142, 161; Evelyn, III, 417–18; Pepys, VI, 120, 124, 128, 140, 205, 207, 210, 233.

86   *'The finest rose'*: Jusserand, 151.
      Ladies dressed as men: Pepys, VI, 172.

87   *The Duke goes to York*: Clarendon, *Life*, II, 406; Reresby, 55.

87–8 *The Court at Salisbury*: CSPV 1664–6, 209; Hartmann, *La Belle Stuart*, 85–7; HMC Rep 6, 336; Pepys, VI, 109.

88   *Pepys's dream*: ibid., 191.
      Oxford, 1665–6: Clarendon, *Life*, II, 425; Wood, II, 46, 48–9.

89   *'I had not such a brutal appetite'*: Bryant, *Letters*, 187.
      Preachers in London: Burnet, I, 411.
      The Five Mile Act: Feiling, *Tory Party*, 131.
      Sandwich's fall: Clarendon, *Life*, II, 466–9; Pepys, VI, 301–2, 321; VII, 26.
      William Coventry: Clarendon, *Life*, II, 255–6, 460.

89–90 *Courtship*: Pepys, VII, 26, 52.

90   *Birth of George*: Official Register of St John Baptist, Oxford, quoted Sergeant, 130–1; Wood, II, 53, 67–8; G. C. Brodrick, *Memorials of Merton College*.

Page

90–1   *The King and Lady Castlemaine :* Pepys, VII, 8.
90   *French unpopularity :* Jusserand, 172.
       The Queen's sore throat : HMC Hastings, II, 146.
       Rumoured miscarriage : HMC Rep 6, 337, 15 February 1667
91   *Work at Hampton Court :* BL Harleian Mss. 1658, f. 129, quoted Andrews, 98.
       The jewelry : CSPD 1665–6, 155; 1666–7, 171, 415.
       Lady Denham and Henry Brouncker : Pepys, VII, 159.
92   *The fire in Lady Castlemaine's lodgings :* ibid., V, 27.
92–3   *Naval battles, June–July 1666 :* Evelyn, III, 437, 441, 445–6, 448; Pepys, VII, 160, 213.
       The quarrel : HMC Rep 6, 485.
93   *The fire of London :* Walter G. Bell, *The Great Fire of London* (1920); Burnet, I, 420; Evelyn, III, 450, 465; HMC Hastings, II, 369; Roche, 37.
       The Duke's lack of concern : Pepys, VII, 320.
       Persian fashions : ibid., 162, 335.
93–4   *Frances Stuart :* ibid., 324, 335, 384.
94   *Lady Castlemaine :* ibid., 324, 404, 409.

Chapter 13: THE FALL OF THE CHANCELLOR

95   *The Duke of Buckingham :* Browning, I, 42; Clarendon, *Life*, III, 145, 147, 237–8, 251; CSPD 1667–8, 159, 258–9; HMC Le Fleming, 44–6; Reresby, 64, 66.
96   *The Irish Cattle Bill :* Haley, 187–92; Milward, 9, 14–15, 54–5, 165; Pepys, VII, 414–15.
       The Proviso : Oliver, 131; Pepys, VII, 399–400.
97   *Castlemaine and the Catholique Apology :* CSPD 1666–7, 171, 361, 415.
       Banishment of Killigrew : Pepys, VII, 336–7; HMC Rep 7, 485.
       Supper at Lady Castlemaine's, January 1667 : The Correspondence of Anne, Viscountess Conway 1642–1684 ed. Marjorie Hope Nicolson (1930), 259.
98   *The betrayal of Frances Stuart :* Gramont, 315–16; Hartmann *La Belle Stuart*, 108; Pepys, VIII, 183–4.
       Money from the Privy Purse : ibid., 324.
99   *Ormonde and Phoenix Lodge :* Carte, IV, 153.
       Lady Castlemaine and the French : Forneron, 21–2, 3 April 1667.
       The Queen's dowry : Hartmann, *La Belle Stuart*, 70.
100   *Audley End :* HMC Rep 6, 337.
       Criticism of the King : Pepys, VIII, 288; Crewe, 8.
       The ladies lie longest in bed : Pepys, VIII, 49, n.
101   *The black boy :* ibid., 33.
       Peace negotiations : Feiling, *Foreign Policy*, 214–16.
101–2 *Clarendon's difficulties :* Burnet, I, 459–62; Clarendon, *Life*, III, 282; Pepys, VIII, 218, 222, 269, 283, 343; Sylvester, III, 20.
102   *The Dutch in the Medway :* Ashley, *Charles II*, 138–9; Pepys, VIII, 255, 282, 291; Reresby, 68.
       The need to call a Parliament : Feiling, *Tory Party*, 119; Pepys, VIII, 292–3; Savile, 15.

Page
103   *Buckingham*: CSPD 1666–7, 428, 431; Haley, 187–9; Reresby, 64, 66;
        Wilson, *A Rake and his Times*, 71.
103–4   *News from Florence*: Bod. Carte Mss. 32, f. 520.
104–5   *The quarrel*: Pepys, VIII, 355, 366, 368, 376, 431–2.
105–6   *Lady Harvey*: ibid., 366, n.
106–7   *The fall of Clarendon*: Barbour, 111–12; Bramston, 256; Burnet, I,
        455–7; Clarke, I, 428–9; Crewe, 9; Pepys, VIII, 404, 409; Marvell, I,
        171, 'Last Instructions', lines 927–942.

Chapter 14: THE RIVALS

108   *The situation after Clarendon's fall*: Pepys, VIII, 404, 409, 416, 417,
        431–2, 447, 525.
108–9   *Bridgeman*: Burnet, I, 464.
109   *Buckingham*. Barbour, 113, n; Reresby, 66.
        Coventry: Foxcroft, I, 54; Pepys, VIII, 415, 2 September 1667.
        Brouncker: ibid., 415–16; Clarendon, *Life*, III, 293.
110   *The King and the Duke*: Pepys, VIII, 431, 447; Clarke, I, 433.
        The King and Queen dine in public: HMC Le Fleming, 52.
        The Lady visits Althorp: Savile, 22.
        The Sunderlands: Kenyon, *Sunderland*, 8–9; Churchill, I, 210–12.
111   *Bristol*: Pepys, VIII, 506, 533.
        Buckingham's activities, autumn, 1667: Barbour, 115; Burnet, I, 464;
        Browning, I, 57–60; CSPD 1667–8, 258–9; Carte, IV, 321–5; Clarendon,
        Life, III, 309–332; Pepys, VIII, 534; Wilson, *A Rake and his Times*, 88.
112   *Clarendon banished*: Milward, 165.
        The Undertakers: Pepys, VIII.
113   *The return of Frances*: Bryant, *Letters*, 212.
114   *The theatre*: Evelyn, III, 465–6; Pepys, VIII, 147.
        Moll Davies: Burnet, I, 483–4; Flecknoe, *Epigrams of all Sorts*; Pepys,
        IX, 19.
115   *The Indian Emperor*: ibid., 23; van Lannep, I, 127–8.
        Horace: BL Add. Mss. 36916, f. 62; Evelyn, III, 504; van Lannep, I,
        128–9.
        Lady Castlemaine still supreme: Pepys, IX, 27.
115–16 *Nell Gwynn*: Findlater, 20–7; Pepys, VIII, 91, 129, 334, 402, 503, 525.
116   *Lady Castlemaine and Charles Hart*: Colley Cibber, *Apology*, ed. R. W.
        Lowe (1889), II, 71–5; DNB Charles Hart; Pepys, IX, 155–6.

Chapter 15: THE WHORES' PETITION

118   *Sheldon*: Burnet, I, 463; Marvell, I, 168, 'Last Instructions' lines
        813–14; Pepys, VIII, 533 n.
        The Bill for Comprehension: Milward, 179.
        The return of Bristol: Pepys, IX, 120.
119   *Riots of apprentices*: ibid., 129.
119–21 *The Petition and the Answer*: Andrews, 131–3; Sergeant 161–2; Stein-
        mann 101–11 (in full); Evelyn, III, 507; Pepys, IX, 153.
121   *The 'rolling out' of officers*: Oliver, 150.
        The grant from the Post Office: CTB, II, 264, 310, 316, 375, 446.

Page

Berkshire House : ibid., 310, 316, 375; E. Beresford Chancellor, *Memorials of St James's Street* (1922), 30, 119; Evelyn, III, 573.

The pleasure boat : BL Add. Mss. 36916, f. 109.

Moll Davies : ibid., f. 102. Moll did not in fact bear a child until 1673 when she gave birth to the King's daughter, Lady Mary Tudor, later to become Countess of Derwentwater. See also, Pepys, IX, 219.

122   *The Queen's miscarriage :* BL Add. Mss. 36916, ff. 95–6; HMC Rutland, II, ii, 10; Hartmann, *The King my Brother,* 216–17; Pepys, IX, 191, May 9, 1668.

Lady Castlemaine out of favour : ibid., 90, 219.

The Richmonds : ibid., 90, 205, 257; BL Add. Mss. 36916, f. 102.

The Countess of Suffolk : ibid., f. 109.

'Ill more in mind than body' : Hartmann, *The King my Brother,* 216.

The King's speech : Pepys, IX, 192, May 9 1668.

Buckingham's behaviour : ibid., 294, 302, 373.

123   *The King follows his own judgment :* Hartmann, *Charles II and Madame,* 218.

The new Treasurers : BL Add. Mss. 36916, ff. 128–9, 133; Oliver, 167–8; Pepys, IX, 341, 346.

Lady Mordaunt : HMC Rutland, II, ii, 10.

124   *Buckingham and Arlington :* Bulstrode, I, 61–7; BL Add. Mss. 36916, f. 114.

The gift to Arlington : DNB Arlington, from Echard.

Arlington and the ladies : Barbour, 153, 159.

124–5   *The Country Gentleman :* BL Add. Mss. 36916, f. 128; Pepys, IX, 462–3, 471.

125   *Coventry retires :* ibid., 470

126   *The secret meeting :* Ashley, *James II,* 97–8; Clarke, I, 440–2, 629–30. Maurice Lee (*Cabal,* 102), is one of those who doubts whether the meeting ever took place. Ashley discusses the authenticity of J. S. Clarke's *Life of James II* in the appendix to his *James II,* 296–301.

Chapter 16: A PARTY AT DEPTFORD

127–8   *The French Ambassador and the ladies :* Forneron, 22–6, 49.

127   *Jane Roberts :* Burnet, I, 475, 484; Haley, 280.

128   *Ralph Montagu in Paris :* HMC Buccleugh, I, 421, 423.

128–9   *The King and Madame :* Barbour, 160, n; Bryant, *Letters,* 234–5; Hartmann, *Charles II and Madame,* 247.

130–1   *The party at Deptford :* Pepys, IX, 468–9.

132   *The Duke of York gains strength :* ibid., 536, 560.

May, Sedley and Buckhurst : Pepys, IX, 335, 336, 338–9.

Howard and the Green Wax : Oliver, 169–70.

Sir William Coventry's release, and the Treasury Commission : CSPD 1668–9, 240; Browning, I, 67; Pepys, IX, 490–1.

133   *The Roos divorce case :* Lee, 110–11; Clarke, I, 439; Milward, 46–7.

The Queen's pregnancy : Bryant, *Letters,* 239; Pepys, IX, 552, 557, 560.

The bribe for Lady Castlemaine : HMC Buccleugh, I, 167.

Further rivalry between Buckingham and Arlington : HMC Report 7, 487; Pepys, IX, 552, 557, 560.

Page

Lady Castlemaine in 'higher command' : ibid., 147.

134   *Severity against nonconformists:* BL Add. Mss. 36916, ff. 177, 180, 183; Pepys, IX, 502.
Negotiations at Whitehall: Feiling, *Foreign Policy*, 304.
Buckingham's illness: Wilson, *A Rake and his Times*, 131.
Madame sets out for Dover: PRO SP 29/231 ff. 189, 208, 239.

134-5   *The Treaty of Dover:* Ashley, *Charles II*, 166–8; Feiling, *Foreign Policy*, 302, 316; Marvell, II, 303.

134   *Lady Castlemaine's part in the proceedings:* BL Add. Mss. 36916, f. 180; Hartmann, *La Belle Stuart*, 176; Margaret M. Verney, *Memoirs of the Verney Family 1660–1696*, vol. IV (1970), 201; Williams Glyn's Bank Ledgers.
The sum of money: Pepys, IX, 536.

135   *Madame's influence over the King:* Hartmann, *Charles II and Madame*, 315; H.MC Buccleugh, I, 487.
The plan to bring over Louise de Kéroualle: Sergeant, 175 and n.

136   *Buckingham in France:* Buckingham, I, 178–80; HMC Buccleugh, I, 442–3, 484; CSPV 1669–70, 248, 272; Wilson, *A Rake and his Times*, 141.
The new titles: BL Add, Mss. 36916, f. 187; Boyer, 48; Steinmann, 122–3.

Chapter 17: SONS AND LOVERS

138   *Nell Gwynn's son:* BL Add. Mss. 36916, f. 183.

138-9   *Jacob Hall:* DNB; Boswell, 348; Pepys, IX, 313; Gramont, 112; Steinmann, 124.

139   *'Madam all I ask of you'* : BL Harleian, 7006, f. 176.
Rochester: Greene, 139; Marvell, I, 149, 'Last Instructions', lines 93–102.

139-40   *John Ellis:* Alexander Pope, Poems, IV, ed. John Butt (1939), 83, 'Sober Advice from Horace Imitated from his Second Sermon'.

140   *Wycherley:* Greene, 178; John Dennis, *Familiar Letters* (1721), 216–17; William Wycherley, *Works*, ed. W. C. Ward (1896).

140-1   *John Churchill:* Boyer, 48; Churchill, I, 51–64; Gramont, 313; *Hattigé, ou les Amours du Roy de Tamaran* (1676); Manley, *New Atlantis*, I, 21–2, 30, 40; G. J. Wolseley, *Life of Marlborough* (1894), I, 68–9; Sergeant 336.

142   *The King visits Nell Gwynn and the Duchess of Cleveland:* Evelyn, III, 573.
Lady Castlemaine at the grand ballet: Evelyn, III, 569–70; Rutland, II, ii, 22–3; Boswell, 194, 350.

142-3   *Sir Henry Wood:* Marvell, I, 151, 'Last Instructions', lines 162–72.

143-4   *Madame intercedes for Arlington:* HMC Buccleugh, I, 474; Dalrymple, I, 124.

144-5   *Euston Hall and the wedding:* Barbour, 102, 186–7; Buckingham, II, 163; CSPD 1671, 592; Evelyn, III, 622; Forneron, 70–1; John Dryden and Nahum Tate, 'The Second Part of Absolom and Achitophel', POAS, III, 331.

145   *Quarrel over the Earl of Euston:* Williamson, II, 62–3.
Proceedings in Parliament concerning Mary Wood: BM Harleian Mss. 5277, ff. 89, 90.

146   *Dr Thomas Wood:* CSPD 1671, 329.
Education of the Duchess's sons: Prideaux, 40, 182.
Evelyn and Lord Henry Howard: Evelyn, III, 592.

Page

Clifford's marriage negotiations : Hartmann, *Clifford,* 250.
Anne Palmer returns : Savile, 30–1.
The genealogical tree : Dorney Court Muniments.

146–7   *Her wedding :* HMC Hastings, 165, 18 August 1674; Bodleian Ashmole Mss., 837, f. 190.

147   *Wedding expenses : Secret Services,* 87, 91, 96, 97, 99.
Titles, arms, money grants : CSPD 1671, 246, 281–2; 1672, 429; 1672–3, 41, 228–9, 263, 589, 617, 621; 1673, 195, 198, 258, 355; Williams and Glyn's Bank Ledgers, S.

148   *Colbert de Croissy and the Duchess :* Forneron, 63.
Arlington and Louise : Barbour, 181; Forneron, 66–8; Evelyn, III, 589, 591, 596.

149   *Gifts and titles for the mistresses :* HMC Buccleugh, I, 320; HMC Report 7, 465; Williamson, I, 109.
The Empress of Morocco : van Lannep, I, 206; Greene, 101–2.
'This making of bastards great' : POAS, III, 478.
The Duchess's coach and eight : CSPD 1671, 271.

150   *Colbert de Croissy's fears :* Forneron, 64.

Chapter 18: LANDLADY CLEVELAND

151   *Landlady Cleveland :* Marvell, II, 311.
151–2   *Sir Robert Howard :* Oliver, 154–161.
152   *The new 'farmers', wine licences, gifts and manors :* Hayley, 293–4; Marvell, II, 310; Williamson, I, 21–2, 38, 130, 136; CSPD 1671, 591; 1672–3, 98, 228, 355, 617, 633; 1673, 138–9, 156, 303, 543; *Essex Papers,* I, 121.
153   *Villiers House :* Haley, 260.
153–4   *Chesterfield and the fountain :* Chesterfield, 159; H. J. Wain, *A Brief History of Bretby* (1964).
154   *Phoenix Park : Essex Papers,* I, 59, 70, 80–1, 122–3, 140; Christie, II, 160.
The Duchess at Oxford : Prideaux, 21.
155   *The Duchess of York's conversion and the Duke's remarriage :* Clarke, I, 452, 484–6; Crewe, 11, 13.
The Declaration : F. Bate, *The Declaration of Indulgence 1672* (1908); *Essex Papers,* I, 121.
156   *The Duke of York misses Communion :* Crewe, 12; Evelyn, IV, 7; Williamson, II.
The Test Act : Browning, I, 98, Clarke, I, 483; Lee, 223; PRO 31/9/100A ff. 223–4, 237.
157   *The fall of Clifford and the Duchess's fears :* Hartmann, *Clifford,* 207; Browning, I, 100.
The satirical catalogue : Haley, 327, from Lady Newton, *Lyme Letters 1660–1760* (1925), 85–92.
158   *'As one whore comes over' :* Wood, II, 363.
The £400,000 : Williamson, II, 62.
159   *'Such small things' :* Feiling, *Tory Party,* 156.
159–60   *Howard and Danby :* Browning, I, 110; CSPD 1673–5, 185; *Essex Papers* I, 241; HMC Laing, I, 402, 404.

Page
160   *The Exchequer books :* Grey, III, 86.
        Sir John Trevor and the Duchess : Danby, II, 82–4.
161   *'The King seems sometimes very earnest' :* Essex Papers, I, 130–3.
        The Duke tries to bring in Shaftesbury : ibid., II, 32.
162   *The strict conjunction :* Feiling, *Tory Party*, 162.
        The Duke of York and the French : Browning, I, 165.
162–3   *The Duchesse de Mazarin :* Forneron, 121; Hartmann, *The Vagabond
        Duchess*, 150; Sergeant, 212.
163–4   *Cleveland to France :* CSPD 1675–6, 532; 1676–7, 25; HMC Hastings,
        II, 169; HMC Rutland, II, ii, 28; Sergeant, 214.

                   Chapter 19: A CONVENT IN PARIS

165   *The convents :* Andrews, 183–4; Roche, 46, 52, from Catholic Record
        Society, 1910; Dorney Court Muniments, 354.
165–6   *Churchill's plan to go to Paris :* Churchill, I, 114.
166   *The great ladies ignore the Duchess :* Rutland, II, ii, 29.
        The old employment: Prideaux, 58.
        The Marquis de Châtillon : Hatton, I, 168, POAS, II, 174.
        The Duke of York's interests : Miller, 138, states that Sir William Throck-
        morton and Peter Talbot each claimed to be James's accredited represen-
        tative in Paris.
        Lady Betty Percy : Browning, I, 223; II, 259–60.
167   *The tutor :* Manley, *Rivella*, 53–4; Prideaux, 58.
168   *Ralph Montagu :* Browning, II, 265–8.
        Danby and Nell Gwynn : ibid., I, 236.
        Honoré de Courtin : Hartmann, *The Vagabond Duchess*, 194.
        His view of the Duchesse de Mazarin : Forneron, 163.
169   *The Duchesse and Anne Sussex :* ibid., 190; Hartmann, *The Vagabond
        Duchess*, 174–5, 186–8, 201–5; HMC Rutland, II, ii, 34, 36.
170   *Buckingham in the Tower :* Buckingham, I, 210–16; Marvell, II, 239.
171   *Order to make the market low :* Browning, II, 326, 18 January 1678.
171–2   *The Duchess's visit to England :* ibid., II, 316; HMC Buccleugh, I, 524;
        II, 316; Luttrell, I, 18 July, 1679.
172   *Henry's marriage :* HMC Rutland, II, 43–4, 45, 47, 50, 67; CSPD,
        1677–8, 694; 1678, 244.
        A new cabal : Browning, II, 344; DNB, Lawrence Hyde.
        Montagu passes information to Danby : Browning, I, 223–5.
        The Sunderlands and the Duchess of Portsmouth : Forneron, 204; Kenyon,
        Sunderland, 18, from BL Add. Mss. 28049 f. 70; Sidney, I, 232.
173   *Sidney and Montagu :* Sidney, I, 67 n.
        The return to France : HMC Bath, II, 162; CSPD 1678, 244, 614.
173–4   *Montagu and the Countess of Sussex :* HMC Bath, II, 166; Hatton, I, 168.
174–5   *The Duchess writes to the King :* BL Harleian 7006, ff. 171–6, quoted in
        full, Andrews, Appendix, 201–11.
176   *George and Lady Betty :* Browning, I, 287; II, 363.
        Montagu goes to England : Hatton, I, 167–8.
        His intrigues : Browning, II, 371–2.
        Sunderland and Savile go to Paris : HMC Bath, II, 165–7.
        Barillon's bribery fund : Forneron .237–40.

9

Chapter 20: THE END OF THE REIGN

Page

177–8　*The Popish Plot:* Kenyon, *The Popish Plot; Anna Maria Crinò, Il Popish
　　　　Plot* (1954); James Corker, *Stafford's memoirs, or the Papists' bloudy
　　　　After-game*; Burnet, II, 147–62; Dalrymple, I, 257–8.

178　　*Traditional fears of popery:* Miller, 67–90. Halifax complained to Chester-
　　　　field in 1680 that he had 'the misfortune to turn papist and yet know
　　　　nothing of it myself'. See Chesterfield 238.
　　　　Montagu produces Danby's letters: Burnet, II, 175; Dalrymple, I, 260.

179　　*The King's 'excellent nature':* Oliver, 219.
　　　　The Duchess returns: HMC Buccleugh, I, 331.
　　　　Her match-making: CSPD 1678, 244; HMC Fitzherbert, 19. It was said
　　　　that Cleveland was the 'marriage maker' in a plan to marry the Duke of
　　　　York's daughter Anne to 'the Dolphin of France'.

179–80　*The remarriage of Grafton:* Evelyn, IV, 190: HMC Ormonde, IV, 504;
　　　　HMC, Bath, II, 162; Luttrell, I, 77.

180　　*Cleveland House:* Evelyn, IV, 190.
　　　　The King's high spirits: Reresby, 182.

181　　*The election campaign:* Burnet, II, 81–2; HMC Fitzherbert, 13.
　　　　Cleveland House made ready: Luttrell, I, 127.
　　　　The Duchess of Portsmouth in Paris: Hatton, II, 11; Forneron, 255–6.

182　　*She returns:* Bryant, *Charles II,* 266; Forneron, 256–7.
　　　　Cleveland returns: HMC Rutland, II, ii, 67, 75; HMC Buccleugh, I, 344.
　　　　Portsmouth's activities: Churchill, I, 156–7; Clarke, I, 592, 645, 665,
　　　　726; Reresby, 202, 228; Dalrymple, I, 343, 346.

183　　*The King in 1680:* Jesse, IV, 270–1.
　　　　Honours for his sons: Hatton, II, 12, 6 December, 1681; Reresby, 238–9.

184　　*At the altar rail with his sons:* Evelyn, IV, 374–5.
　　　　Charlotte Lichfield: Archaeologia LVIII, 176–87.
　　　　Houses for Anne and Charlotte: ibid., 184; HMC Rutland, II, 75.
　　　　Birth of an heir to Grafton: ibid., 81, 6 November 1683.
　　　　A fund for the family: Bryant, *Charles II,* 284; *Secret Services,* 91.

185–6　*The death of the King:* Bramston, 164; Clarke, I, 746–9; Chesterfield,
　　　　273–4; Lady Cowper, *Diary* (1864), 94–5; Dalrymple, I, 155–8; Evelyn,
　　　　IV, 395, 403, 413; Hatton, II, 51–2; HMC Portland, III, 383; Strick-
　　　　land, V, 678.

Chapter 21: COUNSELLOR CASTLEMAINE

187　　*The Duchess of Portsmouth's difficulties:* Forneron, 290–1.

188　　*The King dedicates himself to the cause of toleration:* PRO 31/9/100A,
　　　　f. 397; 100B, 527.
　　　　Moderation of the new Court: Evelyn, IV, 415.
　　　　The money grant: Ashley, *James II,* 164–5.

189　　*Dr Fell and Dr Massey:* Singer, II, 472; Hugh Trevor-Roper, *Christ
　　　　Church* (1950), 15.
　　　　The printing of Catholic books etc.: Churchill, I, 219–20; Reresby, 416.
　　　　The Committee: Oliver, 252–3; van Lannep, 348–9, 353.
　　　　Count d'Adda's reception: HMC Report 7, 504.

190　　*Castlemaine's character:* Kenyon, *Sunderland,* 146; Lee, 109; Boyer, 39.

Page

190 *His imprisonment and trial:* Hatton, I, 200; HMC Le Fleming, 150, 176; Savile, 62.

191 *His mission to Rome:* Child's & Co. Ledger for 1686; Nahum Tate, 'On the Earl of Castlemaine's Embassy to Rome', POAS, IV, 112; HMC Downshire, I i, 72, 113, 128, 133–4, 252, 283; PRO 100B, ff. 8, 32; *Ragguaglio della solenne comparsa fatta dall' illustrissimo conte di Castlemaine* (1687), Michael Wright, *An Account of his Excellence Roger Earl of Castlemaine's Embassy* (1688); Godfrey Anstruther, 'Cardinal Howard and the English Court', *Archivium Fratrum Praedicatorum* XXVIII, 352. *He returns to London:* Kenyon, *Sunderland*, 128–33, 171, 191; HMC Downshire I, i, 283.
Catherine Sedley: Churchill, I, 219.

192 *Grafton's duel:* HMC Buccleugh, I, 344; Rutland, II, ii, 102; Fitzroy, 44–6.

193 *Northumberland's marriage:* Ellis, I, 67, 71, 86, 94; Alice Fairfax-Lucy, *Charlecote and the Lucys* (1958), 164–7, HMC Rutland, II, ii, 102; HMC Downshire II, i, 135–69; Luttrell, I, 373; III, 39.
Cardonnel Goodman; HMC Rutland, II, ii, 107; Oldmixon, II, 576.

194 *Grafton and the papal nuncio:* HMC Report 7, 504.
The Declaration of Indulgence: Clark, 126.

194–5 *The Bishops petition the King:* Evelyn, IV, 583, 586; Churchill, I, 237–8.

195 *Churchill's letter to William:* ibid., 240.
Churchill, Grafton and other defectors: ibid., 260; Bramston, 336; Reresby, 534; Clarke, II, 218–19.

196 *Castlemaine escapes to Wales:* Roche, 71, 75.
Catherine Sedley's complaint: HMC Finch, III, 219, 351.
Cleveland House lent to Dutch Ambassadors: Roche, 246.

197 *The King dissatisfied with Grafton:* Foxcroft, II, 208.
Grafton at Beachy Head and Cork: Churchill, I, 288, 291; Fitzroy, 74–84; HMC Finch, III, 450; POAS, V, 223–5.
Isabella: Barbour, 260 n.

198 *Castlemaine:* HMC Downshire, I, i, 321; HMC Report 7, 198; Roche, 78.
The Earl of Arran and Barbara: Evelyn, IV, 640; Hatton, II, 143; Rosalind K. Marshall, *The Days of Duchess Anne* (1973), 168–88.

199 *Cardonell Goodman:* Luttrell, III, 483–4.
The Duchess at Tunbridge Wells: HMC Hastings, II, 281; HMC Portland, IV, 118; Darney Court Muniments.

200 *Castlemaine in 1696:* HMC Downshire, I, ii, 681, 704; HMC Hastings, II, 264.

201 *Financial payments:* BL Add. Mss. 5755 ff. 71, 246; *Case of her Grace the Duchess of Cleveland* (1690); Sergeant, 290.
The Duchesse de Mazarin's pension: Hartmann, *The Vagabond Duchess*, 262–3.

Chapter 22: HANDSOME FEILDING

202–5 *Feilding:* Francis Atterbury, *Correspondence* (1783), II, 31–2; Boyer, 49; BL Harleian Mss. 5808, f. 135; Luttrell, VI, 70–1, 83, 94, 100, 115.

205 *Charles Hamilton:* Sergeant, 317–18.

206 *'Cleveland, I say, was much to be admired':* POAS, I, 427.

Page
206–7   *Her character and beauty:* Burnet, I, 160; Boyer, 48; Oldmixon, II, 270; Reresby, 41.
207   *The Duchesse de Mazarin's sister, Madame de Soissons:* Chesterfield 231. *The mistresses:* Barbour, 260.

INDEX